TRUE BLUE

Also by Lt. Randy Sutton

True Blue

A Cop's Life

TRUE BLUE

TO PROTECT AND SERVE

Lt. Randy Sutton

ST. MARTIN'S PRESS ⧟ NEW YORK

www.stmartins.com

Library of Congress Cataloging-in-Publication Data

True blue : to protect and serve / [compiled by] Randy Sutton.—1st ed.
      p. cm.
  ISBN-13: 978-0-312-38354-1
  ISBN-10: 0-312-38354-1
  1. Police—United States—Biography. 2. Police—United States—Anecdotes. I. Sutton, Randy.
  HV7911.A1T77 2008
  363.2092'273—dc22

2008009457

First Edition: May 2008

10 9 8 7 6 5 4 3 2 1

Contents

Acknowledgments

True Blue: To Protect and Serve is the work of many people. The contributors are currently serving or former law enforcement officers who have opened their hearts and memories to us and chosen to share their experiences with the reader. In many cases, these memories will open emotional wounds, which are often as painful as physical injuries, suffered in the line of duty to be faced once again. I salute the courage it has taken to put pen to paper and allow us a glimpse into their world.

I wish to personally thank my editor, Patrick Lobrutto, who in agreeing to work on this volume has opened himself to the pain of others and selflessly brought these stories to life. The business of giving birth to a book is never fun for an author, but my agent, Laura Rennert, and George Witte, editor in chief of St. Martin's Press, made this process as painless as possible. Finally, the support of my close friends and family has given me the belief that this book would become not simply a dream, but a living thing capable of touching the lives of many. I owe more than I can say to my mother, Lillian, Jeannie Watson, and the memory of my father, Arthur, whose presence never wavers.

"In Valor There Is Hope"

I stood transfixed before these words carved in the mottled granite. Candlelight reflected from thousands of badges gleaming proudly on the chests of the uniformed men and women. As I watched, the words began to expand and undulate in time to the chorus of bagpipes as homage was paid to the thousands of names these few words would guard through eternity.

I shivered despite the warmth of the May evening and felt an almost eerie sense of protection in the company of the souls of heroes. I looked away for a moment as the solemn sea of uniformed police officers raised their candles. There was something besides sadness to be read in these faces, be they smooth or craggy, yellow, black, white, or brown. It was the look: the steely look of resolve, visible through the tears flowing freely down their cheeks and onto their uniforms.

I didn't bother to wipe away my own tears, for they bonded us together. Each one of us knew that we would never betray the trust placed in us by those we serve and those we serve with. We would never yield to those who would threaten or attempt to destroy our country or our way of life through crime, violence, or terror. We as a people will prevail over those who would harm us.

None of us doubt the truth of these words: "In valor there is hope." I saw it in the faces of our nation's police officers as they stood surrounding the National Law Enforcement Officers Memorial and heard it in the silent voices of those whose names lay forever carved upon its sacred stone.

Introduction

The stories in this book fall loosely into five categories and are identified as:

The Beat

Some walk a beat in the inner city, others patrol rural highways or small towns. Some wear blue uniforms, others wear khaki. Their patches are as different as their badges, but what they have in common is that every time one of them puts on his uniform, straps on his gun, and pins on his badge, he knows that he will be facing the unknown. The hours of his shift may crawl along with nothing more than checking out a broken burglar alarm to break the monotony. Or time may sail by with lights and sirens from one emergency to the next. You just never know, and that's why it takes a certain kind of person to do the job. There are some certainties: heartache, cruelty, and death are constant companions in the career of every law enforcement officer. So are humor, irony, and courage. At the end of the day there are stories to tell. Stories from "the beat."

The Fallen

The lone bugler will stand tall among the silent headstones. He will be ramrod straight, uniform crisply pressed, badge polished and gleaming. A salute will be passed and the mournful melody of taps will tear into the souls of all present. The flag of our nation will be folded by those who have chosen this solemn duty and handed off, as the ultimate symbol of sacrifice, to widow or parent, child or spouse.

Uniformed arms will rise in final salute as the piper plays "Amazing Grace" and seven rifles will fire as one, each of the three volleys causing the survivors to flinch.

This sad scene will take place today in one part of our country and tomorrow in yet another. The ceremony is always the same, yet as different as the individual officer being honored. It is the one time in law enforcement when all personal differences and politics are forgotten and empathy unites those who share the profession.

It is the time we honor those who have given their lives in the line of duty; we call them "the fallen."

War Stories

Every cop has them. You will hear them in the locker rooms of police stations in the largest cities, in the station parking lots in the smallest towns. You will hear them in neighborhood bars and hangouts where off-duty cops let off steam after the end of their watch. They're called "war stories." These are the tales that will work their way into private conversations with other cops, and with those lucky enough to be taken into their confidence. Some are poignant, some absurd; others might offend delicate sensibilities. Some will make you laugh out loud; some will make you shake your head in amazement. These stories are a cop's way of sharing the moment, a snapshot from his album of memorable moments in a long and riotously varied career.

Line of Duty

Much of a police officer's work is routine; it is simply interacting with people who have problems, or issues, or even illnesses. The truth is, the majority of the calls won't even be remembered at the end of the week. But there is always that one call, the one that changes your life. The revelation experienced may come from inside when suddenly the cop *sees* something in someone or in himself that he never saw before. These stories are epiphanies—they are the stories from a cop's life that will never be forgotten by those who have lived them. What these stories have in common is that they define the "line of duty": the line that separates cop from civilian, the line that no cop can retreat from, where every cop makes his stand, no matter what it costs him.

Deadly Force

"Dropping the Perp," "Smoking the Punk," "Dropping the Hammer," "Lighting Him Up." When the gun smoke clears, the phrases are legion. These are all euphemisms for the ultimate action a cop is called to perform, the taking of a human life. Most cops know that they are expected to be prepared to kill, yet will be judged when they do. Judged by the public, the press, their department, the courts, even their family and, most importantly, themselves. The act takes but a moment. The moment, however, lives forever frozen in time. Officers will question their courage, or perhaps be convinced of it. They will fear the uniqueness of their feelings or be comforted by them, or, perhaps, suppress them. The world will be different forever.

The reality of killing another human being is never what we expect, despite the hours on the firearms range and the intensity of our training. The changes may be subtle, dramatic, destructive, or inspiring, but change is inevitable. Most law enforcement officers know that the taking of a life is the most foreign yet compelling experience of their career. Despite Hollywood's portrayal of America's cops as trigger-happy, troubled men and women, the reality is that less than one in two hundred will ever fire a weapon in combat during an entire career. Many of the bullets fired will never find their mark, never leave a legacy of blood, but even the act of pulling the trigger will change the course of an officer's life. The decision may mean their own life, their partner's life, or the lives of the people they are sworn to protect. It is called many things, but a cop calls it "deadly force."

TRUE BLUE

A Senseless Act

BY RANDY SUTTON

Lieutenant, Las Vegas Metropolitan PD, twenty-two years, Princeton Borough PD, New Jersey, ten years.

The man who killed Sergeant Henry Prendes did not hate him. He couldn't have; they had never met prior to the moment the killer dumped three 7.62mm bullets into his chest, leaving Sergeant Prendes lying mortally wounded on the cold concrete walk leading up to a nondescript family home in suburban southwest Las Vegas. "Why?" is always the question in the depressing aftermath. The reply we've come to expect answers nothing at all: "It was a senseless act." Can we make sense out of something meaningless? Maybe for the sake of Sergeant Prendes's memory we should try.

2:20 P.M.: A Diner on Charleston Boulevard. I had been having coffee with an old friend, another cop from a neighboring department, when his cell phone rang. He listened for a moment and then his eyes sought mine; I caught the briefest hint of despair before his expression hardened and his jaw set. I felt the clenching in my gut as I set my coffee cup back down on the table and waited for him to finish the call.

"Sorry, brother, there's been a shooting," he said. "It's one of yours."

"How bad? Dead?"

He nodded. "Another officer wounded. He's en route to the hospital."

"The suspect?"

"Your guys returned fire at the scene. Put him down." My friend's gaze turned steely, but his knuckles were white where he gripped his coffee mug. "That takes care of that complication."

We seemed frozen there for those few seconds, each staring down at the table, distracted, enveloped in the normalcy and fragrant warmth of the small diner. I looked around; everyone was enjoying their meal, their afternoon, their life. In here you could almost imagine that nothing bad ever happened. But it had.

"I've got to get over to the hospital," I said, standing up. He nodded and grabbed his coat. I threw down a twenty-dollar tip for our two cups of coffee; maybe it was guilt money for sitting snug in a diner while one of my own paid the ultimate price for doing his job.

We both stood up and walked outside; he stood at his patrol car door and I stood at mine. I knew what he was waiting for. There are almost four thousand cops in my department, and though I don't know at least half of them, the question had to be asked.

"Did you know who it was?"

"They said it was Sergeant Henry Prendes. You know him?"

A chill swept through me, and my chest and jaw grew tight.

"Yeah, I did."

Our eyes met and held for a moment in the manner of old warriors, and then we went our separate ways.

One Hour Earlier: 8336 Feather Duster Way. It was a domestic violence call. Several neighbors had called 911 to report that a man was beating a woman in the front yard with a stick. The woman, they said, was his girlfriend. A few minutes later the girlfriend called in.

GIRLFRIEND (*screams*): He just broke my car window!
911 OPERATOR: I can't hear you. What?

GIRLFRIEND (*sobbing and screaming*): Oh! He just broke my
    car window—
911 OPERATOR: Are you injured?
GIRLFRIEND: Come quick! He's got a gun!

Sergeant Prendes arrived at the residence, three backup units close behind. He was met in the front yard by the tearful girlfriend, her mother, and her brother. The suspect, they told him, a young man in his twenties whom newspapers later described as "an aspiring rap artist," had retreated inside the house. The front door had been left wide open. The officers approached cautiously, by the book. But they hadn't even gotten halfway up the walk when the suspect, deep inside the shadows of the open doorway, opened fire with a high-powered knock-off assault rifle, striking Prendes point-blank. He reeled backward, shouting "I'm hit!" before he collapsed. Under the barrage of automatic weapon gunfire, the other officers were forced to take cover behind an old Volvo at the curb in order to return fire, but not before the gunman had fired three rounds, execution-style, into Sergeant Prendes's head.

The suspect, it seemed to everyone at the scene, had gone mad. He ran upstairs and continued firing down at the officers out of the windows, firing, reloading, firing and reloading: forty-two deadly rounds. The cops returned fire, sixty-three rounds, but the gunman had an advantage with his shielded position.

Bystanders, screaming, scattered and tried to take cover. One officer threw himself over a prone bystander even as the bullets tore into the ground around him. No one there thought, or would let themselves believe, that Prendes was dead. Rescuing the wounded officer was foremost in their minds, more than subduing the gunman or getting out of this alive. They decided, to a man, to rush the house.

Two Hours Later, University Medical Center, Trauma Center. I stood among almost a hundred other cops, some in uniform, others in street clothes, outside of the trauma center. We milled around numbly, sometimes shaking hands, sometimes hugging each other, all united by a feeling of disbelief and unreserved sorrow. For hours cops kept arriving to stand with one another, drinking in not just the sorrow but warming themselves through the sense of unity such tragedy brings. Now and then bursts of laughter could be heard as those who had known Henry related funny anecdotes about something he had said or done, making him alive again, if only for that moment. Sergeant Prendes was one of the few officers who were Las Vegas natives, a hometown boy who'd been the captain of his high school football team. He was a family man, married, with two teenage daughters, and very active in his church. He was an avid golfer, an outdoorsman, a Dallas Cowboy fan, a joke teller with an irrepressible sense of humor. We all knew him as a fourteen-year police veteran and a good cop. He was just thirty-seven years old.

In the growing crowd I came upon one of the officers who had been at the scene. His pants were torn at the knees where he had dropped down into a kneeling shooting stance. The acrid smell of gunsmoke wafted from his shirt.

"What finally happened?" I asked him. He told me.

Every cop at the scene of this raging gun battle knew that their ballistic vests would not protect them from the power of an assault weapon, the unrelenting fusillade such a lethal weapon let loose. Each man knew that the next moment might very well be his last. But their comrade, their fellow officer, was lying on his back in plain sight, a pool of dark blood spreading across the walkway beneath him. They prepared to advance, to break cover. Then, like a scene out of an old Western movie, a plainclothes officer with the Gang Crimes unit arrived. He was armed with an assault rifle, an AR-15. He started firing almost before he got out of his car, and he kept firing even after he was shot in the leg. The tide turned. The suspect was ballistically overpowered; the six cops on the scene advanced; and the suspect ran down the stairs and into the front yard, spraying the neighborhood with lethal rounds. But the wounded officer shot him, staggering him. Despite his wounds, the suspect stood and continued his assault. Another officer armed with a 12-gauge broke cover and calmly marched toward the gunman, firing blast after blast until he was out of ammo, then reloaded on the move, continuing his march into the sights of the gunman. Other officers were firing from their positions, and suddenly the gunman fell, his body coming to rest just a few feet from the motionless body of Sergeant Henry Prendes.

The cop now standing in front of me told me he ran to his fallen friend and pulled him to safety, out of the kill zone, in case there was a second armed suspect. But there was no other gunman and Prendes was already dead.

It was over as suddenly as it began. Pungent gunsmoke filled the air. Nothing but absolute silence until one of the bystanders started whimpering and one of the cops shouted, "Is anyone else hit?" Then, of course, a chorus of approaching sirens.

The cop stopped the story there and looked away, shrugged. I didn't know what to say. One of the bosses came out of the trauma center to let us know that the wounded officer, the Gang Crimes Bureau officer, was going to be okay. There was scattered applause at this, some good news in a bleak day. I turned to my companion, but he was already headed back to his patrol car, his gait unnaturally stiff. I called after him but he didn't turn around.

I was scheduled to work the graveyard shift that night. I arrived early at my area command to find most of the cops in my shift already there, glued to the TV in the briefing room, where news coverage of the shoot-out continued unabated. Sergeant Prendes was the first cop in our department murdered in the line of duty in nearly two decades, which was just a few years less than most of these young officers had been alive. This was their first experience with the shooting death of a fellow officer, and the tension, an almost physical entity, enveloped me as I walked through the door. Some of the younger cops muttered oaths each time a reference was made to the killer or his "aspirations." But it was the older cops who caught my attention. They simply stood or sat, their posture rigid, their eyes downcast whenever mention was made of Sergeant Prendes. The young ones felt the anger; the older ones felt the sense of loss.

The undersheriff stood with our captain at the front of the briefing room. Though each had experienced this type of tragedy before, the strain was evident on their somber faces. I thought, for the first time, that the undersheriff looked older than his years. The two did their best to calm the young ones, to bring a sense of normalcy to the briefing, but when the cops filed out to their patrol cars, they were seething with an anger and a grief they couldn't put words to. My friend from the diner and I had once tried to dissect this feeling and had decided, one long evening over a lot of beers, that a change happens in cops when one of their own is killed. It is a grief without a name or a border, a pervasive sadness that sinks into your soul so deep it can never be exorcised.

I could only watch, share their grief without acknowledgment, and hope that one day each would be able to come to terms in his or her own way. For I have learned as a cop that no one can really share his pain with others; at best, we can just experience the same thing silently, side by side.

I buckled my worn and creaking leather holster and headed into the parking lot. But before I stepped into my supervisor's wagon, I stopped and looked around and, just to be sure, I yanked my .45 out of the holster, slipped the magazine out, and drew the slide back, making sure I had a round chambered before I seated the magazine and reholstered.

"Just relax," I told myself. But it wasn't going to be easy, not tonight. I knew that no cop could be ready when up against someone who really wanted to kill us. This is where we differ from the military. We have to switch from being Officer Friendly to Rambo in about an eighth of a second. We have to go from smiling to pulling the trigger in less than two seconds. We have to be lucky or have some weird sixth sense guiding us into the most banal-to-deadly situations imaginable. Even though I've lived the life of a cop for almost thirty years, I felt the adrenaline begin to pump as I began my patrol.

Somewhere around two A.M. I walked back to my car after conferring with an officer and a witness to a minor burglary and I saw the clouds part. There was one bright, even radiant, star blazing away through the gash in the cloud cover. I leaned against the open door of my black and white, gazing at its brilliance. "Here's to you, Henry," I saluted him. "I won't forget you, my friend. None of us will." And that's a promise.

Six days after his gruesome death, Sergeant Henry Prendes was laid to rest.

Funerals, it seems to me, are the one occasion when cops truly honor each other. All petty animosities and jealousies are forgotten. The rituals that walk alongside our deaths are vital, not only to the families of our fallen but to all who wear a badge and who share its joys and burdens. The mournful wail of the bagpipes as "Amazing Grace" fills the heavy air becomes our collective tears. The glint of sunlight sparkling off the bugle as taps plays causes us to blink as one, momentarily blinded by our almost illogical faith in humanity. The twenty-one guns fired in unison by the stone-faced honor guard breaks their reserve and their falling tears betray their rigid posture and stoic expression. Even those of us who do not pray, pray. We pray that our fallen fellow not be forgotten; we pray that our presence on this earth will not have been in vain.

More than five thousand people joined together in the memorial service for Henry Prendes, and more lined the procession route, proudly holding their hands over their hearts as the miles of police cars, from every corner of the nation, filed by with their overhead lights flashing in silent homage. It was during these brief and beautiful moments that our community and our cops were one. One in spirit, one in all the beliefs that mattered. So when I heard one earnest young newsman call the killing of Sergeant Prendes a senseless act, I thought to myself that he was wrong. Senseless means in vain and that's the worst way to condemn a good man to obscurity. In the death of our brave cop we must search for sense. We must embrace the unity that his death inspired, for it is that unity that can defeat "senselessness." Even the most insidious evil can be faced, battled, and overcome when the righteous stand strong and together. The killer? No one will remember his name. Obscurity is *his* eternal condemnation.

I refuse to believe that Sergeant Henry Prendes died in vain that blustery Las Vegas day. His sacrifice stands for all that we as law enforcement officers embrace: courage, duty, and, above all, honor.

Nothing Is Ever Routine

BY STEPHEN "STEVE" BERG

Lieutenant, Del Rio PD, twenty-five years.

One of the duties we had in the small department where I worked was checking the houses of citizens who were out of town. When the citizen left town, they filled out a card providing information about when they were leaving and when they were returning. The card also provided space for the citizen to let us know what lights would be on, vehicles on the premises, pets, any damages to the structure, and any items in the yard. These checks had to be made once a shift by the patrol officer assigned to the area where the residence was located, and the check was recorded on the card the homeowner had filled out for us.

I was working the midnight shift and came to work at 2200 hours. I received an out-of-town request for a check from my supervisor. I studied the request and saw that there would be a van parked in the driveway, no lights would be on, no damage to the exterior of the structure, and no pets.

It was approximately 0300 hours on a cloudy night, with no moon visible, when I arrived at the house. Immediately I noticed that there wasn't any street lighting available in that neighborhood. It was so dark I could hardly see five feet in front of me. I exited my patrol unit and listened for any sounds, but the night was quiet. To be tactical I lowered my portable radio volume and decided not to use my flashlight, as I did not want to give my presence away. I waited until my eyes adjusted to the darkness. I was totally focused, totally on guard. This is the way it's supposed to be.

I started by checking the front of the residence and then the carport. Everything was as it should be. I proceeded down the east-side wall of the residence, and again everything was fine. I was extremely careful about every detail, walking slowly, making as little noise as possible when I moved. I stopped and listened for any sounds before I turned to the corner to check the rear of the house. Again I heard nothing to cause any alarm. I started to check the rear of the residence.

I was starting to become complacent, since the check seemed routine, just like the hundreds I had done before. I began to feel safe and no longer was so careful about making noise or checking my surroundings.

As I reached the patio I sensed movement. I didn't hear anything, but a quick jolt of adrenaline told me something was wrong. Before I could react something struck me on both shoulders, a blow so hard it knocked me flat on my back.

I saw two eyes staring at me and felt hot breath on my face. I attempted to remove my service revolver but was unable to grab it while falling backward.

My life begin to flash before me, but I was determined that I would not go alone. When I hit the cement of the patio the weight of my attacker pinned me to the ground. I struggled to break free, when suddenly I felt a large wet tongue licking my face.

The biggest and blackest Labrador retriever I have ever seen lay on top of me, joyfully playing and licking me.

The next stop was home to change uniforms . . . for more than one obvious reason.

Nicky and the Mustard Gas Caper; or, How Two ATF Agents Saved South Central Los Angeles

BY KEN CATES

Special Agent in Charge, Department of Homeland Security, U.S. Immigration and Customs Enforcement, Dallas, Texas, retired, thirty-three years.

It's not at all unusual for a special agent to work for a couple of different agencies during his career. Truthfully, the most fun I ever had as a federal criminal investigator, the most effective and the most meaningful work I ever accomplished, was while I was employed as a special agent for the Bureau of Alcohol, Tobacco, and Firearms. ATF, an agency of the Department of the Treasury, had evolved out of the old prohibition days. It had a rich history of agents who were independent, innovative, freewheeling, and aggressive. While federal gun laws had become ATF's primary jurisdictional focus, we were daily involved then in investigating bombings and arsons, and street gangs and in locking up badass felons caught by us or by the local police for possessing weapons. It was exciting and challenging work and I know it goes on today, despite the Homeland Security reorganization after 9/11 that moved ATF into the Justice Department

In those days of the seventies and eighties, all ATF street agents will tell you, a really good "1811" (the federal job series number of all criminal investigators and special agents) had to be able to do it all . . . be a generalist in everything and excel in a few things. On any given day an ATF street agent might have to be a firearms expert in court in the morning, an evidence collection technician at lunch, a case and investigative funds manager in the afternoon, a moving surveillance expert in the evening, an undercover operative that night, and a SWAT or raid team member at six A.M. the next day. ATF agents pretty much all worked at least some undercover from time to time, usually on the most violent and mean crooks on the street. Hell, they all carried guns, weren't afraid to use them, and many had been in prison at least once before we ever even targeted them for investigation.

We learned to be cautious, manage our risks, plan our cases, and, to the extent possible, always live by the motto: "You run the case; the case doesn't run you!" But sometimes the shit would hit the fan, and it would be all "elbows and assholes" out the door on some caper or arrest or raid because "shit happens and it happens a lot in the ghettos of LA." That's really where this story begins. Shit was happening *all* the time, and my partner, Jimmy Cannia, and I had gotten ourselves shit-deep in a continuing special operation called Project Watts. It was really just a way for Jim and me to do what we liked best back then—work undercover (U/C), stay out of the office, stay away from our obnoxious boss, and have some fun while we locked up gangsters in and around Los Angeles. Project Watts was an umbrella investigation that let us develop targets with some seed money, then open new cases on them individually. We had developed one of the best informants a South Central LA agent could hope to have. Old Nicky was his name and he was simply "the best." He was about sixty-five-years old when we knew him, and had worked as a confidential informant (CI) for LAPD, LASO, the Secret Service, the FBI, and who knows who else, so he had a solid reputation for reliability and productivity. He cruised around the LA ghettos in an old beater "good times" van, knew everyone, heard everything, and knew that with the right agents working with him, he could make money while actually making his own neighborhood safer. Honestly, Nicky just disliked the gangsters and what they did to his community. Don't get me wrong, though. He believed in getting paid for his efforts, too.

Nicky's wife, Daisy, was the live-in cook for comedian George Carlin (and a great cook she was!), so she was out of their house six days a week and that let Nicky work the streets for cases. Nicky was referred to us by some other agents that just didn't want "to work that hard" and we three really clicked as a team. Nicky was constantly finding some gun deal to do in the ghetto and Cannia and I were constantly struggling to find ways to pay him for so many deals. ATF was pretty stingy with informant money back then so, being the innovators we were, sometimes all we could do was fill up his van with a government gas credit card, but he kept the cases coming. If Nicky said this crook had a shotgun or was a felon with a pistol for sale, well, you could take it to the bank. Cannia and I would round up some cover agents from our group, have a quick briefing on either buy-walking the gun (letting the crook go to do a bigger, better deal a few days later) or buy-busting the guy when the deal went down. Jimmy and I would get in the van with Nicky, head to a liquor store for a six-pack and some menthol cigarettes since they always took the "edge" off a U/C meet with a gangster. Nothing like getting out of the van drinking a cold beer, giving your target a beer and a cigarette, bullshitting him about how Cannia (dressed in a loud silk shirt half unbuttoned) had mob connections who needed guns or how Cowboy (dressed in cutoff shorts, a big cowboy hat and no shirt—I was skinnier back then!) needed guns to sell down in Mexico, and tape-recording the whole thing.

Yeah, when Nicky said he had a deal for us, we jumped on it. That's why on a particular fall day in 1985 when Nicky called in to say he had a crook that had a case of army mustard gas grenades, well, we took note. Granted, my experience and training and prior military service as a military intelligence specialist told me that mustard gas hadn't been around since World War I! But this was Nicky, and he was never wrong when he put us on a deal. He was able to describe in explicit detail to me how he had seen the crook in possession of a whole case of these mustard gas grenades, how they were packaged in a heavy tan cardboard box with army writing all over it, how inside the case, the mustard gas grenades were further packed in heavy round dark cardboard two-piece cylinders that twisted apart, and how the grenades themselves were dark green and had some kind of black block army letters written on them. He hadn't been able to hold one since the Watts or Compton gangster would only let him look at the case and its contents. Nicky, knowing we would be interested in *any* grenade for sale or in the possession of a gangbanger, had worked the crook and arranged a U/C meeting for Cowboy and Cannia with the target for that evening.

We really didn't have time to do much if any research on military mustard gas grenades, since just believing they were out there in the trunk of a car poses a huge risk to civilians. Our boss was ecstatic! He could see big headlines of the heroic ATF effort that he was leading. Our group supervisor took the bold step and called our special agent in charge direct to alert him to the impending glory and all was now in motion for a huge ATF bust and the recovery of a *case* of army mustard gas grenades!

Cannia was a much more experienced ATF agent than I and . . . well, let's just say that he had learned over time to be a tad more cynical. Still, even Jimmy was a little pumped because this was one of Nicky's deals. So, as usual, we called for an LAPD bomb tech to be on standby, and Jimmy, Nicky, and I set out to meet the crook and do the deal. I was wearing a concealed "nagra" tape recorder. Jimmy had a "kell kit" transmitter so the cover agents could hear the undercover negotiations with the violator and also hear the pre-arranged bust signal that would call them in to help overwhelm the crook and ensure that the mustard gas grenades didn't slip away. When you are working undercover with typically armed and violent targets, no feeling is better than hearing those "plain wrapper" cars come screaming in to the arrest location and seeing the "cavalry" charge up to back your play. Of course, since ghetto gangsters were so damn good at countersurveillance and "making" any cops that were in the "hood," Jimmy and I usually went out of our way to lose our own cover team, then call them on a handy-talkie radio to tell them to set up several blocks from where we were really doing an undercover meet. That kept them close enough in case the deal broke bad, but it kept them from getting us "made" during a meeting and it covered their asses since they were set up exactly where the undercover agents told them to be. It usually worked great. This time, however, we decided to risk it and have the cover team close, as close as possible, to ensure they could hear our transmitter, see our backup visual bust signal, and make damn double sure that, no matter what, we got the mustard gas grenades.

So the deal was set. I had the Project Watts buy money, only about $400. Ghetto contraband was dirt cheap back then—$40 would easily buy a nice automatic or big revolver or even a pipe bomb—so four hundred bucks was a *big* deal! Jimmy and I drove in the van with Nicky to meet the crook on a residential street in Compton, just as Nicky had arranged. Cannia was silk-shirted, I was cowboy-hatted, and Nicky was nervous, unusual for him, as he was always a cool, calm, and collected CI. Nicky being nervous made me nervous and it made the likelihood that we were about to be confronted with a *real case* of *fucking grenades* all the more scary.

Jimmy and I both had "hideout" five-shot revolvers (highly concealable pistols) and I know without a doubt we were primed to use them if it came to that. We pulled up behind the suspect's car and waited while Nicky got out and walked up to the crook to kick the deal off. He waved to us in the van to come on up and meet the crook. "Here we go," Jimmy told the wire after reading off the license plate and vehicle description for the cover team. We got out of the car, drinking beer, smoking Kools, and walked up for one of the biggest undercover gigs in the history of the LA Field Division of ATF—maybe one of the biggest deals ever done by undercover ATF agents anywhere.

We were introduced to Johnny or Ronnie or whatever the crook said his name was, which of course was always a lie, and started bull-shitting with the dude. We gave him the standard cover story about buying guns to sell in Mexico and laid out a solid story about why

Johnny-Ronnie should do business with us. We would get the stuff out of the country fast so it would never come back on him. Plus, doing business with us always led to more business and more business and more business and Johnny-Ronnie would most certainly make tons of money dealing with the two of us from now on. Johnny-Ronnie said that was way cool with him because he had stolen the case from the National Guard armory where he worked and he didn't want to get caught. He went on to assure us that he had stolen a case previously and had sold it to some gangsters for a "party" and that he could get more. Johnny-Ronnie motioned us back to the trunk of his car to take a look. Jimmy and I followed closely, ready to take the guy down or out if anything went south while we looked at the mustard gas grenades. The cover agents were ready, poised to roar in as soon as one of us undercover guys gave the bust signal. Johnny-Ronnie opened the trunk.

There it was, just like Nicky had described it, a tan heavy cardboard case, black army block printing. The case was open. I could see the dark canisters neatly set inside the cardboard case . . . metal-top, black-cardboard cylinders, just like army grenades had looked when issued to us during my military stint . . . and there, printed right on the case, was the military nomenclature: 24, each, Standard Grade, 24 Liquid Ounces, Lot Number 2816753-1A6901-MUSTARD. Yeah, that's it . . . *mustard*. Not mustard grenades, not fragmentation grenades, not grenades of any kind . . . just . . . *mustard!* A case of twenty-four OD green cans of U.S. Army field kitchen mustard.

Jimmy started laughing so hard he almost fell down. I was laughing so hard I couldn't speak to the cover team, the crook, Nicky . . . nobody. Nicky was really, really perplexed, not understanding what we were laughing at, not understanding why the bust had not gone down, not understanding anything that was written on the case. See, turns out his reading skills weren't the best, something we didn't know up until that time. And the crook? Well, he just got mad. He had come all the way to the meeting, ready to do some big deal, apparently not understanding how much money Nicky had negotiated for the sale of the case of mustard, and not appreciating why two weirdly dressed white guys were laughing their heads off. So he threatened to do us bodily harm with his pistol, which of course saved the day. He was a felon. We hooked him up without the benefit of the cover team; we recovered the stolen National Guard mustard from the armory where Johnny-Ronnie worked cleaning up, and South Central LA was made safe from the ravages of a stolen case of standard-issue army mustard by the heroic special agents of ATF's Los Angeles Field Division, LA Metro Group. Just doing our duty.

Oh, yeah, our boss was a long time getting promoted after that.

Mr. Martinez's Christmas

THE BEAT

BY MICHAEL HAHN

Sworn Officer, San Jose PD, California, twenty-six years.

The man who called us said he'd found a guy stuffed into a shopping cart. The call taker asked him to stay there, with the dead guy in the shopping cart on the sidewalk in front of his house, but the man said he had to go inside because the football game was starting. Also, he said, it was too cold. He was sure right about that.

So the dead man, lying on his back with legs as stiff as boards, just sat there in the early morning fog and waited for us to come to him.

Being dead can be a lonely thing.

I got there after the fire department had come and gone. My officer told me the fire captain hadn't gone through the usual motions performed on the more recently dead, the chest pounding and defibrillation and the cutting off of clothes. No paramedics hooking up a pint of saline, no airway established, no oxygen administered. Death is legally "pronounced" reluctantly in a nonclinical setting, and it's best to be sure the person is *totally* dead before you "pronounce." Sometimes, cops or firefighters jump the gun, and a person literally wakes up in the morgue.

You need to have stopped breathing to be *really* dead. The oxygen that feeds your onboard computer must have been cut off for several minutes. There are major clues that help us determine when folks kick off: fixed, unresponsive pupils, cold blue skin, the lividity or pooling of blood on the gravity side of the body. Stiffness—rigor mortis—comes. Joints lock into place, and if the body is moved, it will stay in the position of death for hours. There's automatic pronouncement in cases of decapitation, or when full rigor has set in, or if the victim gets blown up or shredded.

So, his stiffness was how we knew he'd died somewhere else in the wee hours of the Christmas Eve morn. If he'd died in the cart, his limbs would have been folded, hanging out of it before the stiffening began. His hands were clenched into folded claws. With toes pointed upward, his rigid body had been placed unceremoniously in the cart on his back, causing the head and neck to tilt forward at a most uncomfortable-looking angle of repose.

Somebody had found him dead, probably a partner in a homeless encampment who didn't want the heat and scrutiny of a death investigation and so had decided to move him. The neighbors said he hadn't been there when they'd come home around twelve. The night had been a cold one, upper thirties, low forties, and foggy. The lingering dampness still seeped through my thermals and vest in the emerging sunshine at nine. I looked down at the young man's face— unshaven, deeply tanned, lips blue, eyes open just enough for me to see the clouded dead milkiness of his glassy orbs.

I think of the person who had loaded him into the cart; the grunting strain of moving stiff dead weight. The sounds of the body going into the cart, the thud of the head sliding down onto the crosshatch of bright metal bars. Had they been friends, this cold passenger and his strange porter? Was the final move an act of compassion, to allow the dead one to be found and given a decent burial, rather than bloating and rotting at the fringe of some smoky camp? Or was the pusher the literal kind, who'd sold him his last hit of heroin, moving him only for some kind of criminal avoidance? I imagine what had it been like, guiding the dead man *clackety-clack* down the dark, misty sidewalk, boosting the wheels up curbs, crossing streets *clackety-clack*. Was the cart a wobbler, the kind you hate to get at the market, whose careening imbalance makes you turn around to exchange it for another?

I wondered if he'd talked or sung softly to his quiet charge as they navigated through the sleeping neighborhood, the living people safe and warm inside their homes. Did he shed a tear, say a prayer, laugh, or babble?

I did my job, asking the young cops to knock on doors, write down license plate numbers, talk to any homeless they could find camped nearby.

No one had seen anything.

I made the proper calls, told my boss what I'd seen and deduced. No obvious signs of trauma, of a struggle. He'd died somewhere else, been moved, found. I next talked to the Homicide commander, who told me to go ahead and call the coroner, and to call back the crime scene crew if the on-scene investigator deemed the death suspicious.

The coroner arrived about ten minutes after I called. We shook hands. His grasp was firm, his hands oddly warm. From a pocket he pulled a pair of rubber gloves, thrust them onto his hands expertly, then put over them another pair. He snapped some photos from different angles before he moved the bulky tan corduroy jacket covering the body. Across the street, outside the barrier of the orange crime-scene tape, people lingered, watching, mute. They spoke in chopped whispers, as if they might disturb somebody. The investigator took off the man's baseball cap and placed it on top of the coat, which was folded now on the bottom shelf of the cart.

"This guy," he said, smiling as he strained to bend the left leg at the knee, "is *really* stiff. Probably gone less than twelve hours." He looked at the pants, lifting a worn denim cuff to find that the man wore two socks on one foot, only one on the other. He had dark blue sweats over thermals under the dungarees. These things confirm that he did his living on the streets, and spoke to the constant search of the homeless for warmth in winter. The investigator moved to the deceased's hands, clenched so tight, and gently pried open finger after finger to see if he clutched some clue to his life or death. I could hear popping sounds as the knuckles were forced; nothing was inside the palms but cold air. The coroner next searched the front pant pockets, discovering exactly two bus passes, two quarters, and a dime. One of the quarters slipped, spinning to the ground, and slowly the coroner bent, retrieved it, placed it in a manila envelope.

Scissors, the kind the paramedics use, appeared in the investigator's hand. After feeling around a bit, he cut the man's left rear pocket, removing a worn brown trifold wallet. A lefty myself, I knew that the dead man was, too. The wallet was packed with business cards, no cash, a probation officer's reminder to come in next week, a medical card, and a driver's license telling us the man's name, Andrew Martinez. With that, something changes. The discovery of his identity allowed us to affirm his humanity. What he was called in life—the mere idea of it—served to anchor the moment, to annul a bit of the indignity of his final circumstances. Carefully, the investigator removed from the wallet a picture of a pretty woman and a little girl, faces scrunched together in a carnival photo booth. He flipped it over. "To Dad. . . ." The rest of the inscription I don't see, my eyes drifting down to his gray face.

Just then the cart rolled forward as the coroner leaned into it, tipping man and conveyance precipitously over toward the cracked sidewalk. As one, we all lunged for it, caught it just in time to keep it from spilling him onto the concrete. We allowed ourselves a small laugh, dissipating the tension of the moment. Around us, front and back and across the street, people stood watching quietly. Next, the man's shirt was pulled up, revealing no signs of cuts, bruises, wounds of any kind. There was the slightest pooling of blood at the surface of the skin, indicating perhaps that he'd died lying on his stomach and was later moved onto his back.

The investigator cradled the head stuck in the corner of the chrome wagon, weaving his fingers through the hair as though shampooing, feathering it back to see underneath. I saw a Ford minivan approach, and one of the officers lifted the orange tape strung across the street to let it in. As it rolled up, I saw the county permit on the dash.

It slowed and parked. The driver emerged first, a tall, genial man who could be anyone's dad, early sixties, kind face. His partner, in his thirties, had the look of a person who hadn't done this too long. He smiled nervously and I focused on his crooked teeth. The men smelled like cigarettes. The windows on the van were tinted darker than normal, and as they turned to extract the unfolding gurney from its depths I found myself wondering how many dead a van can carry. The two worked together silently, unfolding a white plastic sheet over the stretcher, which had thicker padding in the torso region. After the plastic came a muslin sheet, long sides brushing the ground. As they finished preparing the gurney, they turned and regarded the shopping cart, speaking softly to each other, sizing up the mechanics of the transfer from his chariot to theirs.

Suddenly from the silent sky, down through the misty sunshine came a flock of perhaps thirty pigeons. They arrived in a rush, a flurry of feathers, turning around us so tight I could feel the breeze from their beating wings. Their motion startled me, the suddenness of their appearance accentuated as they made a tight turn, then a second lap of the cart, and were gone. The cop across the sidewalk from me stood momentarily transfixed, tilting his head back, squinting into the low winter sun, tracing the birds' progress skyward.

The investigator and the body snatchers were ready then, asking our help. We carefully tilted the cart forward as the two men, with surprising grace, lifted their new charge onto the gurney. With snapping flair the sheet was folded up and over the man's face, finally covering him from the curious eyes of the neighbors. A short roll to the van, straps fastened and checked, the lift and slide up onto the platform, and the doors slammed.

It was done.

Andrew Martinez finally made it off the streets.

Slowly, the van pulled away. Clothing and change bagged and

tagged, the investigator thanked us. We shook hands again, and he, too, was gone.

The cops rolled up the orange tape.

I noticed how cold the wind felt as I watched the neighbors drifting back inside their homes.

One of my guys asked what we should do about the cart. For a full minute we looked at each other and at the cart. I thought of the football fan inside the house, and how important his game had been. I thought of what the dead guy might have wanted.

Merry Christmas, Andy.

The sun was gleaming off the bars of the cart as it got smaller in my rearview mirror.

I was rolling, very slowly, down the street toward the next call.

Pigeons and Monkeys and Snakes, Oh My!

WAR STORY

BY THOMAS J. CLINE
Sworn Officer, Chicago PD, thirty years.

I was very lucky in the seventies to have worked with a unique group of cops. In all of our diversity there was a lot of love, hate, scandal, triumph, tragedy, and vengeance. There were about seven cliques of guys on our watch, each messing with the others. We had hunters, drinkers, lovers, bikers, boaters, skiers, and dogs. Individuals were often members of several groups because of working relationships and shared interests. Make no mistake, there was plenty of friction in our crew, but when it came to getting the job done, dislike, animosity, or hate were cast aside. We'd pull together, cover each other's back, and even put our lives on the line for each other. We may have appeared a shrill and screaming dysfunctional family behind closed doors, but in public we looked like the Cleavers.

Practical jokes were standard fare for reasons of fun, vengeance, boredom, or a combination of all three. Jokes ranged from dangerous to cunning. Like the time Polish Bob and Harold were pulling away from a job shared by another car and Bob decided a cherry bomb would be an appropriate farewell note. When the unsuspecting boys entered the street, returning to their car, Bob lit a cherry bomb, intending to toss it at their feet as he pulled away. He flicked his Zippo closed as soon as the wick started spritzing sparks and tossed the bomb in their general direction. All would have gone as planned had he opened the car window. Harold barely had the words, "You asshole!" out of his mouth when the firework hit the clean glass and bounced back between his legs. A shrill scream and a reflexive flick of Bob's fingers sent the fizzling object to the floor between the pedals. Before Polish Bob could get the car in park and grab the door handle it ran out of wick. All Harold could do was cover his head and ears as he turned toward the door in a curl. *Kablooooie!*

Hearing the report, the would-be victims dived for cover. Peering from behind their shields, they saw Bob and Harold, exiting their smoke-filled vehicle shrieking in tongues. Bob's pants were shredded from the inside ankle to the knee. When the intended victims realized what had happened, they laughed at their bloody buddy Bob and his half-deaf partner Harold.

As they drove to Evangelical Hospital, the only sympathetic words Harold could muster over and over were: "You stupid motherfucker." Since both were excellent working cops, the bosses just rolled their eyes at the reports and didn't investigate further.

For many of us it confirmed our suspicions. Polish Bob hadn't been right since Officer Tony rolled over his head with a souped-up minibike the previous year.

You would think that pranksters might back off after near castration by explosion, but no. They turned away from pyrotechnic pranks to things they knew better—animal pranks. Their favorite marks were the guys who used the car on the following shift. Kenny and Wally were jokesters, too, and well aware of the risk in using a car inhabited by Polish Bob and Harold for eight hours a day.

We were trained to expect the unexpected from the citizenry but less apt to detect things awry after carefully inspecting a vehicle at the beginning of a tour. All it takes is finding one back-from-the-dead wino in your trunk to make you more adept at vehicle inspection.

One night after giving their car the once-over Ken and Wally confidently headed toward their beat. It wasn't until they parked to sip coffee and write a report that they discovered their car was inhabited by a creature not native to Dodge Monacos. It was a good thing the season was summer. Wally was holding the hot coffee out the window as Kenny wrote. He felt something strange hit his shoe and move over his ankle. He jerked a bit, spilling just a little coffee. He looked down and threw the cup while screaming the Lord's name in vain when he realized there was a snake in his car. It was a garter snake. After the initial shock they both realized there was no real danger. The snake was tossed in the nearest prairie.

Less than ten minutes later two more serpents came out of hiding. The car was infested. In all they recovered at least a dozen snakes from under the dashboard and seats and in the glove box.

Kenny and Wally continually threatened the boys they relieved, but never pulled a coup de grace. They just weren't as devious.

One very cold midnight shift Bob and Harold spied a lone pigeon in the middle of the street. They surmised the bitter cold had grounded the poor pigeon. Feeling sorry for the flyin' rat they brought him in the car, placing the critter on the back windshield deck. There he sat for a few hours, ruffled up, with his head buried in a wing. By quitting time they had forgotten the bird was there.

Taking over the car 10-99 on the day shift, Kenny did his outside inspection and pulled out the rear seat looking for weapons or drugs. He never saw the bird. Pulling out of the station lot, he must have taken the corner too fast for the feathered friend. The bird took flight, banging into the windows and shitting all over the place. Kenny almost hit a few parked cars and cussed and almost shit on himself.

I've saved the monkey tale for last. This made the front page of the *Chicago Sun Times* absent these details.

Bob and Harold were about to get off shift when Del the dispatcher asked if they would take a quick one on the way in. They consented, and they were sent to an address in Canaryville to check on an intruder in a lady's garden. The lady met them in front and told them, "He's in my backyard ruining my cucumbers."

They, of course, asked, "Who?"

She snapped, "That damn monkey."

They laughed a bit and said they'd take a look. Sure enough, there was a monkey in the garden, a ring-tailed monkey.

Not really wanting to catch the monkey, they mused out loud in front of the lady about what they could do. Harold mumbled, "Gee, if we only had a monkey net."

Her eyes lit up and she said, "I've got a fishing net in the basement. You could use that."

Bob just wanted to go home. He said, "Oh, I don't think so, ma'am. He'd probably tear a fishing net to shreds. We really need a monkey net."

"I don't care about the damn net. I just want that monkey outta here. I'll go get it."

She wasn't about to take no for an answer and rushed to the basement. Returning, she thrust her arms out, handing the boys the net.

They shrugged and took it. None too carefully they "snuck" up on the dining primate, hoping it would bolt. It didn't seem too concerned about being netted. Taking him to the car they figured they would put him in a dog cage in the station. He was fine till they got to the station and were about to bring him in. He jumped from the net and scooted under the car seat.

They had been wondering what type of radio code to give the dispatcher for recovering a malicious monkey, and when he took refuge under the front seat they decided on a 5-E, Edward.* Without even trying, they were going to stick it to their favorite marks again.

They turned over the keys to the unsuspecting, you guessed it, Kenny and Wally.

Right out of the box Kenny and Wally got a traffic accident call on the Damen overpass, a ten-block stretch that rose above trucking companies and railroad tracks built to relieve rush-hour traffic.

---

*5-Edward, an alphanumeric radio code that signifies: "Disturbance, other, perpetrator gone on police arrival."

Still hiding under the seat, the monkey must have been shaken by the change in the angle of the floor when the car ascended the hill of the overpass. He screeched, left his hiding place, and hopped on the dashboard. Both coppers screamed. Kenny hit the brakes, and as the car was fishtailing to a stop, both were opening their doors to bail out. This was in the days when our radios were still attached to the dashboard. Wally had the presence of mind to grab the mike on his way out. He slammed the door on the cord.

Both looked at the monkey inside, then at each other, and in unison exclaimed, "Those dirty sons of bitches."

Unfortunately, the Channel 7 news truck was stopped next to them.

It was about 5:10 P.M. Harold was sitting down to supper. The phone rang. Bob's voice was on the other end saying, "Harold, when the phone rings again, don't pick it up. You got that? Don't pick the damn phone up."

"Bob, what the hell are you talking about?"

"You'll see, Harold. You'll see on the Channel 7 ten o'clock news." The phone went dead.

Harold called back. It rang and rang. Bob was taking his own advice.

Sitting back down to supper, his wife knew something was awry, and she asked what the call was all about.

Harold could only say that he had to watch the news at ten.

Many of us know that sick feeling of waiting to see something you said or did on the news and not knowing how they'll spin it. It sucks your energy as you wait for the worst.

This happened in the days before everyone had answering machines and little jacks that easily disconnect the phone. Harold forbade his family from answering. He stared at the phone when it rang. His family stared at him.

At ten all eyes were glued to Channel 7 *Eyewitness News*. The lead story showed the ring-tailed monkey on the dash of Beat 907's car, backlit by the setting sun. Interviews with Kenny and Wally made them sound like Clinton's crew or Sergeant Shultz from *Hogan's Heroes.* "I know nothing!"

Harold and his wife roared. After the news Harold tried calling Bob again. The phone just rang and rang and rang.

Little Johnny on the Front Porch

BY CLINT W. McKEAN

Sworn Officer, Hobbs PD, seven years.

had been on patrol on my own for about two years. I was in the phase of career where I wasn't a rookie anymore, and I thought I already knew just about everything there was to know about law enforcement. I had gotten past the initial shock of seeing my first dead person, homicide victim, child abuse case, and so on. I had made it through all of these situations and thought I was pretty "hard." I had survived my first fight, high-speed pursuit, drug raid, and ass-chewing from my lieutenant. You hear stories of how police officers lose sleep and have to seek counseling due to the trauma and stress of the job. I had made it through all of this and never felt depression, anger, or sleeplessness. You had to be hard to be a police officer, and the guys who experienced those things were just not cut out for the job. This was my considered opinion after my first two years.

My perception of the job and maybe more importantly my perception of myself was about to change.

It was a nice summer evening in August and I was working the swing shift (two to ten P.M.). It had been uneventful, and I was heading home for my lunch break. A call from the dispatcher came over the radio of a female down, unconscious and not breathing. I was only about two blocks from the address. All I could think was,

"Damn it. I'm going to miss my lunch break again." It was probably some elderly lady who had passed away and I was going to catch another report and be stuck on scene all night waiting for the coroner to show up. It was my job, though, and I knew this is what I had signed up for, so I responded.

I beat the paramedics to the scene by several minutes. For a cop, this is not always ideal. Sometimes you roll up into a situation that you're not capable of handling, because you do not have the medical expertise needed. You carry a gun and not a trauma kit. Applying pressure to a bleeding wound or starting CPR is just about all you are trained to do as a police officer.

When I rolled up on this scene it was different. The only thing I saw was a little boy—we'll call him "Johnny." Johnny was sitting on the front porch with his face in his hands. Johnny was nine years old and looked to be your typical little boy, dirty blue jeans and sweaty hair, a bicycle sitting next to him. I assumed that Johnny's grandfather or grandmother had passed away. As an inexperienced cop you seem to jump to conclusions and think you have it figured out before you even have any of the facts. In your mind you think you know everything because you made it past rookie year. All Johnny could tell me was that it was all his fault. Over and over again Johnny kept saying it was his fault. "I knew I shouldn't have left her and went outside to ride my bike." I wasn't real sure what I had on my hands at this point and asked Johnny where she was. Johnny still crying and without lifting his head pointed in the front door of the house. In the master bedroom I found a thirty-year-old woman hanging lifeless from the ceiling fan with a rope around her neck. It was apparent that she was dead.

I returned to Johnny on the front porch. He was still sitting and crying in his hands. I wanted to comfort him, but I needed to find out if this was suicide or homicide or if the woman was even his mother. I placed my hand on Johnny's back and asked him what had happened. His mother's boyfriend called on the telephone and broke up with her, Johnny said. His mother was very upset and he just wanted to get out of the house, so he went outside to ride his bicycle for a while until his mom calmed down. I'll never forget Johnny's anger at himself as he shouted at me, "I knew I shouldn't have left her alone. I should have stayed with her. She was crying!"

I had never been so speechless in my entire life. I knew there was nothing I could say or do that would provide comfort or relief to Johnny at this point. As a police officer you always think that you have the answers and will be able to provide help to a child in time of need, but I had nothing in my arsenal to help Johnny with his pain.

Johnny was blaming himself for the selfishness and death of his mother. I'm not one to preach, but for a mother to kill herself and leave that sight and responsibility for her son to live and deal with is unconscionable.

Once the dust had settled and things were winding down, I began to feel something I had never felt up to this point in my career. I was totally helpless. What could I do? What could I say? The hard, terrible answer was: Nothing. I could only watch.

I'll never forget Johnny sitting in the backseat of the detective's unmarked cruiser. No family could be located for the boy, and the only thing we had was a counselor from the state. The counselor was trying to help Johnny, but his face was turned away from her with the deepest, blankest stare I had ever seen. I will never forget his face with the mud created from the tears running down his dirty little cheeks. On the inside I was crying, but I had to be "hard" around my peers. In some ways, I have never stopped crying for Johnny on the inside; I have never forgotten that I'm not a god, that I don't have all the answers.

In this one night on the job I learned more about life and myself than I had in the previous two years of my career, or probably any of the years that followed. Throughout my career in law enforcement I was involved in homicide investigations, narcotics investigations, numerous high-speed chases, and two officer-involved shootings, but none of it had the impact on my heart as the night that I found little Johnny sitting on the porch with his tear-soaked face in his hands blaming himself for his mother's senseless death.

All of the training had not prepared me for this. I remember sitting in those critical incident stress classes they give you in the academy thinking, *This is ridiculous. Why don't they just teach us what we need and let us out on the street?* Now I was thinking maybe I should have paid a little more attention. I lost sleep for the first time since becoming a cop. I started to wonder whether I was just one of those "soft guys" who wasn't cut out for the job. Surely that wasn't possible. This reaction must be normal. Just go home, have a few beers, and it will all go away.

Now I know that this is why cops struggle with alcoholism at an alarmingly high rate. Too often we can't admit that something bothered us, got us down, made us helpless. We don't want to be looked upon as soft by the other officers, and it's so hard to admit that something is eating away at our mind and heart and soul. So we drown our feelings in a bottle.

I was no different. I had to take a hard look at myself and my career. I had to face the fact that being tough and capable meant doing my level best, facing my fears and uncertainties honestly. It was a tough process, and scary, too.

None of the emotions I was feeling, though, would ever compare to what little Johnny would endure for the rest of his life. I often think of him, of where he is and what has become of him.

I will have Johnny sitting on the porch with his face in his hands engraved in my memory forever.

Let Me Tell You a True Story

LINE OF DUTY

BY ROBERT V. TREVINO

Sworn Officer, Clinton PD, thirteen years.

Let me tell you a true story.

I had only been a police officer for ten months and I was working the midnight shift on March 19, 1994, a very cold and icy Saturday night. Suddenly I heard the fire tones go off for Hudson Fire/Rescue for an accident involving a car versus tree. I informed our Central Dispatch that I would be en route to assist, as this was just outside our city, and I knew I was closer than the county unit.

The roads had gotten slick with black ice. You could say my patrol car was like a giant skate on a huge rink. I would guess if you went over 35 mph, on the normally posted 55-mph country road, you were going too fast. When I arrived, a few people were trying to open the driver's-side door. As I jumped out of the patrol car I nearly slipped face-first on the icy roadway.

My attention immediately went to the passenger who was trapped in the car. The entire passenger side was crushed inward, and it was quite apparent the passenger would have to be extricated from the vehicle. A man was holding a towel to the back of the passenger's head, and I saw his towel was drenched in dark blood. I leaned into the vehicle and tried to comfort the young female who was obviously scared and trying to hold back her tears. I told her the fire department was coming and they would get her out. I asked her what her name was and she told me she didn't know. There was a girl behind the wheel and she appeared to be unharmed. Thank God both girls had their seat belts on or they would have been calling a coroner to the scene instead of the fire department.

I remember someone saying the two girls were local girls from Hudson and had been in the high school play that evening. I immediately flashed back to my high school days, thinking they had so much ahead of them. I told the man with the towel that I would hold it and he left for his nearby home to get another towel. I was now alone next to the female passenger, and I took her right hand and told her she was going to be fine. I remember her looking at me with these big blue eyes. She had glass fragments all over his face, neck, and arms. She also had knocked out her two front teeth and was bleeding from her mouth. I was scared for her as she could not remember her name and didn't know how she got in the crash. The young girl said she had pain all over. I'll never forget her fear as she squeezed my hand and asked me if she was going to be okay. I knew she was seriously injured because the passenger side had taken all the impact in the crash up against the tree and was crushed in about one and a half feet.

It seemed like an eternity for the fire department to arrive on scene. They had to drive slowly on the icy country roads. I kept assuring both girls that they would get through this. I informed the fire department of the passenger's injuries to the back of her head and they requested an advanced ambulance unit be dispatched because of the severity of the injuries the passenger had sustained. I continued to hold the girl's hand but was asked to step back as they were going to use the Jaws of Life to remove the passenger door. I stepped back and took a final look into the passenger's eyes and told her to be strong.

The female driver was removed without incident and she was transported by ambulance to Bixby Hospital in Adrian, Michigan, as they continued to work on the passenger side. Once out of the vehicle, they placed the passenger in the advanced ambulance and transported her to Bixby Hospital, some seventeen miles away on the icy roads.

One of the firemen walked up to me and said the passenger was his niece and he needed a ride back into Hudson so he could notify her dad of the crash. When I returned, I assisted the County Sheriff unit with the crash investigation. The deputy in charge was Randy Kelly, and he said there was no sign of alcohol and it appeared the vehicle had slid on the black ice while attempting to slow to make a right turn at the intersection.

Afterward I cleared the scene and went to the fire department to clean up and see if anyone had heard how the two girls were doing. I talked with Fire Chief Terry Camp. He said the driver was doing fine, but the passenger was his cousin, and they lost her twice on the way to the hospital; luckily, they revived her both times. She was so bad they didn't think she would make it through the night. Med Flight, an air ambulance was contacted, as they had decided to airlift her to St. Joseph's Hospital (a level-one trauma center) in Ann Arbor. Terry said the helicopter landed and when they went to load her up it would not start. They ended up calling in a different helicopter, Life Flight, out of St. Vincent's Hospital in Toledo, Ohio, and that one transported her there.

Two months later, on May 15, 1994, I got a chance to again meet the wonderful person who had been in the passenger seat. I was on duty in Hudson and stopped a black Pontiac Fiero for a minor plate violation. After talking with the woman driver and the passenger, who was her daughter, I realized that the daughter was the passenger in the March 19 accident on Beecher Road. I told them I was there at the accident and I had held her daughter's hand until the fire department told me to step back. The mother explained this was the first time her daughter had been out since the crash and she would most likely not even remember talking with me today, as she was suffering from short-term memory loss. I told them I would never forget them and their story. Before they drove off I walked over to the passenger side and I held the young girl's hand. It was beautifully soft and warm. I asked her if she remembered me from the crash and she just smiled at me with these big blue eyes. The mother said her name was Jessi Hepker and her daughter's name was Jennifer.

On February 19, 1995, I was getting fuel at the Shell gas station. I looked up into the eyes of a very beautiful young woman. Jennifer had grown up. I was in awe. The first words out of my mouth were, "Boy, have you matured!" Jennifer smiled and her face got beet red as she turned in embarrassment. That young girl had become a very attractive young lady, and I wanted to know her better, even though I was twenty-five and she was only seventeen.

Weeks later I was on my way home from work, and I decided to stop by and say hi to Jennifer. She told me of her life after the crash. While on Life Flight's helicopter, her heart had stopped beating and they had to do CPR on her twice to get her back. In doing so they broke many of her ribs. She ended up staying in St. Vincent's Hospital intensive care unit as she recovered from her injuries. Jennifer said she had major head trauma from hitting the door in the crash, she crushed her pelvis and broke her pubic bone in two places, broke her right hip, broke her right wrist, broke her collarbone in a few places, knocked her two front teeth out, had a black eye, and had many other severely bruised areas on her body. Jennifer explained her head trauma was the worst problem and she had short-term memory loss. She said her head ached from time to time and the doctors had started to put injections into the back of her head to help reduce the swelling. She was studying with a tutor from school because she planned on graduating in June, on time. She was stubborn and courageous; I found it, and her, very attractive. We casually dated, but due to her age it was very low-key.

In June, after Jennifer turned eighteen and graduated from high school, I asked her to move into an apartment with me in Hudson. It all seemed so right; she was a very mature young lady, and I really cared about her in a special and spiritual way. I'm not sure if it was because I was there when she almost died, but I felt very close to her. Soon, I knew that Jennifer was everything I could have asked for in a woman; she had a great sense of humor, she was so damn cute, she had a funny laugh, her energy was tremendous—and she loved eating tacos. She wore these great dark cowboy boots and blue jeans. Standing at five feet eight inches, this blond, blue-eyed young woman with the brightest smile was my girl.

We dated from that June until December 1995 when I asked her to marry me, and she said yes. It was a bit odd having a fiancée who was seven years younger, but Jennifer was up to the task. Jen, as I called her now, had told me her doctors explained to her she might not be able to have children due to the crash. I told her it didn't matter to me as she was going to be my wife and we would get through it. September 7, 1996, we were united in marriage in the Catholic church where I had grown up in Adrian.

In July 1998 our dream came true. Our daughter, Paige, was born via C-section. This was the safest way for Jen's body to be able to handle the delivery. In March of 2000, our son Payton, who was also a C-section, arrived. Both kids have grown up to be healthy, though Jen still deals with many heath issues stemming from the crash. In December 2003, Jen had a pacemaker implanted to help regulate her heart rate and she has severe arthritis.

I don't know if God makes all dreams come true, but I had asked for someone special to come into my life who could love me and understand me as a police officer. Jen was that angel, and I am so thankful we are husband and wife and have a beautiful family together.

There are still times when we pass by that intersection where the crash took place. Our kids usually smile at us. They know the story of how mom and dad met. They have since taken down that tree the car crashed into, but that will never take away my memory of how I met my wife on duty that cold and icy March night in 1994.

Just So You Know

LINE OF DUTY

BY MATT WALZ

Constable, Saskatoon Police Service, two-and-a-half years.

It was New Year's Eve, 2005. I was a young police officer, twenty-three to be exact, and fresh out of field training. So fresh, actually, that this was my first "block," or set of four days on my own, and I had yet to be assigned a partner.

The platoon was shorthanded, just like I'm sure most are on New Year's Eve, and we had an odd number of officers. For that reason I was assigned to work with an acting sergeant I'll call Ken. Ken had nine years of policing under his belt, and was fairly junior to be an acting sergeant, but he was and still is one of the best police officers I have ever had the opportunity to see in action. Ken was fit, strong, smart, intuitive, charismatic, and, most of all, compassionate. He could handle just about any situation with relative ease and exit that situation having achieved whatever the objective may have been: Arrest the bad guy, save the good guy, calm the family, secure the evidence, or simply take the report.

The night started out relatively uneventfully, with Ken driving and me in the passenger seat, barely able to contain my excitement at my first night shift out of training, my first New Year's Eve, my first chance to make a good impression, and with one of the officers I most respected.

It wasn't long until the drunks started to cause problems, and the "drunker" it got, the busier it got. We made our way through the streets of Saskatoon from domestic incident to bar fight to stabbing to medical emergency call, and then it began to snow. We raced through the slick streets as I took it all in; every call I watched and learned from Ken. I strove to be like him and other excellent officers I had worked with: a solid rock of unwavering authority, decisiveness, and compassion in all situations. On the way to each call I would visualize my reactions to the call, trying to apply all that I had learnt in the past ten months and all that I learned that night. Scenarios were running through my head faster than I could resolve them, but somehow I made it through each call unscathed, with a pat on the back for a job well done.

As midnight approached it occurred to me, strangely for the first time, that I wouldn't be celebrating New Year's Eve this time around. I thought of all my friends. They were, at this moment, having a great time at a great party, a bunch of people in their early twenties enjoying life and looking forward to many more New Year's like this one. I chuckled to myself thinking of their antics and thought, I look forward to many more like this one as well.

About thirty minutes before midnight, Ken and I received a different kind of call. It was from the Royal Canadian Mounted Police (our provincial police): There had been a fatal traffic accident just outside Saskatoon and two twenty-two-year-old males had been killed. The father of one of those males had already been notified, and it was our job to find and notify the parents of the second of the two. We'll refer to him as Johnny.

I felt sorry, of course, for this terrible event, but at this point I didn't know Johnny, or his family, and therefore it was not unlike the average person reading of the death of a young man or woman in the newspaper the next day: You are saddened, but, okay, not really touched by the event. I felt that I could face this call easily, I had my training on what to say and what not to, and I had Ken. It was only then I turned to see the lump in Ken's throat.

Ken coughed, then turned to me, and began going over all of the things I had learned in training about these kinds of calls as we weaved through the streets toward Johnny's address. As we pulled up to the house, Ken turned to me and said one last thing: "Boy, I'm glad that you are working with me tonight, Matt, but just so you know, this is going to stay with you forever."

I followed Ken up the walkway and noticed that ours were the only fresh footprints in the snow. I was hopeful at that moment that maybe, just maybe, no one was home, that the morning shift could notify the parents. I stood to the side and slightly behind Ken as he rang the doorbell and knocked several times: No answer. Maybe they really weren't home. After some time had passed and we had received no answer, Ken and I trudged back to the car, both of us breathing a sigh of relief. As I turned to get in the car, I saw a light come on in the house, and I watched through the picture window as a couple entered through the back door, obviously from a party, and made their way up the stairs. For a fleeting second I thought of not saying anything, of just letting Ken drive away, of letting someone else take care of it. But that just wasn't in me; we were the ones they called. I alerted Ken and we made our way back up the walk.

We were met at the door by Johnny's mother, and I could see the apprehension in her eyes. We entered a side room. Ken asked if she could call her husband in and if she wanted to sit down. I watched her eyes change quickly from apprehension to fear to panic as they darted between Ken and me, trying to ascertain some gleam of hope that this wasn't what she thought it was.

Johnny's father entered the room and I saw the same look in his eyes, and also the concern for his wife, who was already in break-down mode. Ken turned to them both and told them in a way that could lead to no confusion, false hope, or misinterpretation: "I am sorry to tell you, but there was an accident on the highway tonight and your son Johnny was killed." There is no mistaking the insurmountable amount of pain accompanied by the scream of utter anguish that came from Johnny's mother. I watched, helpless, as the pain tore her apart, as she cried, and screamed in agony, yelled at us, and God, called us liars, went to hit us and instead struck anything in her path, struggled to breathe or remain standing, and finally collapsed on her knees in tears in the dining room not far from a picture of her now dead son.

We remained there for what seemed like forever, trying futilely to bring some comfort or help to them. Johnny's father, though not much better off than his wife, was eventually able to thank us and let us know that we could go. Ken and I left, got back in to our car, and moved on to the next call. It was twelve-o-five; New Year's had come and passed.

I look back on that night and realize that I learned more on that shift than I did or have on any other. I also learned more on that call than I did or have on any other. I look back and realize that I now understand that lump in Ken's throat and the warning he gave me. He knew that he was on his way to add another set of faces to his dreams and nightmares, but most of all, he knew I would be adding my first. I know that some years from now I will be with some fresh-out-of-training officer on my way to his or her first call of this sort and that I will get a lump in my throat realizing that he or she is going to remember with unmistakable detail the house, the walk to the door, the look in their eyes, the agony in their voices, the finest details of their faces, and, lastly, the warning I will give them before we go in: "Just so you know, this is going to stay with you forever."

Part of the Job

THE BEAT

BY MICHAEL J. WARDEN

Sworn Officer, Department of Defense Police, eight years.

If you're not a cop, it's somewhat difficult to understand what it feels like. Those of you who are, or were, know exactly what I mean.

I had worked at the Long Beach Naval Shipyard as a civilian police officer for just about eighteen months without too many unusual incidents. That quickly changed when I became sergeant. I knew this was quite an accomplishment in such a short time, and my wife was very proud of me. However, cops are always suspicious of others, even other cops. My rapid promotion caused excessive tension among my squad. You cannot imagine the friction that it caused with the cops who were my friends.

Close friends now treated me as if I had the plague. It also meant that the upper management expected me to act accordingly. I didn't have any problems doing my job, but I did lose a couple of friends, or rather they decided they didn't trust me. But I put up with it. It was part of the job.

It wasn't too long before the only lieutenant we had for our department was going out on a medical leave. We didn't have anyone else who could do his job and I figured the Chief was going to give it to one of the military criminal investigators who worked in our office. However, that proved wrong. He tossed the lieutenant bars to me and said, "Put these on, you're now in charge of the department." I didn't know whether to be happy, throw up on his desk, or take a couple of days off. I had only been the sergeant now for about eight months, so you can imagine how that went over with the rest of the department.

It was a lot to handle. More, even, than when I became sergeant. The officers treated me in a different way than when I was their sergeant. I didn't think it mattered much to me, but I was taking out my frustrations at home. Unfortunately, this can be a part of the job. Not a real good thing to do in any marriage, let alone one that is less than three years old. Fortunately for me, I have a remarkably understanding wife. Mind you, we had our skirmishes, but she stood by me, and still does almost twenty years later.

The tensions really took their toll. I finally had enough, so I decided it was time to move on from the federal government and went to work for the Irvine Police Department as a reserve police officer while I continued pursuing my degree in architecture.

It was the last week of my tour of duty at the shipyard that left an everlasting impression on me. Although I have seen many fatal accidents in my career, this particular one hit home. I guess I was really stressed to the max, too.

It was about the end of my shift and the radio crackled with a call from the dispatcher to respond to a 902T, which is an "unknown injury traffic accident." The location was on the highway just outside the base gates. Our jurisdiction and patrol responsibilities, although mainly on the military base, also encompassed any area directly surrounding the outside of the base.

It always seems to happen at the end of the shift, doesn't it? Of course, this call meant I would be there at least another four or five hours depending upon the severity of the accident. I called home to let my wife know I would be late, again. She said she understood, but I could tell by the tone of her voice that she was not happy. I activated my lights and siren, zigzagging my way around the traffic. Responding Code Three with the siren blaring and the unknown situation of the accident my adrenaline was pumping wildly through my veins. I took a couple of deep breaths and tried to calm myself down as I approached the accident scene. Even though I had responded to many accidents, the initial scene always seems surreal.

At this particular accident, I saw a Lincoln Continental sedan that was totally smashed into the front of a semi, steam coming up from the boiling radiator as it spewed onto the hot engine.

My patrol car skidded to a stop directly in front of the wrecked vehicles and I jumped out to check on any injuries to the people involved. The driver of the semi had a little blood trickling down his forehead, but seemed to be okay as he stood in front of his rig. I ran over to check the driver in the Lincoln.

Now this was a big car with a long front end, but it was completely smashed together into the front end of the big rig, just like a tin can. The driver's body was pinned against the steering wheel and the front end of the car was so smashed the car door was jammed.

I reached inside to see if I could move the steering wheel as I called out to the driver, but he was desperately gasping for air, and I could tell he was in no real condition to talk. I advised dispatch that I needed a rescue squad and paramedics on scene right away. Cars were slowing for the accident as people craned their necks to try to get a peek at the gore. I kept talking to the man, trying to reassure him help was on the way. I was not concerned with why or how the accident happened at that particular moment. Normally I would have tried to contain the scene after I knew the victims were stable, and directed traffic around the accident. Standard procedure would have me setting up flares and such if I was not able to rescue the victims myself. This time, my main concern was for the victim. I wanted to make sure he was not alone. You just learn to recognize all the signs, and I knew this accident was that bad and he was not going to make it. It's tough, but it's a part of the job.

You're trained in the academy so that you don't become emotionally attached to the people you come in contact with while you do your job. It's not that easy, even after years of experience—after all, we are human, and we do have feelings.

I could hear the rescue squad rolling my way. "Hey, mister you're going to be okay, help's on the way," I kept telling him. He was still gasping desperately, and looked at me, his eyes pleading for help.

A friend of mine, Collin Bell, was a fireman-paramedic; he was on duty that day and happened to respond to this accident.

"Breathe, mister, just try to breathe," I said.

Collin jumped out of his rig, grabbed his equipment and ran over to the driver's side of the Lincoln. We did not exchange small talk because time was critical; however, I did tell Collin what I knew of the condition of the victim in the car. Collin looked back up at me without saying anything. The look in his eyes told me everything I needed to know.

They covered the victim so that he wouldn't receive any additional injuries as they attempted to extricate him from the mangled wreck. The rescue squad used the Jaws of Life to try to extract the victim, who was barely breathing on his own. They attached the chain to the steering wheel so they could pull it off his chest. I did something I had not ever done before; I held his hand while they did this so he wasn't alone. The victim's eyes had been closed, but when we told him we were going to try to get him out, his eyes opened and locked on to mine. He needed me to do something for him, to save him, but all I could do was hold his hand.

As they started to pull the steering wheel away, the victim screamed out in pain, and what was probably his last breath. His hand squeezed mine with incredible pressure, then his hand went limp and he quit moving. I saw the light go out of his eyes forever. Collin was right there and they pulled the victim from the car to begin emergency procedures to try to keep him alive.

I looked down at my hands and noticed they were covered in blood. I saw the blood on my wedding band and quickly wiped it off.

I looked down at the victim; his eyes were open and he wasn't breathing. I looked at his hands and noticed he, too, was wearing a wedding band. The victim appeared to be in his mid to late seventies, he was well dressed, and had been driving a nice car. He was a husband, probably a father, maybe even a grandfather to someone.

I finished my investigation at the accident scene and went back to the station to work on the report and make the call to his family. Notifications to the next of kin were probably one of the most difficult parts of my job, but, after all, this is part of the job.

Collin did his best that day to save this unknown man. I did my job, didn't I? Hey, it was out of my hands. God had made the choice that day, and, unfortunately, we could not do anything differently that would have helped save him.

I called my wife and told her not to cook, that I'd take her to dinner. After I hung up, I looked at my wedding band and knew my victim would not be going home to his wife for dinner tonight.

I got home and walked in the house, grabbed ahold of my wife and started crying. She didn't say anything and just hugged me back. We never made it out to dinner that night. I told her everything. I always did. I still do. She never complained, and assured me I was doing what I had always dreamed of doing. I *did* make a difference. I needed to hear that. Losing someone who depended on you to save them is part of the job, too.

The alarm went off at 4:30 next morning and I showered to get ready to go to work. I looked at my wedding band and knew I had made the right choice.

Law enforcement is really the same no matter where you work. A big-city agency, small-town sheriff, or large government, we all do the same job day after day, week after week, and sometimes for many years.

It takes a significant toll on you mentally and physically. You always have to show the brave face. Be above reproach. Do no wrong, as you are the keeper of the law. Unfortunately, the profession has one of the highest divorce rates, and nearly as many suicides. There's a tremendous amount of stress involved. You have to be strong, and make all the hard decisions in an instant. You have to juggle all that with the normal stresses of working with other human beings, your fellow officers.

I climbed into my patrol car that morning, headed out to my beat for the day, and got my first call, another unknown injury traffic accident . . . Well, after all, it's just part of the job.

Just Another Car Stop

DEADLY FORCE

BY DAVID R. DeKAY

Sworn Officer, Waverly PD, New York, eighteen years.

I am thirty-nine years old. I am married and have three children and live in a small village called Waverly, New York, which is located in the Southern Tier of New York State. I am employed by the Village of Waverly Police Department, a ten-officer department. I have about eighteen years on the job now. Waverly, with a population of just four thousand, is generally pretty quiet. It's a nice place to live and not as dangerous as some bigger towns and cities. Usually.

But being a police officer is always potentially dangerous. You can never get careless or sloppy.

It all started on September 18, 2000. I had worked the day shift from eight A.M. to four P.M. I normally work the evening shift, but I had switched shifts with another officer that day. I started my day out patrolling and following up with investigations. Nothing too complicated. I was enjoying the nice sunny day in Indian summer, looking forward to the beginning of a week's vacation after my shift ended.

It was three P.M.—just an hour before my shift ended. Just an hour until I could kick back and relax. The first thing I was going to do was take a seat in the backyard, open a beer, and think about how I was going to spend the seven days.

In the middle of this pleasant reverie, I observed a male subject that I knew was driving on a suspended driver's license. It wasn't much of a big deal really. I followed him, pulled alongside, and waved at him to pull over to the curb. Maybe I could get this over with quickly and get on home.

He looked me with a wild expression on his face and began to slow up. Suddenly he screamed a curse and hit the gas and the pursuit started. I can tell you I was pretty surprised—and pretty angry, too. I just knew, right then, that it could only get more complicated. And it did. When the pursuit started, the fleeing suspect was going so fast he almost lost control of the car. He swerved into oncoming traffic and almost caused several head-on accidents. The suspect then struck a curb, which blew out his right front tire. But that hardly even slowed him down. By this time, a second officer from my department was behind me, and we continued the pursuit at increasingly reckless speeds for about eleven miles outside of Waverly.

During the pursuit, this idiot sped by several school buses that were letting children off, putting citizens and children in grave danger. That got me steamed. Halfway through the pursuit, my chief terminated the pursuit. We had already identified the driver of the vehicle and the risk of some innocent bystander getting killed was becoming too much of a risk. I disengaged my lights and siren at that point, but I continued to follow the suspect at a safe distance. I felt an obligation and my duty to follow this suspect and have him in constant sight until other patrol units arrived from other agencies. This guy didn't seem to care that he was going to kill someone. I had stopped thinking about my vacation. I wanted this guy.

As I was following the suspect, my backup officer was behind me most of the way. He stopped, however, to put out a couple of fires along the way—sparks from the suspect's car rim had started grass fires all along the roadway.

I didn't think about how dangerous this jerk was. I didn't think about the fact that I had no backup. The guy was dangerous. It was my job to stop him. The suspect sped into a highway construction site where there were numerous construction workers. At that time, I don't think either of us realized that the road came to a dead end. When he saw he could go no further and I was blocking the road behind him, the suspect stopped his vehicle. He just sat there. His hands were on the wheel. He didn't seem to have a weapon so I got out of my vehicle with my weapon drawn and ran up to the driver's side of the vehicle. I ordered the suspect to get out of the car and get onto the ground with his arms spread out. The suspect didn't even look at me. He put his vehicle in reverse and stepped on the gas and the front end of the vehicle swung around and knocked me to the ground.

I got up and the suspect drove directly at me. I couldn't get out of the way in time; he just came on too fast. The suspect struck me head-on. I flew up onto the hood of the vehicle with my weapon still in my hand. I yelled at the suspect to stop, and I had my weapon pointed at him through the windshield. When the suspect began to speed up, I fired one round through the windshield. That's when I was thrown from the vehicle onto the ground. The SOB turned and started to drive off, so I fired another round at the vehicle as it drove away. I then radioed for help as numerous construction workers were helping me to my feet. I didn't seem to be hurt too badly. Nothing was broken, I thought. Frankly, I just wasn't concerned about myself. I wanted to nail this suspect.

I ran back to my patrol vehicle and went after the suspect again and found that the vehicle had gone through some bushes and into a yard and stopped about a hundred yards away. I ran up to the vehicle to find the suspect slumped over in the driver's seat. I pulled the suspect out of the vehicle and tried to provide medical treatment and found that I had shot the suspect through the center of his chest. He was dead. Shortly after that, other police agencies were arriving on the scene.

I was transported to a local hospital to be treated for minor injuries and released that night. The New York State Police did the investigation of my shooting and later my case went to grand jury, where I was cleared of any wrongdoing and found justified in my shooting incident.

Whether you live in a large city or a small town, anything can happen in this job. At any time, anything can happen. There is no such thing as a simple vehicle stop. *Nothing* about this job is ever simple. Ever.

If you remember that, you stay safe.

Jesse: A Case Study in Sexual Assault

LINE OF DUTY

BY TRINKA PORRATA

Sworn Officer Los Angeles PD, retired after twenty-five years.

The young woman moved confidently through the early morning chill, oblivious to the traffic and other people around her, caught up in thoughts of her upcoming math test. Life was just fine—her boyfriend, her job and school, her conservative existence in a religious organization's dormitory for young ladies.

Suddenly the tall, thin black man leaped from his parked car, grabbed her, and quickly forced her inside. She wrestled, screamed, and pounded the horn. Assistance came in the form of a hospital security guard who challenged the thin man, withstood his threats of karate violence, and wrote down the license number as the assailant sped away.

It was all over so quickly. A scary interruption in her life. A bit of a delay while making a police report, an explanation for being late to school, and life was pretty much back to normal.

As police reports go, it wasn't much. Attempted kidnap, briefly and casually written. But it did contain that precious license number that for once didn't belong to a stolen car, long since abandoned.

Forget it, my partner insisted. It was nothing. The District Attorney's Office wouldn't be interested. The most I could get was a misdemeanor battery charge from the city attorney, he said.

I would remain on loan from uniformed patrol to the rape investigation team only a few more weeks and, heaven knows, we had two major rapists working our area and (even more important to the bureaucracy) tons of overdue follow-up reports to be made for an upcoming audit.

But something about this "nothing" attempted kidnap case captured me, making it my obsession during my brief investigative loan. The car was registered to a man named Jesse. It would take just a few moments. Run the name for driver's license information; run the name and birth date for a criminal record. After all, criminals do sometimes caper in their own cars.

Bingo. Numerous prior arrests for kidnap and rape or attempted rape, with a few car thefts, and more, thrown in along the way. There was a gap of over five years, then one arrest for assault and another year silent on his record. I ordered a booking photo from his last arrest and began to work frantically on my pile of other cases while I waited for it to arrive. But I couldn't wait. I stumbled through the delays and transfers calling the various police departments involved in his past, trying to locate crime reports, now six years old, hard to find and even harder to read from the blurred copies.

Each case was virtually identical. Each time he had accosted the girl on the sidewalk or parking lot, and each time he had dragged her into a car—either his or hers.

As rapists go, he wasn't highly successful. Half of his victims had been spared the ultimate indignity. Whatever the problems were that drove him to rape also prevented him from leaping confidently into it.

When his photograph arrived, I stared long and hard at his odd, light eyes, the expression on his face.

Great care is required in preparing a photo lineup of six pictures to show a victim so that it will pass the court's test of fairness. Each subject has to approximate the victim's description so that the possible suspect won't stand out like a sore thumb.

My victim looked at it only two seconds, pointed to Jesse, and shuddered. "His eyes. I can't forget those awful eyes." My security guard witness studied the photos, giving proper respect to each, and stated emphatically, "There's no doubt about it; that's him. I couldn't forget those eyes."

Jesse had been imprisoned for the various assaults and thefts in one trial with all pending cases combined. He had done more than five years in prison, had been paroled, and survived only a month before threatening his wife with a shotgun and getting thrown back in for a year's parole violation. He had been paroled again, just seven days before the assault on my victim. He was now living with his wife and infant son (the product of his one month of freedom the year before) in an adjacent division.

Armed with a special arrest warrant, allowing me to arrest him in his own home, we approached the house.

The car was there and a tow truck was ready to take it away for us. I also had a warrant to seize it and search every inch of it. His description and car matched another kidnap-rape so perfectly that I was sure we had him on that one, too. But that, unfortunately, would result in nothing decisive. Her fractured jaw wired shut, this victim would describe his car but with two details significantly different. And she would pick suspects from the photo lineup and live lineup at the county jail most similar in every detail to Jesse, without really looking at or commenting on him.

That case fell by the wayside later, leaving me with the personal conviction, which I never quite gave up, that she was too terrified to identify him.

The man with the eyes of violence opened the door at my knock. The smile faded instantly and the new velour bathrobe must have suddenly become overly warm as his forehead broke into a sweat. I dangled the warrant in his face and gave him the good news. He asked only that he be allowed to dress. My male partners accompanied him upstairs, leaving me alone with his disbelieving wife.

All 250 pounds of that woman shook with rage. What did I mean *kidnap* and *attempted rape?* This man had slept with her every night since his release, she bellowed. Well, he had gone to sleep with her and woke up with her but admittedly she couldn't account for every moment in between, as she, too, had slept. But she *knew* it wasn't possible. Not again.

I thereby resolved that in the future I'd help the suspect dress and let my partners face such wrath. Her desperate grip on her crying son seemed to be all that spared me a physical assault.

The deputy district attorney had been specific in his order to bring the man's wallet along. It hadn't registered as terribly important, but it was an order. At the station, we advised Jesse of his rights under Miranda and gave him his chance to present his side of the story.

He would tell us all, if only we wouldn't tell his wife. Yes, it was true; he had slipped out of the house during the night in question to find a whore in Hollywood. He had found one and had stopped for gas when she grabbed his wallet and ran. Frantically he had cruised the streets looking for her—needing his money and knowing he'd be unable to explain the loss to his wife—and thought he had found her.

Of course, the location he gave for losing her was far beyond walking distance to where he had grabbed my victim, firmly believing, he said, that she was the one with his wallet. As soon as he grabbed her (neglecting the part about her being stuffed inside his car) and just when the security guard approached (disregarding his threats to kill the guard) he realized she wasn't the long lost hooker and willingly let her go.

He paused, and I waited for him to go on, slowly turning in my hand the well-used leather wallet, brimming with his identification and papers. When he failed to continue, I noted, "Jesse, I have your wallet." The sweat was really pouring from his forehead now. Finally he broke the silence and stated weakly, "Well, I saw the right one later and she threw it back to me."

But victory was not to be mine just yet. Before the deputy DA would file this unusual case, I had to have the consent of at least one prior victim to testify against Jesse in order to establish that his intent was to commit rape. Without that, he reminded me, we had only a little old attempted kidnap.

From the standpoint of our justice system, our helpful security guard had been too quick, had interrupted too soon. Good cases are measured by the completion of crimes, by the level of suffering or bloodshed of our victims.

Since my victim had suffered so little, Jesse's prior victims would have to suffer again.

Finding the current addresses and phone numbers of the girls proved easy. Triumphantly, I called the one whose case most resembled mine.

But police reports and court records leave out the human aspects, the gory little details of how one coped, or failed to cope, with the personal assault and the aftermath of a bitter trial. Nowhere did I read how Karen, who was only an attempted rape victim, had been tormented by Jesse's friends, who had possession of her purse, identification, and other personal papers, how she had lost her job, her boyfriend, and even her mental health.

Yes, I knew rape was tragic. It was an evil, painful intrusion into one's most private existence, an unfair robbery of the highest degree. But I had never really examined the long-range effects. My time had come to learn.

Karen had regained her strength and found a new job and a new boyfriend. I cannot express how small I felt when she came unglued over the phone. I apologized, left my name and number, and said I'd never call again.

I stared at that dumb old phone for a portion of eternity before I could dial another victim. The next two were reluctant but agreed to meet the Deputy District Attorney and talk about it, with no commitment about testifying. One step at a time.

Ellen would arrive clutching her Bible. She said simply, "If I hadn't found Him, I'd be in a funny farm right now." Tanya would be our tower of strength, though she insisted she felt more like a "puddle of warm Jell-O."

The Deputy District Attorney would inspire them with the need to put Jesse back in prison for a year or more and thereby spare someone else the suffering they had endured for at least a little longer. It was the best we could do, and we needed them. They would show up for the preliminary trial.

Meanwhile, my forty-eight-hour hold on the suspect, during which I had to file the case or drop the whole matter, had long since expired. Jesse was in jail thanks only to his parole officer, who could hold him seven days pending a report of his alleged violation of parole.

What a patient, trusting man he was. Unable to complete his report until I'd accomplished some sort of action, I know he must have been relieved when I finally called to verify that I'd filed attempted kidnap and attempted rape charges on Jesse. A mere six and one-half days had elapsed.

Police officers, uniformly bitter about the liberal courts that let hard-core criminals walk away from crimes of every degree, are often suspicious of parole officers, who also have a hand in deciding when a criminal sees daylight again. But with Jesse's parole agent around, there's still hope.

Jesse's attorney, with his irritating personality and his unfortunate but distracting stutter, had been annoyed by the delay in filing. He couldn't get copies of the police reports until then, and he was anxious, he said, to contact the victim and get this thing over with. It was, after all, merely a simple case of mistaken identity and he would explain it all and have the victim sign off the case. Did he really believe that? Hadn't he seen the defendant's prior record? I offered to let him read the past cases, but he "didn't have time."

Carefully, I explained to my victim and witness that they might be contacted by the attorney who would offer explanations and possibly even money to drop the case. They had the right to talk to him if they desired to do so. I had to be careful. I wasn't to pressure them on the matter.

I had already told my victim of the search for the other victims and why it was needed to put on an MO trial (to show his "modus operandi," his method of operation). She hesitated, then answered, "Well, I don't think I'm going to talk to him. I guess this case is kind of special. I was really pretty lucky, wasn't I?"

The preliminary trial went smoothly, my victim patiently surviving the defense attorney's attempts to confuse her and reverse her statements. She handled it much better than I would have done, since I have always found it difficult not to react to the absurd statements made by such desperate defense attorneys in the courtroom.

The Deputy District Attorney stated our intentions to call one of the prior victims to the stand to show the suspect's intent, and we waited breathlessly for the judge to decide whether or not he would allow it.

A suspect's prior record as such is not generally admissible in court. This judge didn't need to hear anything more to make his decision, and he had made it clear he was in a hurry to get out early. He listened to the defense attorney's objections and studied the expressions on my face and the Deputy District Attorney beside me.

Though there was no communication before or after, I'm sure he knew our thoughts. If denied in the preliminary, we might have a tougher time getting the testimony admitted in a trial before another judge.

Tanya testified calmly and effectively.

The attorney made a motion to dismiss the entire case as it was a big nothing and we hadn't proved any sexual intentions. The judge merely replied, "Now for what other reason does a man drag a woman off the street? Defendant is held to answer."

Clearly defeated, Jesse would plead guilty on his trial date and hope for a lenient judge at sentencing time. My victim could now blank out this interruption in her life, and the prior victims could move ahead cautiously, wondering how long before they would be called again and be reminded of what they'd never be able to forget anyway. I certainly didn't want to be the one to call them again.

While searching Jesse's car, I had read his letters to his wife, written while in prison, full of promises to be a good father and husband, never to stray again. He would be a different man, he wrote just two weeks before his release. I also read his own notation that the psychiatrists did not want him paroled because of his extremely violent tendencies. I had read his thoughts, seen inside his soul.

Maybe someday I'll pick up my typewriter again, drag my old journalism career out of hiding, and write something about this creature I had come to know so well—well enough to know that those haunting eyes of violence would surface again someday in the photo lineups of other rape investigators and in the nightmares of his victims yet to be.

NOTE: True to form, this suspect indeed was arrested repeatedly after his release on this case for ongoing sexual assaults and various other crimes.

The Men Who Never Leave Your Side

THE FALLEN

BY JERRY D. WOLSEY

Sworn Officer, Sikeston PD, Missouri, two years; Chaffee PD, Missouri, two years; Perry County Sheriff's Department, Missouri, one year four months; Scott County Sheriff's Department, Benton, Missouri, fifteen years active duty; Scott County Sheriff's Reserve Unit, four years; Wolsey Investigative Service, thirteen years.

In law enforcement, you don't forget the men who never leave your side.

On the evening of June 2, 1978, Trooper Jim Froemsdorf and I were preparing to run radar in Perry County, Missouri. I was the traffic safety officer with the Perry County Sheriff's Department, and Jim was with the Missouri State Highway Patrol. Our primary mission was to enforce the 55-mph speed limit, not only on Interstate 55, but also on secondary roads throughout the county. It was a warm summer evening that began uneventfully, as many of our shifts often did.

At that time, there were certain areas of Perry County where the law hadn't been enforced in years. We came to discover that there were quite a few people in those areas who didn't want the law enforced. Our sheriff was a young man by the name of Gerald Pingel. Early in his career, Sheriff Pingel had mounted a campaign against underage drinking in the county. We had a high fatality rate among teenagers in traffic accidents, the majority of which were attributed to alcohol. Working with the Missouri State

Highway Patrol, we began a very strict traffic enforcement program. That's how Trooper Froemsdorf and I began working together. Jim lived about a mile from me with his wife, Sarah, and their three little girls. My wife and I had two young sons, and the kids were all around the same age. Jim and I got to know each other very well while we were on duty, and our families quickly became friends.

We were preparing to work a section of the highway that June evening when I got a call from Sheriff Pingel advising us that they had gotten word about a big party taking place in a field in the northern part of the county near the Perry County—St. Genevieve County line. We needed to go out there, shut the party down, and make the necessary arrests. They had already done some preliminary surveillance and found that there were a couple of hundred people there and a few rock bands had already begun playing. It was the weekend of Perryville High School's graduation, and with two beer wagons set up inside the party, there was a lot of drinking being done by the largely underage crowd.

Sheriff Pingel, Jim, and I took off down Highway 61. It was dark as I wound my patrol car down the one-lane gravel road deep into the woods. The sounds of live music and raucous revelers got louder as I came upon the open field, where I found a sea of trucks, cars, tents, and a huge flatbed trailer that I assumed was for the band, whose amps were blaring loudly into the rowdy crowd. There were two young guys standing at the entrance charging admission. We immediately arrested the two gatekeepers and put them into the back of my patrol car.

As soon as the partygoers realized that we were there to shut them down, they turned their energy on us and started throwing rocks and beer cans. It became obvious that this crowd was not going to peacefully accept that their party was over. To make matters worse, the mass of people seemed to be growing by the minute. Sheriff Pingel advised me by radio to head back up to where the dirt road intersected with a county road and block the entrance to the field where we had just raided the party.

As I blocked off the road, I realized that the crowd had gathered into an angry mob around me. I radioed Sheriff Pingel, who was seventy-five yards due west of where I was, and requested that he send Jim down to help me with crowd control. It wasn't a few minutes before I saw Jim coming down the dark lane on foot. Because of the vehicular traffic and swarms of people jamming the gravel road, it was the quickest but also the most dangerous way to get to where I was, at the center of the crowd. I kept my eye on Jim, and as he approached me, a huge fence post hurtled through the air and crashed directly through the front windshield of my brand-new patrol car.

A guy in his mid-twenties sporting long hair, tattoos, and a leather biker's vest jumped up on the hood of my car. I would later learn that he was a member of the Outlaws motorcycle gang, which had a club in the Perryville area. I pulled my shotgun out of the car, jacked one up in the chamber, and took aim. He immediately jumped down and disappeared into the crowd. At that moment, I realized that I had just made a huge mistake. Jim and I were far outnumbered by the unruly mob. We had our service revolvers, but we both knew that we didn't stand a chance against a group of four hundred angry rioters.

The partiers continued to throw rocks, beer cans, and whatever else they could find. They also began to chant, "Kill the pigs! Kill the pigs!" There was no question that the situation was out of control, and we were in desperate need of assistance. My keys had been taken out of the ignition and thrown into the woods and the fence post was still lodged through the windshield of my patrol car, so Jim and I ran on foot to the one-lane dirt road to talk to Sheriff Pingel and radio for backup.

That's when my patrol car blew up. Someone had poked holes in the fuel tank and let the gasoline run out into a fuse line. When the fuse was lit, the rear half of the car exploded as if a bomb had gone off. There was a lot of yelling and screaming, people running in all directions. By the time I took the radio mike and advised Perry County we had a riot in progress and needed the fire department and surrounding agencies for assistance, my patrol car was fully engulfed in flames.

The fire department arrived after about fifteen minutes to put out the fire, but officers from the surrounding agencies weren't familiar with the area and were having trouble locating us so far back in the woods. It was the longest forty-five-minutes of my life from the first time the call for assistance was made before officers from the surrounding police departments, sheriff's departments, and the Missouri State Highway Patrol started to arrive. During that time Trooper Froemsdorf, Sheriff Pingel, and I made every attempt to control the rowdy crowd. Once the backup officers arrived, the crowd finally dispersed, only to converge again on the city of Perryville, where the local elected police chief opened the city park up for them to finish their party. I could not believe the chief would make such a decision after the absolute pure hell we had just survived.

Sheriff Pingel, Jim, and I headed back to the sheriff's office in Perryville. We booked the handful of rioters we had arrested and started the investigation to find the people who had torched my car. The next day we received a tip that the two men responsible for the fire were Outlaw bikers, one of whom was the same guy who had jumped on the hood of my car. I'd had the two gatekeepers we'd arrested upon our arrival handcuffed in the back of the car, and learned that the bikers told them to either get out or burn up with the patrol car.

That following Monday, warrants were issued for the two men. I arrested one at a local rock quarry where he worked, but his friend had gone on the run. It took about two weeks, but Jim and I tracked him down and found him hiding in the closet of a mobile home along U.S. Highway 61 approximately three miles north from where my patrol car was burned. Both men were convicted and each received a seven-year prison sentence.

I'm still amazed that we made it out that night without any injuries. I can think of a dozen other situations where I called on Jim for backup and he was always there for me.

Jim was killed in the line of duty on March 2, 1985. He had stopped a car on the interstate and discovered that the driver, a man named Jerome Mallett, had a suspended license and was in violation of his parole for a previous armed robbery conviction. Jim had him handcuffed, but Mallett had a trick thumb and was able to escape from the cuffs. A struggle ensued inside the car, until Mallett got Jim's sidearm out of the holster and fatally shot him three times. Jim was thirty-five-years old. Jerome Mallett was found guilty by a jury and was sentenced to death. He was executed on July 11, 2001, for the death of Trooper Froemsdorf.

I took Jim's death very hard. I'm still not over it. I will never be over it. Jim was a cherished husband and father, a true brother, and an outstanding law enforcement officer. Those are shoes that can never be filled.

Even twenty years after his death, I can't help but shake the feeling that Jim is still by my side. In 2002, my son graduated from the Missouri Police Corps after twenty-six-weeks of training. Sarah Froemsdorf and one of her daughters were also in the crowd of family and friends showing their support for Missouri's newest police officers. They were there to celebrate another young man from the graduating class; a young man that Jim, whose life was taken when his daughters were still small children, never had the opportunity to meet—his future son-in-law.

To this day I wear an armband in Jim's memory, and his picture still hangs in my home. A section of the highway near where Jim lost his life is dedicated in his name. Jim Froemsdorf was a proud member of the Missouri State Highway Patrol, and I'm very honored to say that I was very proud to work with him and call him my friend. You just never forget a warrior like him. Especially in law enforcement. You don't forget the men who never leave your side in the line of duty.

This story is dedicated to the men and women of law enforcement who have paid the ultimate sacrifice and given their lives in order to protect and serve the American people.

It Was Just Business

THE BEAT

BY PHILIP V. BULONE

Detective, New York PD, retired after fourteen years.

The morning sun peeked through the alleys separating the buildings that made up the labyrinth of the Manhattanville Houses. Mornings in this drug-infested neighborhood were quiet. The evenings made up for the silence of the new day. Jimmy and I were there for surveillance of one of our local drug dealers. We weren't looking to bust him, at least not today. We needed a solid case on this guy. No mistakes; no short cuts. This scumbag had to do time, lots of time, for the shit he sold on the street, the shit that people, mostly kids, were shooting into their veins.

I was circling the block looking for a spot to park when the dispatcher broke the silence of the police radio. "Manhattan North Narcotics Auto 1753, are you on the air? K."

Jimmy picked up the receiver. "Narcotics Auto 1753, K."

"Auto 1753, respond to 631 West 1-4-2 Street and meet the sergeant. K."

"What's up, Central? K."

"Nothing further, I'm getting a second request that you respond forthwith. K."

"Central, be advised we're sitting on a target location. Can you raise another unit? K."

"That's a negative. You're the only narcotics unit available. K."

"Ten-four Central, ETA ten minutes. K."

I looked at Jimmy. "This doesn't sound right. Why would the precinct patrol sergeant call us?"

"Who knows? That's what we get for volunteering on a Saturday."

As I turned the corner from Adam Clayton Powell Jr. Boulevard onto 142nd Street, I counted six radio motor patrols (RPMs), two ambulances, and an emergency service truck parked in front of the building. Several cops were standing around, smoking. "What's up, guys?" Jimmy said. "Got a call to meet the patrol sergeant here."

An officer interrupted. "The boss is down in the basement. Looks like a few dopers overdosed."

Entering the dimly lit basement, I saw the bodies. Some were sitting up against the unpainted concrete block walls. Others were lying on the floor. There were fifteen of them. The room was decorated in typical shooting gallery decor. Several empty milk crates were sprawled around the room. Empty and broken syringes lined the floor, along with dozens of empty glassine envelopes, brown paper bags, and white cardboard containers with half-eaten Chinese food. Bottle caps, pieces of cotton, and several bent spoons were also scattered around. The smell of human and animal piss and feces mixed with the rotting food filled my nose.

The bodies looked as though they were asleep. But the sleep they were in was eternal. Their lives were over, finished; dope was more important than life.

Sergeant Jankoski, a tall slim Polack, waved us over. "Looks like a new batch of smack arrived in the neighborhood. Must be that new shit, China White; I hear it's pretty pure."

"Yeah," Jimmy said. "How'd the call come in?"

"Some skel looking to shoot up found them when he came down. He used the pay phone up the street to call 911."

"Well, at least the pay phone worked," I said. "Is the squad on the way?"

"No, you guys can handle this. It's a narcotics case. My people notified the Medical Examiner and Crime Scene. They should be here soon."

"Come on, Sarge. Dead bodies are usually handled by the precinct detectives, not narcotics."

"Listen, I got a call from your boss, Captain Santangelo. He said to call you. There's going to be a lot of press. Look at the bodies. All the victims are white. And they all died in Harlem."

"That's more of a reason the squad should handle this."

"Don't know, don't care," the sergeant said. "You guys got it, and that's the end of the story. I'll leave a couple of uniforms here with you to help the ME load the meat wagon. When that's done, it's all yours."

I recognized the medical examiner. It was Dr. Victor Pena from the Bellevue Hospital Morgue. "Hey, doc, how you doing?"

"Thought I'd have a nice quiet Saturday; planned to watch the ball game. What do we have? It's like an oven down here."

Jimmy explained the case. The doctor quickly checked each body. "I don't see any visible wounds or blood. You guys think they all overdosed?"

"That's how it looks," I said.

"I'm not making a call on this right away. Let's bag them up and get them to the morgue. I'll call in my backup pathologist and we'll take a closer look. Fifteen people overdose in one room? I have a problem with that. I'm not sure they overdosed."

"Doc, let's not make a big deal of this," I said. "After all, this is a place where people come to use drugs. Drug addicts die from time to time."

"Listen, fifteen people at one time is unusual. Let me check the bodies for foul play."

When everyone left, Jimmy and I went back down to the basement for one more look.

"What the fuck happened here?" I said. "You know we joke a lot about seeing dead bodies. I guess it's a good way to not lose your mind. But fifteen dead bodies in one place? This is gonna be a tough one."

We drove to our office, which was located next to the Two-Six Precinct on 126th Street. Just as I was pulling a stack of pink follow-up reports, the telephone rang. Jimmy answered. "Manhattan North Narcotics, Police Officer Crawford." Jimmy didn't say much—he was doing more listening—and after a few minutes, he hung up the phone.

"What's going on?"

"That was Captain Santangelo. He wants us to go down to the morgue and view the autopsies. He said the chief called him and wants to know the cause of death ASAP."

"Why don't you go, and I'll get a head start on the paperwork."

"No way, man, you're coming with me. I know you aren't a fan of autopsies, but I'm not spending the afternoon alone with fifteen stiffs. Let's go. I'll drive."

I hated the morgue. As soon as Jimmy and I entered the lobby, I could smell death. It got stronger as we rode the elevator down to the basement, to what I called the chop shop. Our victims took up three autopsy rooms. Dr. Pena was already working on one corpse while his attendant was making the Y cut into another. A second pathologist was preparing to start on a third body. I walked over to one of the lab tables and grabbed a bottle of Vicks. I circled my finger around the edge of the open bottle and stuffed the menthol gel up my nostrils. I offered Jimmy some, but he didn't take it.

"That's for pussies. Real cops don't use Vicks."

Always the wiseass, I thought.

We approached Dr. Pena. "Anything unusual, doc?" I asked.

"You guys aren't going to like this. There was strychnine mixed in with the dope. You guys just caught fifteen homicides."

"You gotta be kidding me, doc," I said.

"I'm serious. I'm classifying this case as homicide; actually, fifteen homicides. You can pick up the reports, photos, and prints tomorrow. If you want, you can go through the personal effects for identification before heading back to your office. Someone has to notify the next of kin."

I called Captain Santangelo and filled him in. Then Jimmy and I started collecting the names and addresses of the victims. Fortunately, they all had licenses. Out of the fifteen, two lived within the city limits. The others came from Long Island and Rockland County. That's what made Harlem a good place for drug entrepreneurs: location, location, location. A convenient drive over the George Washington or Triboro Bridge, sandwiched between the West Side Highway and East River Drive; less than an hour from the suburbs. A place where drug dealers could rake in cash, or trade their product for a piece of ass; a place where fifteen kids figured they could drive, buy a bag of heroin, shoot up, get high, and drive home. Only last night would be their last Friday night. They'd never drive home.

Captain Santangelo and Chief of Detectives Timothy Donovan were waiting for Jimmy and me. We had the names and addresses of the victims. Detectives from the Two-Six would make the notifications. Six Manhattan North Narcotics teams were already called in from their regular days off. The chief had a plan to get this case solved quickly. He wanted this scumbag off the street immediately and hoped it wasn't some psycho planning to lace Harlem's entire heroin inventory with strychnine.

The roll call room of the Two-Six smelled of stale smoke. Captain Santangelo was preparing to brief the sixteen officers, four sergeants, and a lieutenant on the plan to get information on the fifteen homicides. Also present for the briefing was the four-to-midnight shift of patrol and anticrime officers assigned to the Two-Six. The plan was simple. Bust balls on the street. Stop the prostitutes from shaking their asses. Chase all the steerers and hawkers from the corners. Bring into the precinct anyone suspicious for a complete background check. Stop all the numbers takers from writing down their digits. "In other words," Captain Santangelo said, "I want any and all illegal business on the street stopped until someone gives up the scumbag who killed those fifteen people."

Jimmy and I called in all our informants, inquiring if they had any idea who could have done this. They knew nothing. An informant is only as good as the cash you have to offer, and today's offer of five hundred couldn't buy anything on this case.

About eleven thirty Jimmy and I headed for 125th Street for coffee. As we turned onto Old Broadway, a young kid waved us down. "You guys cops?" As if he didn't know. Jimmy answered, "Yeah."

"You looking for the guy who works the shooting gallery up on 1-4-2 Street?"

"You got something for us?" I asked.

"Maybe."

"What's 'maybe' mean?"

"My father got busted last month. He shot a guy. It was self-defense. Could you get him out of jail if I tell you who messed with the dope?"

Jimmy opened the rear door. "Get in. Let's go for a ride."

The kid looked at Jimmy. "I ain't getting in no cop car. People see me go with you and not cuffed, they think I dropped a dime or something."

"So what do you suggest we do?"

Suddenly, the kid raised his voice. "Fuck you, pig! I didn't do nothing. Leave me alone." The kid ran in front of the car. He picked up an empty beer bottle leaning against the curb, threw it at the police unit, and smashed the rear window. He yelled, "Fuck you," as he ran.

I put the car in drive. Turning the corner I could see the kid heading toward the river at the end of 125th Street. I slowed down and let Jimmy out. I speeded up past the kid and made a U-turn. The kid turned and ran right into Jimmy's arms. Jimmy threw him on the ground and rear-handcuffed him. Then he opened the rear door of the Diplomat and flung the kid into the backseat.

I turned to the kid and yelled, "What are you, fucking nuts?"

He laughed. "I told you guys I wasn't getting into this car unless

I was cuffed. Now, take me to the station. Can you get my father out of jail?"

Assistant District Attorney Brian Feely arrived about twelve thirty. Captain Santangelo, Jimmy, and I had already talked with the kid, Anthony Greene. We checked his story. His father had been arrested a month earlier and charged with murder. Santangelo had copies of the original UF-61 (Crime Reports) and DD5s (Follow-ups) faxed to our office. From what the responding officers and investigating detectives found, this was a smoking-gun case. Anthony's father killed the other guy. For what reason no one knew. It wasn't self-defense. Trying to make a deal with the DA's Office wasn't going to be easy. Actually, it was going to be nearly impossible.

Brian Feely was a straight-up Assistant District Attorney who played it right from the book. If anyone had a shot at getting him to make a deal, it would be Chief Donovan. The two men entered the interrogation room. The Chief carried two cups of coffee and a manila folder, which contained photographs of the crime scene. Jimmy, Captain Santangelo, and I watched through the two-way glass. I turned up the volume on the speaker so we could hear the conversation. Both the ADA and the Chief knew they were being watched. The Chief flipped us the bird.

"Counselor," the Chief said. "I've got fifteen dead victims, a commissioner who's on my ass, and a mayor who's on the commissioner's ass to find the scumbag who did this. Now, my guys got a kid in the other room who they believe has information on the prick who laced the dope. I believe my officers when they tell me this kid has solid information, and I don't want to screw around here all night trying to convince you to make a deal with the kid's old man who got busted for shooting some street scumbag."

"Chief," Feely said. "With all due respect to you and your officers, I can't just let a murderer walk out of jail because you need to get the name of someone you aren't even sure is your perp. I need more than the word of some kid."

"Okay. Tell you what. You talk with the kid. Tell him if he gives up the guy, you'll at least talk to the district attorney about getting his old man out."

Still hesitant, the young ADA agreed to talk with the kid. The Chief motioned me through the two-way mirror to bring the kid into the interrogation room.

The kid had balls and was a better negotiator than the young lawyer. I whispered to Jimmy, "The lawyer got book smarts. The kid, he's got the real education. Street smarts." After an hour of the kid and the lawyer playing a game of cat and mouse they came to an agreement.

The Chief and Feely left he room. I turned to the kid. "Okay, Anthony. What's the name?"

"I'm not one hundred percent sure he did it, but Angelo Martinez runs dope out of that building."

Jimmy yelled, "Come on, Anthony. That's black man territory. You telling me the other dealers are going to allow some spic from Spanish Harlem in their hood?"

"Yeah, he's fucking some black broad whose brother deals. She's got a couple of his kids, so the spic gets a pass."

"Okay," Jimmy said. "What's the script on this guy?"

"He's a spic, man. You know about five seven or eight, greasy hair, bad breath, and a mustache. A regular-looking spic."

"Where's his crib?"

"I'm not sure, but he hangs out most of the day at the Beavers Den, across from Morningside Park. He likes watching the naked dancers."

I asked, "How late does he stay on the set when dealing?"

"Till the dope's gone or business slows down. What time is it now?"

"Almost three," Jimmy said.

"I'll bet you he's at the location or the Beavers Den. Angelo likes to party on the weekend."

I left the room and went out to my team sergeant requesting he call the Two-Six desk officer and get a couple of uniformed officers to babysit Anthony while we went out, hoping to pick up Angelo

Martinez. The captain suggested we first try making a buy at the 1-4-2 Street location.

The teams set up on 140th Street, two blocks away from the target location. Detective Carmine Padula, the team undercover, would walk the two blocks to the location and attempt to identify and make a buy from the suspect. If Carmine confirmed the suspect was on the set, Teams A and B would cover the rooftops and rear yards behind the subject location. Teams C and D would make the entry. Jimmy and I were assigned to team D. We would arrest the subject and get him off the set, back to the Two-Six. The rest of our team and Team C would detain and identify any others in the location and do a preliminary search.

The undercover was out of our sight for about half an hour before my portable radio crackled and Carmine verified he made a buy from the target. Captain Santangelo was riding with Jimmy and me. He gave the signal and the four Manhattan North Narcotics Teams rolled down 142nd Street. Team C pulled up directly in front of the location with the two officers sitting in the backseat, grabbing the ram in case the door to the basement was locked. As they exited the vehicle, several street people yelled, "5-0, 5-0," which in gangster language is a warning that the police are here.

We entered the building and headed straight for the basement door. We didn't need the ram. The first officer used his foot, kicking the door, which immediately opened. As we descended the staircase, we screamed, "Police!" Someone broke the single lightbulb dangling from an overhead wire, darkening the room. Fortunately, two officers had flashlights. I heard glass breaking and then someone yelling, "Police, don't move!" I tensed, waiting to hear gunfire. "Phil, we got him. Come on, hurry up."

I found my way to the broken window, climbed out, and there, already cuffed, was Angelo Martinez. An easy ID since he had his expired driver's license in his pocket. On the ride back to the Two-Six, Captain Santangelo kept him company in the backseat.

The captain thought it would be a good idea to put Angelo in a lineup, having Anthony Greene identify him. It didn't take long to find five Puerto Ricans hanging out on 125th Street willing to stand in a lineup for twenty bucks. It took less than five seconds for Anthony Greene to finger Angelo. A couple of uniformed officers drove Anthony home.

We sat Angelo in an armless metal folding chair in the middle of the interrogation room. He hadn't said a word since he was cuffed. He looked dirty and stank of piss. I began the questioning. "Any idea why you're here, Mr. Martinez?"

He had a smirk on his face as if his current situation was a joke. "No speaky the English," he said in a phony Spanish accent.

Jimmy wasn't going to play with this guy. He grabbed a New York telephone book, the Yellow Pages, and slammed it against the back of Angelo's head, sending him flying off the chair and across the room. Angelo jumped up, clenching his fists and heading toward Jimmy. I extended my foot, causing Angelo to trip. He jumped up a second time. "I'll kill you pigs," he said, losing his accent and speaking perfect English. Jimmy and I both grabbed him and threw him face-first into the split-pea-colored wall. Captain Santangelo opened the door. "Easy, guys, let's not mess up his pretty face. We want him looking good for the judge."

Jimmy escorted Angelo back to the metal chair, forcibly sitting him down. "Now," Jimmy said, "let's talk about last night. What were you selling?"

"I don't sell nothing. I want my lawyer. I ain't saying nothing to you pigs."

I kicked the chair out from underneath him. He fell hard onto the concrete floor. "I want some answers, you little spic. You ain't getting no lawyer. You're going to tell us what you did with your stash last night. We've got fifteen dead people and you killed them."

"What the fuck are you talking about?" Angelo yelled. "I didn't kill nobody. I just sell some dope, man. You guys know that. I've been busted by Narcotics for dealing. That's it. I sell dope. I don't hurt nobody."

"Then how did we end up with all those dead bodies?" I asked.

"Listen, man, I sell drugs. That's how I make my money. I have customers, regulars who come week after week to score dope. I was shy on the load and my main man was running late."

I asked, "So, what's that supposed to mean?"

"That means I'd be light. I usually move eighty bags. I had fourteen left from the night before. You understand, I needed eighty."

"Yeah. So you cut the fourteen bags with strychnine!"

"Fuck no. I used some white powder that was in a brown bag. It was on the floor. In the corner. It looked like flour or something."

"Oh, it was something. Rat poison."

Jimmy took over the conversation. "You dumb fuck, you cut your dope with rat poison, and rat poison has strychnine in it. What do you think kills those big rats hanging out in the basement?"

Angelo looked at Jimmy, then at me. "Hey, what the fuck did you expect me to do? I had customers coming and they were depending on me. If I stiffed them, they go somewhere else. This is my fuckin' living."

"What the fuck did I expect you to do?" I screamed picking Angelo off the chair with one hand. "You killed fifteen people. Don't you have any feelings about that?"

I threw him back down. He still had a smirk on his face. "Like I said, man, that's the business. It was just business."

Captain Santangelo walked into the room. "Book this psycho. Get him out of here."

Jimmy cuffed the prisoner and we took him down to Central Booking. We booked him then lodged him in the Two-Four Precinct. In the morning, he'd be transported to the courthouse for arraignment on fifteen counts of murder.

On the drive back to our office, Jimmy looked at me. He was shaking his head. "Do you believe this psycho? He kills fifteen people and shows no emotion. No remorse."

I kept my eyes on the road. "Jimmy, this is the reality of the drug world. Like he said, 'It was just business.'"

I Hear Ya, Rick

THE FALLEN

BY MIKE "MOMO" MARTINEZ
Sworn Officer, Hondo, Texas PD, twelve years.

eath. It's been a part of my life as long as I can remember. Cops see more death and dismemberment than most people could ever be expected to tolerate, let alone handle. Sometimes death kinda sneaks up on you and smacks you in the back of the head. March 4, 1997, was a day like that. I was starting the first day of my two relief days lying in bed, watching the sunset outside and listening to the radio. My phone rang. The dispatcher began rattling off information. "Rick went down while running on the track . . . Gibby and Don started CPR . . . He's at Medina Community, AirLife's en route . . . You need to hurry if you're gonna see him before they take him to San Antonio."

"Rick" was Sergeant Rick Taylor, our DARE officer and the answer to our prayers. Rick was training for the FBI National Police Chiefs Academy. He wanted to be our chief and, more important, we wanted him as our chief. Rick as chief would be considered a community policing dream. I've never met anyone who didn't like Rick. Not only did Rick know community policing, he practiced what he preached, and was loved by all because of it.

I grabbed some blue jeans and threw myself into my Ford Bronco. I drove way too fast for the road conditions. It's about ten miles from my house to the Medina Community Hospital; it might as well have been a hundred. Time-to-think . . . can suck, to put it mildly. As I drove, I kept thinking about would-a, could-a, should-a. If I got up when I should have, I'd have been there exercising with Rick when he went down. I would have been there . . . I don't suggest using would-a, could-a, should-a in your daily life; you'll never get out of bed.

As I zipped through the parking lot, I saw the blue LZ lights blink off. I came to a grinding stop and jumped from the Bronco. One of the day-shift guys, Greg came up to me. "He's gone, Mo," Greg grunted through a sob.

No, this can't be happening. I saw Gibby and Don sitting on a curb, crying, with several people trying to console them. The hurt in their eyes burned deep in my stomach. We hugged and held each other and cried. We cried. As each additional officer arrived, we experienced the pain again and again.

The death of an officer deeply wounds each and every department that loses that good man or woman. When your department numbers thirteen souls, the hurt is that much more personal for the officers. It also means there aren't other divisions to fill the gap as you mourn. I distinctly remember how infuriated the officers were when the Chief spoke to the local newspaper on our behalf. He implored the townspeople to bear with the officers during this trying time. He said they need to understand why we might have short tempers. We were very insulted. We're professionals; we could handle it.

Or so we thought.

I was working second shift, two P.M. to ten P.M., and the night was going well. We'd had few calls. Most of our issues had been with each other and not the general public. Rick's funeral was tomorrow and our tempers *were* short. We had no one to take out our grief and anger on but each other. I got dispatched to a keep-the-peace call. This type of call can usually be pretty mundane and is often very boring. We're not supposed to give them more than fifteen minutes.

The woman came rushing outside. I copied down her identification just in case something happened while I was there. *Wow, she's only twenty and she has three kids. Poor Momma.* She was leaving her boyfriend. *Again,* I thought to myself.

"I just need to get my clothes, some of my stuff, my kids' clothes, and their toys," she yelled as she ran back toward the house.

"I can only stay for about fifteen minutes," I called after her. "817 . . . 811" My handheld radio crackled to life. "811, go," I answered.

"You gonna finish anytime soon?" The sarcasm in his voice made me angry, and he continued to tap-dance on the land mine. "I would like to take my lunch before all the restaurants close." I looked at my watch. Six twenty-eight P.M. Restaurants didn't close for hours. What he was really saying was, "I don't want to take any calls, and the longer you stay out with the bullshit call, the greater chance I'll have to work."

Momma was racing furiously back and forth between house and minivan, shoving things into every empty crevice.

"Ma'am, we need to get a wrap-up on this. I've been here for over twenty-two minutes." *Hello, I'm bored . . . Can't you see that?* Momma pushed her hair back from her face and quietly said, "I'm just trying to make sure I get the kids' stuff."

"Alright, just hurry."

Momma returned to her frantic pace.

Excuse me, sir." A young man about twelve years old walked out of the tree line.

"Yeah?" I answered.

"I just had a question," he timidly asked.

"What's that?" *This should help to pass the time.*

"Are you a friend of Mr. Rick?" *Aw, crap.* Not one of the usual questions we got from kids. "Do you shoot people? . . . Have you killed people? . . . Do you drive fast? . . . Why do you hate my daddy?" Those were easy compared to "Are you a friend of Mr. Rick?"

I felt my temperature rise and my spine tingle. Somehow I kept the tears from crashing over my eyelids. My head ached and my stomach turned. "Yeah, Rick was a friend of mine," I whispered as I tried to clear this huge lump from my throat.

He pretended not to notice the tears welling up into my eyelashes. "I just wanted to say I'm sorry. We loved him so much and we miss him a lot. So, you must miss him a lot, too."

Just as quickly as he arrived he was gone. I cupped my hands over my face trying to regain my composure. I began laughing. I laughed until I cried, and then I did both at the same time.

I dried my tears and looked up to the sky. I walked back to the minivan. Momma was even more flustered than before. "I'm hurrying, I swear," she called out quickly.

"Stop. Look at me," I told her as I touched her elbow. "Make sure you get *all* the clothes and toys for your kids, OK?"

She quietly nodded and returned to the house. Lunch was going to wait a little while longer.

I looked up at the sky and said, "I hear ya, Rick."

How Do I Find the Words?

LINE OF DUTY

BY PAT JENKINS

Deputy Sheriff, Okaloosa County, Florida, fourteen years.

The public does not realize that beneath the uniform, the badge, and the gun, there lies a heart filled with compassion. Police officers carry within them for their entire lives the memories of the tragic events they have encountered while walking the thin blue line. Law enforcement officers around the world agree that the notification of the sudden death of a loved one to a family member is one of the most difficult of our responsibilities. All the hours of training help little when it's four A.M. and an officer is about to knock on a door to give the news no one wants to hear.

One such event took place in March 1995. I had been working as a patrol deputy for about a year. The night started out uneventfully, but the details would soon imprint themselves on my memory for the rest of my life.

It was around one thirty in the morning and the weather was still cool. The forecast was for patchy dense fog throughout the early hours. I had been checking the closed businesses in my beat when the radio came to life, "Unit 147." I could sense the urgency in the dispatcher's voice. I replied with the customary, "Go ahead," and was given the details. "Unit 147," she said, "Be en route to the area of Emerald Coast Parkway near the Gulf Power substation. We are getting multiple calls in reference to a possible traffic crash." I acknowledged the call and began heading east on Emerald Coast Parkway. I could hear my shift partner also key up his radio and say that he would be en route to assist me.

I thought some fool hadn't paid attention to his surroundings and had run off the road. I pushed through the fog faster and faster. My blue lights probed through the darkness as my mind went down a mental checklist of what to do: Get the vehicle off the roadway, avoid another accident, check for injuries or impairment on the driver. With my luck this joker will be as drunk as Cooter Brown and I would have three hours of paperwork ahead of me.

As I neared the area, I reduced my speed and began to scan ahead. Straining to spot any reflection or headlights to help guide me to the accident, I saw what appeared to be a small piece of metal in the roadway. "Slow down, Pat, you're close," I thought. The fog impaired my vision. Then more metal parts appeared, larger ones. I had to be close to the accident. I came to a complete stop and turned on my high beams. What I saw in front of me made my heart leap into my throat. My mind was trying to register all the visual information I was taking in. I picked up the radio mike, took a deep breath, and told dispatch I was on the scene.

Sitting in front of me was what used to be a car, now reduced to a mangled mass of metal, wires, and glass. It seemed as if the car had just exploded, leaving debris scattered in a twenty-five-foot radius. As I sat mesmerized by what I saw, my peripheral vision picked up figures approaching my patrol car through the fog. Everything was moving in slow motion. Their faces were eerily illuminated by the flashing blue lights, and their features became more defined the closer they came. "She's in the car!" a lady shouted, and from that point on everything seemed to move at the speed of light.

I ran toward the car and could see smoke rising from the engine compartment. The smell of gas and antifreeze was in the air. As I moved closer, my attention was drawn to the tree line to the right. I saw a large orange and black utility truck. The truck had heavy front-end damage, but nothing compared with what I saw in front of me. The reason for the accident became all too clear. One of the vehicles was traveling westbound in the eastbound lane. This was a head-on collision at a high rate of speed.

I turned my attention back to the car in the middle of the roadway. Sitting behind the steering wheel was a raven-haired woman. She looked to be in her early twenties. She was slumped over to her right. I tried to open the driver's door to get to her, but due to the extensive damage the door was jammed. The back door was partially open, and with adrenaline surging through my veins, I yanked it the rest of the way open. I climbed through the back door and immediately began talking to her. "I'm with the Sheriff's Office," I said. "Everything is going to be alright."

I could feel my heart pounding. My mouth was dry. I reached over the seat and felt the side of her neck for a pulse. There was none. I placed my hand over her nose and mouth to see if I could detect any breathing. There were no signs of breath in her. I looked up and saw my partner, Deputy Paul Goldsmith, running toward me. He leaned into the car and asked, "What do you need?" I shouted to him, "No pulse, no respiration. I need an ambulance here now!" As I shouted my request to him I became aware of a small crowd of people gathered around the car. All of them were staring at me. Although they were silent, their expressions and eyes screamed, "Do something! You're the police! You're supposed to know what to do! Don't let her die!" How could I make them understand that I was doing all that I knew to do.

I spoke very softly in her ear, "My name is Pat and I'm here with you. I need for you to breathe." My heart was pleading and praying that she would be alright, but my mind was telling me there had to be massive internal injuries. Where was the ambulance? Where were the other rescue personnel? Shouldn't they be here by now? I needed help. I couldn't do this alone. I reached down and took her hand in mine and asked her to please squeeze my hand. Maybe she couldn't hear me, but maybe she could feel my touch.

As I looked down at her hand I could see that the tips of her fingers were turning blue, a clear sign of a lack of oxygen. On the floorboard I noticed several boxes wrapped in brightly colored paper. Floating free in the confines of the car was a round helium balloon with HAPPY BIRTHDAY written on it. I found what appeared to be the contents of a purse scattered on the seat. It must have been spilled during the collision. Among the clutter I found her driver's license: Jennifer Smith of Niceville, Florida, twenty-three years old yesterday.

In the distance I could hear the faint wail of the ambulance siren. Suddenly I felt Jennifer grab hold of my hand and squeeze tight. Her eyes fluttered open as she drew in a big breath. She then exhaled slowly, her eyes closing for the final time. Her small delicate hand gently released mine and her body slumped forward.

The emergency crews took over from there and I walked quietly away. The unbelievable serene atmosphere that Jennifer and I shared was shattered. The scene was now awash in noise and light. The firemen yelled to one another for equipment, the Jaws of Life ripped at metal, there were more sirens, and the constant flash of red and blue emergency lights. I sat on the hood of my patrol car and questioned my decision to become a law enforcement officer.

Two hours later the vehicles had been towed off and the fire department had hosed down the asphalt to remove any hazardous fluids left behind by the crash. The small parts scattered in the roadway had been swept up and there was hardly any trace left of what happened. The Florida Highway Patrol had taken over the investigation and they had found evidence that the large truck was heading in the wrong direction. It was quite possible that the driver was under the influence of alcohol. The trooper needed to run the driver in to complete his investigation and paperwork, which left the question: "Who was going to make the notification to the next of kin?"

I felt a duty and responsibility to make the notification. I was with Jennifer as she drew her last breath. I needed to try to assure her loved ones that she was not alone when she passed away and that a prayer was said for her. Everything that could be done had been done, and she was treated with the utmost respect and dignity. I know that if it were one of my family members I would want to know the answers to these questions, no matter how much it hurt to hear them.

The drive over the Mid-Bay Bridge to Niceville didn't take as long as I wanted it to, and I was still searching for the right words. All too soon I found myself pulling into the driveway of the Smith residence. I turned off the engine and quietly got out of the patrol car, being sure not to slam the door. I noticed that the lawn of the two-story brick home was manicured, and the only light on was the front porch light. I remembered that my mom used to leave the front porch light on for me, too.

I stood at the front door, praying, asking for some sort of divine intervention to help me find the words. "Lord, help me to fight back the tears that are already welling up in my eyes." I took a deep breath and rang the doorbell. There was no turning back now. The instructors in the police academy never told us about this side of the job. I saw a light come on in what must have been an upstairs bedroom. Oh God, I was shaking! What would I say? How would I say it? Where would I begin? The doorknob slowly began to turn.

How would I find the words?

Even though this incident occurred eight years ago, it is still imprinted on my memory as though it happened yesterday. Never in my life have I felt so helpless and alone as I did standing there in that living room at four A.M. I was stumbling through the words, trying to give the account of the heartbreaking events that unfolded that evening. It doesn't matter if you're a fresh-faced, wide-eyed rookie, or a seasoned old veteran; the notification to the next of kin never gets any easier.

How did I find the right words? I guess I truly never did.

Heroes

LINE OF DUTY

BY THOMAS E. SCHULTE JR.

Sworn Officer, Overland PD, Missouri, twenty-four years; St. Louis PD, Missouri eleven years.

Before that dreadful day in September 2001 it appeared that sports figures and actors were the world's heroes. Many people have said that the world became a different place because of the events of that day. They say that the world has been changed forever.

I believe that the world remained the same; it's the *perception* that people have of the world around them that has changed. I *know* that society's way of thinking changed; as a police officer for thirty years, I have had an up close and personal view of it. Not only could I *see* that the people around me had changed, I could *feel* it.

The firefighters and police officers who gave their lives without thinking had now become prominent heroes, and rightly so. No longer were these public servants taken for granted; now they were looked upon as beacons of strength and hope. Even with all of the devastation surrounding them, these brave men and women performed their daily duties with no thought for their safety. That is the true embodiment of the word "hero."

I would like to take a moment to recognize the heroes in *my* life. These people aren't the ones we all see on the news every day, being interviewed and given special recognition for their bravery. The people I'm speaking of are the people who just do their jobs quietly with no thought of reward.

Twenty-five years ago I was one confused and hurting individual. I used every type of substance I could think of to try and fill the hole that was in my soul. No matter what I tried or how much I ran away, nothing seemed to work. That hole in my soul was fast becoming a void that threatened to engulf my entire being.

I had reached a point in my life where nothing made any sense. I could see, as if from a distance, everything good in my life being tarnished or disappearing, like a row of dominoes falling, but I had no idea how to stop one domino from crashing into the next. I stood by helplessly and watched my life spin out of control, and yet I still had the arrogance to think that I could make myself better on my own.

At this point, I was a police officer in a large city and had tried to ignore the pain of the job, to forget the wary faces of the children I had failed to protect when their mommy or daddy beat them so bad that they had to be hospitalized. I looked away and tried to become hard in order to protect my own sanity. What was impossible to forget, I allowed the alcohol to dull. I drank until thought was no longer possible. My life went on this way too long.

Then one day I was ordered to go to an older officer's house to see why he had not come into work that day. His name was Andy, and he was always quick with a joke.

Despite the carefree front, I could always see an underlying sadness about him. His wife and children had left him long ago, and he was facing his pending retirement alone.

His was a sad but common case. Something happens to cops during the course of a career. Most of us become moody and sullen because of the many negative and stressful aspects of our job. We never talk at home. Wives can only take this for so long; this is why the divorce rate among cops is so high. The same thing had probably happened to Andy. He was one of the many old-timers who could be found at the local watering hole after a long day at work.

The sergeant and I went over to Andy's house and found the back door unlocked. We found Andy slumped at the table with a bottle of scotch and an empty pill bottle. He had been dead for some time. My sergeant threw away the pill bottle and the scotch and then called for an ambulance.

I wrote his death up as a heart attack, and no autopsy was performed. It was just another old cop who died. Andy had spent his entire life serving and protecting others until the city that *was* his life said, "Thank you very much for your service, but we don't need you anymore." Andy couldn't stand to go into retirement alone. He had been a cop his whole life, and that's exactly how he wanted to go out—still a cop.

Andy's death hit me hard. I had spent some time with Andy and could not figure out why he would want to end his life without a fight. Cops aren't supposed to be that way. Then I began to think about the emptiness Andy must have felt, the way *he* must have seen the good things in his life disappearing one by one. Just like me. I began to have an inkling of what had driven him to this drastic act.

Questions began to torment me every day. People called us all the time in order to solve their problems, but who were we supposed to call? It was then that I began to face the fact that my own worst enemy was myself.

I kept on going for a while longer, but eventually the drinking got the best of my police career. They had no choice but to let me go.

I was devastated. Being a police officer was all that I knew. As bad as the loss of my job was, it did not teach me anything. I was on my way to losing my family next. No matter how I tried to run, I couldn't escape my inner demons. I was so out of control that my wife and daughter needed to escape *me*.

I had to do something, for without them I could not go on. I continued to try and change on my own, but I was sick and couldn't heal myself. One day, when I thought I couldn't spiral down any further, I decided that I was sick and tired of being sick and tired, that it was time for me to change. I obviously had no idea of how to accomplish this, and so I was directed to a place where the coffee was terrible but the help was free. This was when I encountered my heroes.

There weren't just one or two of them; there was an entire group of them. I was afraid to trust them, but they understood and helped me in spite of this. They opened up and helped me with no thought of their own needs or comfort. That is the true definition of the word "hero." I began to form a type of superdependence on them that was not only tolerated, but in fact was nurtured. No longer was there a *suck it up and deal with it* mentality. These were people I could share my darkest fears with, and I trusted them with my spiritual and emotional well-being. This was something I had never done with anyone in my entire life.

I believed that I was in a safe, protected cocoon. With my new-found friends surrounding me, I no longer trusted my ability to make decisions on my own. Like the true heroes that they were, they then let me go. I was told that I had been taught all that I could be taught. Now it was *my* time to give. I started to understand that in order to continue to grow as an individual, I must be willing to give away what I had learned to others who were like me. I would need to be able to make the sacrifice of opening up my experiences and inadequacies to strangers who came to me for help just as I had reached out to the friends who were my heroes.

Lately I have begun to think of ways that I could repay these heroes for saving my life. I tried to think of what I could do to show them how much they mean to me. How could I thank them and give them something special, so that the whole world would know what they had done for me?

The greatest thing that I could do for them is to inspire *you* to stop for a moment, look around, and find the everyday heroes in your own life. It could be the friend who listens to your problems without judging you. It may be the parent who loves you unconditionally no matter what mistakes you make. It might be the pastor who can guide you through a tough spiritual time. A hero is any person who takes the time to give you strength and hope when you have none of your own. Open yourself up to these heroes. Trust them. You may be surprised at what a difference it will make in your life.

I now realize that my heroes do not need or want my thanks. All I need to do is pass on the hero message—what you are makes me who I am. That is all the thanks that heroes need.

Heartbreaker

BY JACK M. COMEAUX

Sergeant, Rogers PD, Texas, seventeen years.

One summer afternoon in 1997, I was on patrol between Rockport and Aransas Pass, Texas, on a killer stretch of highway called the "Bypass." My partner was a rookie, fresh out of the academy. Sean Johnson was a hometown boy, big, good-looking, and ready to clean up the streets. He was strong as an ox, smart as a whip, and never met anything that could throw him too far. He answered every call with that fire in his heart and the can-do attitude that all rookies have. He didn't feel there was anything he couldn't handle.

He and I were about to be educated.

The call crackled over the radio and sent a chill down my back. A small child was facedown in a pond not far away. I built a fire in that big Chevy cruiser, switched on the lights and siren, and roared down the Bypass at about 120 mph praying, "Please, oh Lord, please let me be quick enough to make a difference." Sean keyed up and called en route as well. He was a little closer, but we both arrived in about three minutes.

When I turned in the driveway of the rural farmhouse, Sean was already out of the car bringing the little three-year-old boy out of the stock pond. Unknown to his parents, the child had slipped out of the house and toddled the short distance to the water chasing a duck. The boy had stepped off the edge of the pond and had fallen facefirst into about two feet of water. Apparently the mother looked out the door and called 911 dispatcher.

Sean took command on his own and began to administer CPR to the child while I coordinated EMS and tried to secure the scene. EMS arrived almost immediately and took over, working feverishly to save the child. The hospital at Aransas Pass was about seven minutes away, and Sean and I broke policy and escorted the EMS unit, blocking streets, clearing a path, doing whatever we could to speed up the arrival.

The emergency room trauma team responded instantly and kept working on the boy, doing everything they could. We prayed outside the doors to the ER treatment room and kept looking through the glass as the ER team poured it on.

Sean looked back and smiled. "He'll be okay, he'll be okay, I know he will."

My experience told me we were a long way from winning this one. But I prayed my partner was right. Rookies are faithful. And this rookie was tough to boot.

Then the ER team paused, a slight response from the child was seen, or so we thought. Sean smiled again and said, "See? I told you." The team continued, and I actually began to believe that all was well.

Then, all of a sudden, everyone stopped in the treatment room. There was a small pause. The technicians began putting equipment away; all the machines were switched off. The boy lay faceup, arms outstretched. It was intensely quiet. For just a moment, there was no sound at all.

The spirit of that child passed us on his way to heaven.

The nurse turned off the big light over the treatment table, and all the team members filed out of the room. I watched the doctor, head down, walk over to the trembling parents. I heard the screams of the mother and father as the doctor brought reality home to them.

My partner's face saddened as reality hit him as well. His strong body, supported by young, firm muscles slumped, and I felt him sway.

Almost immediately, he took a deep, deep breath, and it all came flooding back in. He handled it like a seasoned officer, and I was damned proud of him.

"You did all you could, buddy," I told him.

He said, "I know, but I thought we were going to win this one." He looked down at me and shook his head.

Two things happened that day. A rookie grew up, and an old guy got a reminder of who really runs the show down here on earth. This one was a heartbreaker, but one good thing makes me smile, that sweet baby boy sleeps with God now, and his worries are over.

I wish the same could be said for all of us.

He is safe forevermore.

God bless him.

Almost There

LINE OF DUTY

BY JOSEPH LOUGHLIN

Deputy Chief, Portland, Maine, twenty-six years.

As I round the bend under Tookey's Bridge the sun catches my eyes, bouncing off of a calm, indigo Casco Bay. I can see it up ahead as I run to that peaceful place and slow down to a walk, heart pounding, sweat running down my back until finally I stop. Surrounded by photos, a candle burns through a red and gold urn. Stuck in the earth of the embankment, it never goes out. I stare at the granite and recite the names I know so well now: Jason Carr, Crystal Young, and Nathaniel MacConnell, who died here January 13, 2002.

I remember getting the phone call that night, one of many over the years, awakened by death . . . again. Lieutenant Bob Ridge was upset this time. Three dead kids! I will spare you the lurid details. "Ya better have a debriefing on this one!" which was a rare statement from this man. Three! The officers at the scene, all very experienced with death, were shattered. Then the notifications to the parents.

Imagine.

There have been many deaths like these since, as classmates, parents, friends, loved ones, and communities gather to mourn . . . and to learn? But again and again, the wailing returns.

Graduations, proms, and then summer is upon us and the cops know what to expect . . . again. It seems so hard to tell kids, "Listen, this really can happen to you." They're in that invincible period of their lives. Studies have determined that teen brains are still developing into the twenties. Those parts that differentiate danger, safety, and judgment are not fully installed in teens. How do we handle these killers among us: alcohol, speed, and cars mixed with young folks?

My brother didn't make it. Tony boy, as my mother called him, was killed in his own drunk-driving accident. Dead, now in the dirt, many years ago. The pain and suffering it caused my parents, siblings, and friends are beyond description.

Getting a driver's license is a significant milestone; however, car crashes are the main cause of death for this age group. Roughly six thousand teenagers are killed each year in these horrific events. Drivers age 16–19 have a fatality rate approximately four times as high as drivers age 25–29.

We must be vigilant with our youth and continue to look at their privilege to drive. Education and law enforcement play a big part. Portland police have teamed up with the local high schools to conduct reenactments of horrible accidents, which are powerful for the students to see. We have conducted aggressive enforcement operations, but what else? Several states have developed some form of a graduated driver's license (GDL), which places restrictions on time of day, go anywhere, anytime licenses. It seems to work, especially when restricting nighttime driving. States have demonstrated that establishing a curfew, a longer waiting period, and restricted driving licenses does make a difference.

It is difficult to change thinking unless there is a horrible event involving someone they know. Then people seem to get it.

Parents can be ambivalent, and of course there is the statement officers constantly hear: "Not my child." This is followed, too often, by another statement," I can't believe this happened to us!"

People like to believe crashes and deaths are isolated incidents, but just ask the cops: We know. I flash back to so many times, arriving on scene in that initial silence, and listening to the ding-dong of the electric door going on a flipped-over car and watching the blood ooze out of the vehicle and pool in the street. No, thanks, I don't want to see that anymore. Younger officers must continue this process over and over.

Inspired by these three who died under Tookey's Bridge, I write to challenge your thinking and bring attention to this issue.

Recently, some rotten individuals spray-painted the bench, knocked down the candle and photos at this memorial, and destroyed the site. Nice, huh. I ran there immediately and shouted angrily into the wind . . . We never found the culprits. I put a police patch on a board there soon afterward as the memorial items emerged again from the dirt.

I learned recently that Nathaniel MacConnell's mom is the one who keeps this light going. I had the opportunity to talk to her recently. She is a very strong woman.

For some reason, after all this time, I finally recognize the date of their deaths as I stare at the bench. January 13, my brother's birthday. It hits me like a rock.

I believe Nate, Crystal, and Jason have made a difference in their short lives and remind us of this problem. It is our responsibility; it's time for all of us to make a difference.

The Recidivists

WAR STORY

BY DICK KIRBY

Sworn Officer, London Metropolitan Police, twenty-six years.

The Recidivists, a luncheon club composed of old and dissolute former detectives from London's Metropolitan Police, meet four times a year. The only rules are that we eat, drink, and thoroughly enjoy ourselves. You can't ask for better than that, can you?

None of us—not one—could exist in today's politically correct, touchy-feely, let's-be-nice-to-everybody police farce (not a spelling mistake, I assure you). The present Metropolitan Police has been shown the way; Bill Bratton came from across the pond and pointed out how assertive policing and zero tolerance could turn the tide, could reclaim the streets from the hooligans who now effectively run them. Our politicians and police chiefs listened politely before slinking away, showing the whites of their eyes, rather like disobedient dogs. No, they said. Absolutely not. That sort of policing costs politicians votes and denies police chiefs access to Her Majesty's honors list.

We old-time detectives saw some of the toughest aspects of police work, which is why we enjoy each other's company so much; and when the wine starts flowing, so do some of the stories.

In 1960s London, practically every weekend, the biggest social unrest came from anarchic students who demonstrated, often about the most preposterous of subjects. This enabled them to display their loathing of the establishment and in particular any form of authority.

Police Constables Green and Brown were just two of the hundreds of police officers bused into central London to police one such demonstration, on a warm public holiday. They, like most of the officers, were bored out of their skulls, listening to the whistling, chanting, jeering layabouts. PC Green was a brand-new, squeaky-clean, and keen-as-mustard young copper who had the misfortune to be standing next to PC Brown, surely the fattest, laziest, and most uncommunicative police officer whom God had ever blown breath into.

And then it happened.

Green suddenly felt he was being scrutinized. He looked around and saw that he was receiving full eye contact from the dirtiest, most repellent student he had ever seen, who was sauntering along the street toward him. And as he came nearer, the student took a bunch of keys from his pocket, put them ostentatiously between his fingers and proceeded to deliberately and malevolently scratch the entire length of a parked car. Having completed this gratuitous act of sabotage against the expensive property of one of the despised upper classes, the student smirked at PC Green and slipped the keys back into his pocket.

The young officer darted forward, keen to arrest this lout for his gratuitous display of vandalism but was brought up short, as the outstretched, meaty arm of PC Brown struck his chest, barring his way.

Let us examine the situation.

A criminal offense had been committed, that was clear. But this incident had occurred before the days when a police officer simply called up on his personal radio, to instantaneously receive details of the owner of a motor vehicle. In those days, a manual search had to be carried out in one of the four London County Council offices who then housed those records, and it was difficult for this task to be accomplished when a murder had been committed on a working day, let alone for a case of malicious damage on a public holiday.

PC Brown knew this, and more besides. He knew that if PC Green carried out this arrest, the prisoner would be taken to the nearest police station and because Green was just a kid, he'd tell the sergeant that Brown had also witnessed the offense (as indeed he had) so he'd be dragged into it as well. By the time they'd finished processing the prisoner, they'd have missed the coach home. Then the car owner would have to be traced, a statement taken, an estimate for the damage prepared, followed by a series of remand hearings at court, miles away from Brown's suburban home. These would seriously disrupt Brown's second (and completely unofficial) trade as an electrician, a service which he carried out whether he was on duty or not. But most of all, Brown knew that because the student was an upper-class little delinquent, his parents would be able to afford some silver-tongued lawyer to convince a jumble of Muppets on the magistrates' bench that the alleged offense was no more than an accident. The easily deluded Muppets would instantly dismiss the charge against the prisoner.

Brown knew all this as a result of years of accumulated ducking and diving, whereas all Green could myopically see was an arrest. But for those of you who like stories with happy endings, Brown also knew that retribution was called for. Stepping smartly forward, he seized the student by the nape of his neck, swiftly marched him around the corner and smashed him, face-first into a brick wall. Released from the hamlike hand, the student staggered off down the road like a drunk, blood spraying from his nose. During this short, five-second piece of action, not one word was exchanged. Not only did PC Brown not discuss his volatile action with PC Green, he did not condescend to ever talk to him again.

As you well know, Keith," I added, as I concluded the story to my drinking partner, and fellow Recidivist, "there's all different ways of dealing with antisocial behavior; it's just a matter of striking the right balance."

Keith laughed and poured the rest of the bottle of Chilean red into my glass. "London in the sixties," he chuckled, reminiscently.

"The swinging sixties, remember? All that free love, flower power, the Beatles—"

"And the drugs," I interrupted, as I raised my glass to him. "And the hippies."

"Why do I feel there's another story coming up?" Keith said.

This tale also involved a newcomer to the force and how the scales were lifted from his eyes, courtesy of a more experienced colleague. It involved Police Constable Jones, a knowledgeable officer, who forty years ago was teaching Police Constable Smith, a green-as-grass rookie, the art of "learning beats" around London's Chelsea. What PC Smith did not know was that his contemporary had been an aide to Criminal Investigation Division; in other words, a trainee detective. He had been returned to uniform in somewhat mysterious circumstances. What follows perhaps explains, in part, the reason for Jones's removal from plainclothes duties.

Jones suddenly spotted a youth, dressed in the habitual "Hippie" garb of that era advancing toward them along the King's Road. He muttered to Smith, "Let's give him a pull; I reckon he's got drugs on him."

A search did indeed reveal a few amphetamines in the young man's pocket, a discovery which didn't faze him in the slightest. "I do hope you realize," he drawled, "that I'll allege that you planted them on me?"

PC Jones raised his eyebrows. "Really?" With that, he produced a small plastic bag, containing a white substance. "Here—have that on me."

The young man had suddenly lost his savoir faire. "What is it?" he inquired, nervously. PC Jones replied, "Uncut heroin."

"I'll take the pills!" stammered the white-faced, upper-class delinquent.

The following morning at court, the youth pleaded guilty to possession of the amphetamines and was fined.

Afterward, Smith, red-eyed as the result of a sleepless night, whispered fearfully to his mentor, "Where did you get the heroin?"

"Baking powder," laconically corrected Jones. "Works every time!"

Keith was in the act of swallowing his wine when the punch line came, and he suffered a choking fit in consequence. "Gentlemen!" called Colin, our host. "Take your places. Luncheon is served!"

Keith and I strolled over to our table. We were joined by Nipper Read, the man who arrested the infamous Kray brothers and smashed up their evil empire. Ray, who fortuitously looked nothing like a cop, since he was one of Scotland Yard's most daring undercover officers sat down as well, and Sandy, my old mentor from our patrol days, with a fund of stories from the time when he ran a coffee plantation in his native Kenya, completed the quintet. It was the best company in the world.

The food and drink served at a Recidivists luncheon is magnificent. The stories are everything.

The Ride of a Lifetime

THE BEAT

BY RICK JAMISON

Chief of Police, Converse, Texas, twenty-eight years.

My career in law enforcement began on August 23, 1979, at the ripe old age of twenty-two. Fresh out of the police academy and eager to protect the public, every rookie dreams of getting into a high-speed chase and catching bank robbers like on TV. But what you see on TV is not how things happen in real life.

The day was November 27, 1979, the time was 10:59 A.M. I was working patrol in Converse, Texas, a small city of about 3,500 people with only seven police officers. People always say nothing really happens in small towns. But this day was different. As I was patrolling the streets, I attempted to stop a brown Lincoln Continental that was speeding. As I pulled in behind the vehicle, which had two occupants, and turned my overhead lights on, the vehicle took off like a shot. The driver didn't care that he was endangering innocent drivers, and speeding through residential streets where children played. With my lights and siren on, we traveled through numerous neighborhoods, passing young people outside along the street; the driver ran numerous stop signs and then finally got back onto the main roadway of Toepperwein Road.

The chase was in full course. I notified dispatch of the chase, and other cities on around the surrounding area joined in. We traveled up Toepperwein Road into the city of Live Oak, turned along the access road to IH 35. The vehicle crossed the median and got onto Pat Booker Road in Universal City where other officers had traffic stopped at the intersection of Pat Booker Road and Loop 1604 in hopes of slowing down the car. It didn't work.

As we cleared the intersection of Pat Booker and Loop 1604, the driver turned left and headed onto Loop 1604. The passenger leaned out the passenger window and fired several shots at me. It was terrifying—no one had ever shot at me before. Despite the fact that I carried a gun and had been trained, despite the fact that I'd heard hundreds of war stories, it never occurred to me that anyone was going to actually shoot a gun at me. I was a rookie and not real sure what to do (nobody told us about this in the academy), so I ducked below the dashboard; if the glove box had a window I could have driven that way. As we got up onto Loop 1604, an officer from the city of Selma fired several shots from his shotgun at the fleeing vehicle, but this did not stop them. We traveled on Loop 1604 in excess of 100 mph, swerving in and out of traffic, and I was right on the bumper of the vehicle. The driver did everything he could to get away—he made screaming, sharp turns at the last minute down so many roads I almost lost track of where we were. I was *not* used to seeing these usually familiar areas fly by at this speed. I found this as scary as being shot at, but I wouldn't let him shake me off. I was scared, but I wanted to prove myself, too. Also, I was getting a little mad—these assholes didn't care who got hurt; they thought they could just run right over anyone who got in their way—even the police! By this time I had a lot of other officers involved in the chase with me, but they were some distance behind.

As we drove down Classen Road, the driver of the Continental decided to do a 180-degree turnaround and go back the way he came. The driver hit a patch of loose gravel and was able to make the turnaround. I thought since he did it, I could do the same thing. Well, I hit the brakes but instead of making a 180 turn, I slid right up next to the driver's side of the Continental. The driver and I just looked at one another for what seemed like a lifetime; I was screaming in anger and he just grinned at me like we were on a ride in a damned amusement park. The passenger started to raise his gun toward me, and I stopped yelling and ducked down by the glove box again. I floored the car and was able to spin out of the way. I was really mad now.

As we got back onto the highway, the passenger leaned out and fired more rounds at me. He had missed by a long way before, but this time I heard the huge roar of his gun—what was he shooting? a cannon?—and bullets pinging off my patrol car, but I was too mad to care. As we got back up on the highway I was advised by my chief of police that he and a Live Oak officer and Selma officer had set up a roadblock, for me to back off of the fleeing vehicle. Unfortunately, we arrived too quickly for the roadblock to be set up properly. Traveling about 60 mph, we both went through with barely an inch of clearance on either side. Unknown to me at the time, a Live Oak sergeant had stopped traffic on Loop 1604 and had an eighteen-wheeler park his vehicle across the roadway.

Apparently the driver saw what was happening and had plenty of time to react so he did another "bat turn" in the middle of the roadway and headed back toward the roadblock. By this time I was some distance from the vehicle. As it came back up on the roadblock, the Live Oak officer and the Selma officer fired numerous rounds from their shotguns at the fleeing vehicle, hoping to stop it. I could see a window blown in and glass flying, I could hear the impact on the body of the car, but it had little effect on these two fugitives—they were desperate and highly dangerous. I was able to get through the roadblock and catch up with the car. We were again traveling in excess of 100 mph. Because of the narrowness and conditions of the road I wasn't able to keep up at a close distance with the Continental. As I slowed down, an officer behind me advised me by radio that I had a flat tire. I yelled and pounded the wheel in frustration. I didn't want to give up the chase. I wanted these two, but when I realized I could no longer keep up, I had to pull over and let other officers finish the chase and catch my "bad guys."

That wasn't the end of it. As I was changing the tire I was advised by radio that the vehicle had been spotted in a nearby shopping center. I changed that tire like I worked in the pit crew for an Indy 500 race car driver. Though my uniform was filthy and my hands a greasy mess, I went to the area and found the vehicle I had been chasing. The vehicle had been shot up pretty good and the front windshield had been hit several times, along with the hood, and one of the passenger-side windows had been blown out.

I was advised that two subjects had been taken into custody in a pizza parlor just across the street from the shopping center. San Antonio Police Department wanted the officer who had started this chase to come up to the location and ID the suspects. I was able to ID both men as being the ones inside the car and the ones who had fired several shots at me.

At the scene of the arrest, I was advised by San Antonio police that their helicopter spotted the two walking in the area and noticed them go into the pizza parlor. Officers surrounded the pizza parlor and called the manager and advised him of the situation and told him and his employees to get out. Once they were outside, the police yelled for the only two people inside to come out with their hands up; they complied. The tense situation was over. Two "bad guys" were in custody and no one got hurt . . . although I *did* get my uniform dirty.

All the officers involved in the chase were told to report to the San Antonio Police Department Homicide office to complete their reports. While I was writing my report, a detective came in and wanted to meet the "kid" who caught the bank robbers. I was advised that the names the two bandits gave us at the scene were false, that the FBI wanted both subjects for bank robbery up in the Dallas area, and one was wanted for federal bail jumping along with our charges of attempted capital murder. The Continental had been stolen in Austin. The detective told me that when they inventoried the stolen vehicle they found ammo, weapons, other license plates and a briefcase with a book on how to make bombs.

The San Antonio Police Department was directly across the street from the Bexar County Detention center. Since I was the person who had started this adventure, I was given the "honor" of walking the two over to the jail for booking. As I exited the PD I was stunned by the amount of media that had gathered wanting to see the two suspects. I got home about ten P.M. that night and called my parents to tell them the exciting news. My dad answered the phone and I asked him if he had seen the news today. He said, yes. I asked him if he saw the chase that occurred, and he asked me if I knew the officer involved. I told him it was me. That was a mistake. Parents are parents, and they wanted me to get out of the business. I laughed and said, "No, I'm living my dream."

I have never regretted that decision. I have been involved in numerous pursuits, but none as exciting as that first one. I am proud to say that I have stayed with the same department and have been the chief of police for the last seven years.

The Road Race and the Fly

THE BEAT

BY JIM ARCHULETTA

Sworn Officer, Decatur PD, Alabama, six years.

Around two in the morning dispatch called my number for an alarm at a liquor store on the far edge of town. It had been a quiet night and the alarm was one I had heard before. It usually didn't have much legitimacy: "alarm indicating general," not "glass breakage" or "door tampering," just a general alarm.

The liquor store was out toward the county line, far away, the type of store that was your last chance to buy alcohol before you entered the neighboring dry county. There was a long stretch of highway as you approached the store. It stood all by itself, with a few stores farther down the road, with woods and fields all around.

As I approached the business, even though it was just a general alarm, I still approached tactically. I turned off my headlights about a half mile before reaching the business. When the store came into view, I didn't observe any vehicles at or near the place. I quietly eased my patrol car to an angle off of the front of the business and got out. Once I was out of the car, I gently closed the door and began to walk around the store. I didn't see or hear anything, and everything appeared to be alright.

Probably just another false alarm, I thought.

As I walked around to the rear of the store, there was an extremely large black male standing at the rear store entrance trying to break down an iron door with a sledgehammer. I'm of average height, and here I was facing someone who looked to be about eight feet tall—a slight exaggeration—holding a damned sledgehammer. The second he saw me, he dropped the sledgehammer and was off to the races. Thank God he didn't turn on me. I yelled for him to stop, but as you can probably guess, that didn't make him stop.

I was instantly on the radio broadcasting that the alarm "was a hit," and that I was in foot pursuit. By the time I got around to the front of the store, he had already bypassed my car and was running away on the highway pavement. He was running in the direction that I had just arrived from in my car, which was headed into oncoming traffic. I quickly thought to jump into my patrol car and give chase since he already had about a hundred-meter lead on me, but I decided to keep running after him on foot. My patrol car was parked facing away from the direction he was running. I figured that if I jumped into my car, cranked it up, and turned around to start pursuing him, he would run into the woods somewhere and I would never find him again. In a foot chase I would be able to see him at all times and be able to see if he ran into the woods.

I radioed the foot chase (direction and location), but the cavalry was on its way fast. It was also on the radio, along with dispatch, so no one heard me. Damn, I thought, why don't they just shut up and listen? The radio traffic was bad; everyone was stepping on everyone, and no one heard where I was. Meanwhile, I was slowly gaining on the subject. There wasn't much traffic on the highway at three A.M., but there still was some. There were two cars coming as we ran and I was afraid that a drunk or even a sober person would come along and run me over. I was wearing my dark uniform and he was wearing all black. As the cars approached, we were both running along the side of the road, and I took my flashlight, turned it on and ran with it pointed over my shoulder. I figured that maybe someone would see it and slow down or, better yet, see that I was a police officer chasing a guy down the road at three A.M. (that's not normal, is it?), slow down enough and render help by running into the guy for me (just enough to stop him, not turn him into a pancake). Well, the cars never slowed, and we kept on running.

As we ran, I continued to gain ground (the guy was fast for being such a large man), and then we ran into a closed Shell gas station. That's where the chase finally ended . . . and the fight began.

The gas station was built on a downgrade, so the parking lot was a lot lower than the highway and not very visible from the highway lane heading toward the store. When we got to the Shell station, and I could see that I had him, I quickly radioed that I was at the Shell station and got out my pepper spray. Again, no one heard me. Everyone was now starting to arrive in the area, asking for my location, and dispatch was trying to check my status. Too many wanting to help, when just listening would have helped out the most. It really began to piss me off. I needed these guys and they were talking to each other.

When we got to the parking lot, the guy finally stopped running, turned to face me, and said, "All right, man, ya got me!" I responded with a blast of pepper spray directly to his face.

It was as if I had sprayed him with water; it had absolutely no effect on him. I had never had this happen before. He just kind of squinted up his face and took off running again farther into the Shell station parking lot. Meanwhile I could see the police cars racing by to my original location at the liquor store. When the other officers arrived at the store, all they found was my empty police car, an obvious burglary at the rear, and no radio contact with me. They began to search the area of the store, ditches, woods, and so on.

As the subject ran farther into the parking lot, I quickly holstered my spray and pulled out my expandable baton (my ASP). I am five foot eight, 135 pounds. This guy was later booked in as six foot one, 240 pounds—as I said earlier, he looked a *lot* bigger than that. I yelled at him to stop and to get on the ground. Again, he didn't want to listen to me for some reason. (Go figure.) I cracked him in the side of his knee, and that stopped him . . . for about seven seconds.

He turned to face me and again said, "All right, all right, you got me, man. You got me." He said it a little more desperately this time, though. I thought I might be getting his attention. I responded with "Get on the ground!" as I hit him again in the elbow area. He repeated, "You got me" as he advanced toward me. Maybe getting his attention wasn't such a good idea.

I repeatedly yelled, "Get on the ground." I hit him a second time in the knee, and then struck again up around the elbow. I tried to maintain good distance, and to "stick and move." The whole time I was backing up while striking and he was advancing, I thought, "Oh, shit." The guy didn't appear to feel any pain to spray or to impact weapons. He had to be on something! Here I was, fighting a giant who didn't feel any pain, with an army of cops a half mile away and they didn't know where I was. I didn't know whether I was more terrified than angry, but angry started to win out.

After I had backpedaled and struck him a total of four times, I tried to keep distance, but he was pretty close, and I went to strike him a fifth time. He stepped into me, took a little of my blow, but caught my baton up under his arm. He then reached out and grabbed the baton with both hands. There was an extremely brief tug-of-war for my baton, and then I let go. I needed to keep my distance, and if that meant giving up my baton, then so be it.

He was now armed with my weapon, but the second I let go of the baton, I had my Beretta 9mm pointed right at his chest. I told him to drop the weapon or I would shoot. He raised the baton above his head as if he were going to strike me with it. I yelled at him again, "Drop it or I'll kill you." This whole time officers and dispatch were squawking away on the radio wanting to know my status and where I was. My status was "Kind of busy at the moment"; my location was "Up shit creek without a paddle."

After I said to drop it or else I would kill him, he kept the baton raised as if to hit me and seemed to think for a moment. I guess he had to decide if he wanted to die or if he wanted to hit me. He made up his mind. He threw the baton away and took off running again. I thought for a moment how I'd just love to shoot him in the back and end it all, but I holstered my weapon and gave chase. (What I would have given for a taser!)

He ran through the parking lot and back onto a main road and started running toward the site of our previous marathon—the highway. I didn't have a baton anymore; pepper spray didn't work; and I didn't carry a taser . . . so what to do? I was faster and caught him quickly this time and got in front of him. I sprayed him a second time with my pepper spray. This time I gave him enough to knock down an elephant and yelled for him to get on the ground. Again, it was as if I'd just sprayed him with cool water. It had absolutely no effect on the man.

I went to holster my spray as I backpedaled. He had stopped running, but kept advancing toward me, and he grabbed hold of my left arm. There was a brief tug-of-war with my arm as I tried to get him to let go. This guy meant business. Again, no baton, spray didn't work, and no taser, but I still had one more gadget on my "Batman belt" . . . That's right—my trusty old Maglite! Not just the C-cell battery type, but the rechargeable one that weighs a ton. As he grabbed my left arm I hit him full force, directly in the face, with a little Maglite justice. *That* got through to him. He let go of me immediately, turned away from me, and started running. I then held my Maglite like a samurai sword and chopped him on the back of his head. This blow was full force, with both hands, and was devastating. It dropped him all the way to the ground, and I yelled at him, "Lay on the ground! Stay on the ground!"

Unfortunately, it didn't knock him out. He was on the ground for a second, and was already trying to stand back up. He got to all fours, and I kicked him directly in the stomach with everything I had. I was a little worried about the kick. Not about hurting him or anything, but I had a flash of worry that I didn't want him to lunge at me or be able to grab my foot and begin a wrestling match. If a wrestling match were to ensue, there would be no way for me to overpower him, and the bullets would immediately start flying.

The kick connected perfectly and hurt him, just a little bit. He remained on all fours and raised up his arm to defend himself from another kick or another flashlight attack. I rapidly holstered my flashlight and armed myself with a set of cuffs. Within a second, I had a cuff on him. It was only one cuff, though. We were face-to-face with me holding the cuff that was attached to him in a death grip. I was going to be in serious trouble in about one minute. But like I said, I got angry. I yelled at him to get on the ground repeatedly and yanked him down by the cuffed hand. I was able to get the better of him, and he went forward to the ground. Once on the ground, I couldn't attempt to secure the other hand because he was instantly struggling and trying to stand back up, so I just kept yanking on the cuff while he continued to tug and stand up.

The events of the night caught up with him—finally. I wasn't feeling too chipper either. He was exhausted and stopped trying to resist—*finally*. He lay on his belly as I dragged him down the road by his cuffed hand. I stopped dragging him once I felt he had stopped resisting enough for me to get that other hand secured. Now I had the complete upper hand. If I went to get the second cuff on and he fought, I could begin dragging him down the road some more.

When the struggling stopped, I hopped to the side, knelt down on his back, and was able to secure the second cuff. No sooner had I got the cuff on him than he started back up again. Now he was completely cuffed, yelling at me, and trying to work his way back up to standing. I stayed on top of him and began driving his face into the pavement with my forearm to the back of his head and yelled for him to stop resisting and to stay on the ground. With a giant sigh of relief, I keyed my radio and let everyone know that I was by the Shell station on the roadway, and had the subject arrested. It was an even half mile from the burglarized liquor store. (Yes, this time everyone heard me.)

The subject was requesting water, which naturally he didn't get, and it was discovered that where I had samurai-sworded him on the back of the head, he had a huge gash with some meat hanging out of it. During the struggle I hadn't even noticed it. I walked back and retrieved my baton and then received a ride back to the liquor store as the suspect didn't go directly to jail, but was transported to the hospital to have his head taken care of.

Now that all of the action was over, the fun stuff began. I was taken back to the store and the owner was there. I began to get my report book and paperwork and someone said to me, "Are you sure you're alright. Your arm is bleeding all over." I looked down, and sure enough, my right arm was bloody. I used the store's outside hose and washed my arm off to find that I wasn't hurt. It was the burglar's blood from the back of his head; as I was making him eat pavement, it got all over me. Well, it just so happened that I had a new baby kitten at home that I played and fought with and that bloody arm of mine was covered in scratches and cuts from my kitten. So, after my paperwork at the scene was completed, my shift was officially over, and I was off to the hospital to meet with a supervisor.

At the hospital, I found the subject was there being treated, too, as a host of officers stood by him. Here we were, only moments ago, struggling to kill or be killed, and now we were sitting next to each other being treated by nurses. This is a weird job.

The hospital determined that he *wasn't* under the influence of anything; he was sober! He was just some big muscled-up dummy who felt no pain and did not want to be caught.

I ended up being fine medically, but I did have to keep on being seen at the clinic for the next year. There were about four visits, and each time they had to stick me with needles, run tests, and take my blood. I didn't know if he had given me something, or if my wife or kid could get it. So for a whole year I was reminded of this guy and that night.

Many officers have said, "I would have just shot him." I didn't feel that it had reached the point of a shooting. Granted, once he took my weapon, I would have been very justified in shooting him, and had he given the slightest sign that he was going to strike me with that baton, I would have opened fire, but things worked out well for me that night. I never felt scared at any time; things were contained and I felt determined. All I was thinking back then was "I'm not going to let this guy get away."

Chalk one up for the good guys for once. I kind of compare the encounter to a fly at a picnic. Large humans have all this food, and this little fly just keeps on swarming around, keeping his distance. He will stick and move to get at the food, get swatted at, and know the danger is there, but he just keeps on coming and will not quit. Well, on that night I was the fly that irritated the man, would not go away, and would not give up . . . and I got what I was after.

The Sadness of It All

THE BEAT

BY BRENT LARSON

Sworn Officer, Dallas PD, Texas, twelve years.

If you're any good at the art of being a cop—and it is an art—you learn to be a problem solver, which involves being a police officer, a priest, and a counselor. I refer to myself and my fellow officers as "the Band-aid guys." I'm not an expert, but I have gained some experience and learned a few things over the years. However, we can't solve every problem.

Several years ago, my sergeant and I responded to a domestic distrubance call. Once there, we learned, through the halting English of the Hispanic husband, that his wife had been having an affair and she was now leaving the house *and* her family. They had two young children together, a girl who was about eight years old and a boy who was six. The girl was upset, but she seemed to understand a little of what was going on. The boy was another story. He was very upset, crying and sobbing that his mother was going away, that his mommy was leaving him. There was no consoling him. His sister tried, but was unsuccessful. So did we. The sergeant and I were just about in tears—that poor little baby was losing his mother, and he couldn't understand why. But he did understand that she didn't love him enough to stay, and I have to say it did piss me off. The father was just angry, and unable to help. It was painful to listen to the boy crying so—and I didn't even have children then; it would have been harder for me to take, I think, if I had been a father. The sarge had kids, and I practically had to hold him up. We could see this was going to haunt this child for the rest of his life. What could we do about it? What could an *army* of psychiatrists do to help?

Then I remembered the stuffed animals that most of us in law enforcement carry in the trunk. I went out to my car, and digging through the bag, I found an especially cute Kermit the Frog, which also happened to be a puppet of sorts. I went back inside the house, where the crying little boy was sitting in the living room with his sister, hiding the frog behind my back. Pulling the frog out and manipulating his mouth to open as I did my best Kermit voice imitation, I talked to the boy, trying to get him to understand what was happening, trying to get him to understand that his poppa loved him and that his sister loved him and that his mama would come to see him all the time.

It seemed to work. He stopped crying and got a smile on his face. I talked to the boy for several minutes as Kermit the Frog and then I gave him the frog. He was happy for a few minutes, then the reality of the situation got the best of him again and he began to cry again.

Unfortunately, there wasn't anything to be done about it; as much as I wanted one, I did not have a magic wand. Sarge and I had to leave. We got to the door, and both turned to look at the boy sobbing on the floor. Neither of us said a word. There was nothing we could say to that child. I just didn't have the skills to bring some solace to the little boy; I'm not sure anybody does. I'm glad that I was able to give the boy some brief happiness, but I went away sad, too. Thinking about the incident, even now, makes me emotional.

Sometimes we have to experience the pain of it all right along with those who are going through it. You can't keep it out. Those are the ones that get to you. They don't happen every day, but they build up. Sometimes they build up into a wall between you and the rest of the world. That wall is as dangerous for us as anything else in this job. It's a terrible balance we have to maintain: Get too involved, and you lose your ability to be effective. Don't get involved enough and you become emotionally constipated, and you'll choke on the poison building up inside you.

Do the most good you can. Do your best. Don't look back. Don't second-guess yourself.

I sure wish I could have helped that little boy, though.

The Shooting

DEADLY FORCE

BY CORY HATCH

Sworn Officer, Utah, ten years.

I was working the swing shift, 1600 to 0200 hours. I have worked the swing shift for several years. Swings are the busiest shift for a cop, and I like being busy. It had been a pretty normal day of taking calls and making a few traffic stops. At about 0200 hours, I was called to assist a juvenile caseworker. The caseworker needed to pick up a juvenile who had a warrant for his arrest. The juvenile was actually eighteen, but was on probation with juvenile court. I arrived at the location, a low-income housing project where I met with the caseworker. He told me the juvenile I was to help him arrest was a good kid who had nothing involving violence on his record. He told me the kid had really come a long way; the warrant was just for missing a court date, not a big deal. The caseworker seemed very passive and showed no hesitation or worry.

We walked to the apartment complex, and when we arrived at the door, the caseworker knocked. We were greeted by a friendly female who had called us about Eli, her nephew. She knew he had the warrant out on him and wanted him to get it taken care of. She also told us Eli was expecting our arrival and knew he was going to be arrested. She invited us in and showed us the stairway to the basement where Eli was supposed to be. The caseworker and I went down a long, narrow flight of stairs to a dimly lit room. As we walked into the room, we saw Eli and what appeared to be some friends. They seemed to be just hanging out, waiting for us to come. Steve, the caseworker, and Eli started up a very friendly conversation. They even shared a hug. After some small talk Steve told Eli he would have to be taken to juvenile detention because of the missed court date. Eli agreed and said "okay." The caseworker pointed to me and told Eli I would be making the arrest. Eli calmly walked to where I was standing . . . and the mood changed.

Eli, "the friendly kid with no violent tendencies," snapped. Something deep in him came screaming to the surface and was about to ambush me. When I told him to turn around so I could handcuff him, Eli did as he was told for the moment and turned around. He allowed me to take his left hand. I took hold of his wrist and attempted the control hold, when he immediately swung around, facing me . . . with a seven-inch knife blade pointed toward my chest. I was only about two feet away from him. He spoke to me for the first time, saying, "I'm not going anywhere with you, motherfucker." Startled, shocked, surprised—and let's not forget scared—I pulled my weapon and took several steps backward until I reached the stairs.

I put myself right into a very bad position. As I quickly backed up, I forgot there were stairs behind me. I hit the stairs and fell backward, landing on the second stair in a sitting position. I jumped up, yelling at him to drop the knife. I knew I was more than justified in shooting him, but the caseworker was right behind him. At such a close range, I didn't want to take the shot for fear of hitting the caseworker.

So I was climbing backward up the stairs for what seemed like an eternity. I had also hit the emergency activation button on my radio, which opened up the radio receiver so everyone on the channel could hear what was going on. I also yelled 10–33 into my radio. That means "help me quickly." This code is only used in the most dire of circumstances, usually when an officer's life is in jeopardy.

Eli, who was still climbing the stairs with the knife, had a cold, empty look in his eyes. I knew he was more than willing to kill me. I yelled at him over and over to drop the knife or be shot. His response was, "Fuck you, pig. You ain't taking me nowhere."

I finally reached the top of the stairs and the solid kitchen floor. Everybody was yelling—his three friends, the caseworker behind him, and his aunt and uncle in the kitchen where I was. Eli came up into the kitchen, cold and hard, and just then, the caseworker ran up from behind and grabbed him. He tried to wrestle with Eli, which was fruitless—it lasted about three seconds. The caseworker was a little pipsqueak of a guy, and Eli was a big eighteen-year-old "future killer," and he had killing and escaping on his mind.

Eli tried to stab the caseworker but missed. He then broke free and looked at me for a split second, deciding whether to take me or run. With a .40-caliber handgun pointed right at him, he decided to make a run for it. He took off through the living room and out the front door of the apartment, knife still in hand. I stood there, thinking that I was safe for the moment and that I shouldn't run after him. But then I remembered, "Oh, yeah, I'm a police officer. I have to chase after the bad guy." I gave an update to dispatch, and to the front door I went. I cleared the doorway as I exited, in case he was lying in wait for me just outside. I looked through the complex and saw him running toward the street. The chase was on. He ran until he was out of the apartment complex and hit the city streets. I surprised myself at how fast I closed in on him. I was just thirty feet behind.

I had been in a shooting three years prior to this incident. It was over much faster than this one. I didn't really have time to do anything but react. Here, I felt like this screwed-up situation had been going on forever. I heard sirens coming from all directions. I continued to give dispatch an update on our location by opening the receiver every thirty seconds or so.

When we got about a block away from the apartments, Eli quickly turned on me. He was out of breath and couldn't run anymore. Pointing the knife at me, he yelled, "Leave me alone, motherfucker. Leave me alone, or I'm gonna kill you." I yelled at him to drop the knife or be shot. Meanwhile my fellow officers were in a panic trying to get to me as fast as they could. They were taking in every word and action through the radio.

Hitting the emergency button on my radio wasn't only so everyone else could know what was going on, but also to protect myself from other problems—such as civil actions or being fired by my department. My department had recently been hanging officers out to dry for political and other reasons, and I was not about to be hung out to dry. Looking back later that day, I thought: What kind of environment do I work in where not only could I get stabbed or have to kill this guy, but I also have to worry about being sued or fired for having to do it? This guy is forcing my hand. Should I let him go, I could also get punished. He could run off and harm someone else, and I would be to blame for that, too.

As he was facing me, I had no doubt in my mind he was more than willing to kill me to get away. I guessed he was thinking I wouldn't shoot him because I had not shot him yet. In the movies he would have died in the first few seconds, or he would have been shot in the back while he was running away. Maybe he thought I was unwilling to pull the trigger.

He was about fifteen feet away from me when he stopped and turned. He stopped so suddenly I ended up much closer to him than I wanted to be. I knew I needed to be more than twenty-one feet away to be safe. I saw an evil look in his eyes and his hand clenched around the knife as he said, "What ya gonna do, motherfucker? Gonna kill me?" Then he lunged at me. I quickly pulled the trigger and hit him in the midsection. I was aiming a little higher, but I was backpedaling and shooting at the same time and dropped my shot a couple of inches. He fell to the ground immediately, rolling himself into a ball, holding pressure on the gaping hole I had just put in his stomach. The situation ended with him being worked on by the paramedics and me being transported to the station house to sit, wait, think, and hope I did everything right.

The times I have been forced to shoot somebody do not weigh heavily on my mind. Yeah, there are three or four sleepless days in which the incident replays in your mind hundreds of times over. You ask yourself if there was anything else or different you could have done. I didn't want to pull the trigger. I don't go to work thinking, "Hey, maybe I can kill someone today."

I hope I never have to pull the trigger on another human being again. That is my hope, but the profession that I and six hundred fifty thousand of my bothers and sisters in blue have chosen, leaves us all with the possibility of having to kill or hurt someone. The choice doesn't make us ruthless, evil, or even unkind people. It is others who force our hand and give us no choice.

Police officers are all heroes. Big city cops or rural county cops, we protect the weak and oppose the evil in hopes of preserving a little bit of sanity in an insane world. I hope and pray every day that not one more officer has to die for just doing his job.

Suicide by Cop

LINE OF DUTY

BY ROBERT MLADINICH

Detective Second Grade, New York PD, twenty years.

I've been retired from the New York Police Department for five years, and it still angers me to read so many articles about the law enforcement community's alleged disregard for human life, especially in minority communities. After nearly every police shooting, the media paints cops with the broad brush of racism they claim to detest. Having been a police officer and a detective for twenty years, I personally bear witness to several instances in which officers could have justifiably fired their weapons but chose not to for a variety of reasons. On one such occasion, it happened to me. Not surprisingly, there was no mention of it in the news.

Back in the early eighties, before crack cocaine became the scourge of the city, my partner, Michael Whyte, and I were working as patrol officers in the 42nd Precinct in the South Bronx. We couldn't have had more than two years on the job when we turned out for midnight shift in full uniform in a marked department vehicle.

As we turned onto a road that ran through the heart of a housing project, we heard two shots and observed muzzle flashes from a distance of about a hundred feet. At the same time, a screaming, panicked crowd ran from the area. Whyte and I did what cops everywhere do on a daily basis. We raced toward danger as everyone else raced away.

Never once did the gunman, a black man in his late thirties, leave our field of vision. We screeched to a halt just a few feet from him, took whatever cover we could from our vehicle, extended our .38-caliber service revolvers in a combat stance, and ordered him to drop his weapon. At the time his eyes seemed feral, but looking back, I realize they were more blank and lifeless than anything else. His revolver was pointed directly at us. To this day, I question why we didn't shoot him immediately. We had every reason to believe he was a danger to us as well as to the community. He made no attempt to flee when he saw us coming, so a reasonable conclusion would have been that he wanted to engage us in a gun battle.

"Drop the gun!" we shouted in unison. It's amazing how many thoughts can run through your mind in such a short time. I actually considered the fact that he was a black man, and also concluded that there would probably be no controversy associated with shooting him. Cops develop their street instincts quickly, especially when working in high-crime precincts. My mind told me to shoot him, but instinct told me not to. One thing a cop needs to trust more than anything else—except perhaps his partner—is his instinct.

Whyte and I repeated the order for him to drop the weapon six or seven more times. He continued to fix us with a steely glare. Although armed with what was a presumably loaded gun, he seemed more desperate than dangerous. Suddenly the same crowd that had fled earlier, nearly all of whom were black, began to regather. As they watched, they grew braver, more raucous, and even meaner by the minute.

"Smoke the motherfucker!" someone yelled.

"Cap him!" screamed another.

"Kill him!" were the last words we heard before charging and disarming the gunman in one or two spine-tingling seconds.

While we processed the arrest of the gunman at the precinct, his daughter came in and ardently thanked us for not shooting him. In her late teens or early twenties, she was wise beyond her years. It was obvious that she had seen a lot of pain in her life, and much of it came from her father's condition. The indomitable love that she felt for him was apparent as she explained that he was a brain-damaged Vietnam veteran who had spent time in a prisoner-of-war camp. After serving his country so valiantly, he returned home, only to be taunted by young punks because of his occasional oddball, but innocuous behavior.

Years after this incident occurred, a phenomenon called "suicide by cop" made its way into the fabric of American culture. Looking back, I have no doubt that was the vet's mission that night. Had he wanted to harm those who taunted him, he certainly could have shot at least one or two of them. After all, he was a combat veteran. Although I could never be sure, I think he carried that gun with him often, waiting for a golden opportunity. He had too big a heart to kill one of the taunting kids, but if he shot *at* them in the presence of two police officers, the cops would have no choice but to take him out. After speaking with his daughter about how despondent he had been in recent weeks, that seemed to be a likely scenario.

I still reflect on that night more than twenty years later. If this man had murder and mayhem on his mind, he undoubtedly could have shot his adversaries and still had a few bullets remaining for responding police officers. Only later did I learn that cops who are in lethal or potentially lethal situations are inveterate second-guessers. The what-if scenarios that run relentlessly through their heads can be maddening. However, what-ifs aside, one thing street cops learn fast is to trust their own instincts. On that potentially deadly evening, I trusted mine, Officer Whyte trusted his, and we both lived to talk and write about it.

Every time a cop is wounded or killed in a shooing incident, I can't help but wonder if their instincts betrayed them. Did they hesitate to shoot for some reason we will never know? Contrary to what many would like the public to believe, nearly all cops are good people who want to do the right thing. They find no joy in taking someone's life. Even when that is completely justified, the scrutiny they are put under and the intense investigative process that follows might have them second-guessing themselves for all eternity.

More times than not, cops don't shoot, even if they have the legal right to do so. Perhaps they fear hitting an innocent passerby. Perhaps the thought of political backlash and possible indictment is stronger than the need for self-preservation. I would hate to think that the latter comes into play, but I have been told by many officers that it does. In a city like New York, where race is always an issue, it was at the forefront of my mind when I was pointing my gun at a black man. I wonder if that factor had any effect on what my instincts were telling me.

The fact is no one was hurt—not the kids who instigated the matter, not the gunman, not I or my partner. I'd like to think the gunman got help and is living a much happier existence today, but that's something I'll probably never know. Sad to say, despite the indelible impression the incident left on me, I don't even remember his name.

One thing I do know is this: I personally made nearly eight hundred arrests during my career and assisted in many more. I executed hundreds of search warrants and sent a lot of criminals to prison for long sentences. Yet, out of everything I've done in my police career, I commend myself most for not shooting that man.

Trapped While Wearing the Badge

LINE OF DUTY

BY ARTIE RODRIGUEZ

Deputy Sheriff, Walton County, Florida, nine years.

My name is Artie Rodriguez and I have been a deputy sheriff with the Walton County Sheriff's Office in the Florida Panhandle since 1999.

It was July 11, 2002, at approximately midnight, one of those Florida nights where you could cut the humidity with a knife. The night was slow, so fellow deputy Aaron Brown and I met at a gas station to decide where to get something to eat. While standing outside by our patrol cars, I received a call from dispatch stating I needed to be en route to a Signal 75 (shots fired) at a nearby residence.

As I listened to the orders I could feel my heartbeat speed up as it pushed adrenaline through my veins. I had a feeling about this call. I couldn't put my finger on it, but something was telling me this was trouble. I got into my patrol car and advised dispatch that I was en route. I overheard Deputy Brown state that he was coming to back me up. We were pretty much flying blind, as no one knew what might be unfolding at the residence. We did not know if there were lives at risk, so I stepped up the speed. I was a good deal ahead of Brown, and my heart was thumping even harder than before . . . and my brain was screaming, "Danger!"

As I neared the location of the call, my speed reached 92 mph. Suddenly, I observed a small black truck run a stop sign to my right. I hit the brakes, veered to the left, and sent up a string of prayers and curses as I tried to avoid the truck. Despite my frantic efforts, the truck slammed into the passenger-side door of my patrol car. I bit down as I spun like a top down the six lanes, turning around three complete times and traveling 364 feet while the smell of burning rubber and asphalt singed my nostrils and eyes.

Several cars had to drive off the road to avoid hitting me. My patrol car finally came to a rest on the other side of a six-lane road. My head was spinning and everything hurt. I felt numb, though, and I thought, since I wasn't in pain, I must be okay. I tried to get out of my car, afraid that the twisted hunk of metal might be on fire. I smelled smoke and this began to make me frantic. I began trying to get out, but I couldn't move my arms. I was trapped. My airbag had deployed, pinning me to the seat, and my lungs were filled with the rancid burning, which seemed to be worsening. All I could think about at the time was: Which would be worse, smothering in the fumes or going up in flames? I quickly realized how dangerous that kind of thinking could be and I forced myself to think of concrete ways to help myself. With desperate strength I tried moving my body back and forth, but I couldn't seem to get free.

As I struggled, I pushed the panic that was threatening to overcome my thinking down and out of my mind. I realized that I was pinned underneath my shotgun and the dash. Nothing was working in my car. There was no radio, no lights, and no sirens. The only two things that were working were my portable shoulder radio and seat belt. Thank God for that!

At that time, I heard Deputy Brown come over my shoulder radio stating he was coming up on a major accident and would check to see if there were any injuries. I yelled, hoping to get his attention, but he was too far away, and I couldn't get my hands free to get him on the radio. I could only hear him. Deputy Brown only saw the black truck and did not see my smashed-up patrol car down the road. When he finally saw my patrol car, he radioed dispatch and advised them that I was involved in a major accident. Deputy Brown stated he did not know if I was hurt or dead. Over the radio transmissions you could immediately hear supervisors and deputies working special details on the beach leave their stations to check on one of their fallen brothers. I was sure happy to hear this, but if my car was on fire, it wasn't going to do me any good. I screamed for Brown to come and get me out, the panic rising again.

Swinging wildly back and forth, I tried again to get free. That's when I began to feel the rising tide of pain in my back. At first there was no pain, and then the pain was overwhelming. The thought that I could burn to death drove me to push through the pain and pull my arms free. Eventually I freed my left arm from the piece of metal pinning it and was able to get on the radio. Now that I could communicate, I did not want anyone to know how panicked I'd been just a few moments before. In a calm voice I told dispatch that I was alive, but I was hurt and trapped inside my patrol car.

I sat clinging to my handheld radio, as my little lifeline squawked and chirped with the voices of my fellow officers. I made myself concentrate on that chatter, knowing my friends and colleagues would get me out in time.

My car never caught on fire, and South Walton Fire Department had to use the Jaws of Life to cut me out of my car. From the time of my accident to the time I was cut out of my vehicle was approximately thirty minutes. It seemed like days.

I suffered a fracture to one of my vertebrae and compressed-disk injuries to my back. I was given the Law Enforcement Purple Heart for injuries in the line of duty from the American Police Hall of Fame. Mr. Dennis Wise, president of APHA, presented me with the award in front of Florida's assistant attorney general and representatives from Mothers Against Drunk Driving.

As for the driver who struck me, he had a blood alcohol content of .254, over three times the legal limit in Florida.

Oh, his injuries, and the shots-fired call? Well, the man only suf-fered a minor concussion.

The shots-fired call was just some drunk idiot who still thought it was the Fourth of July.

Unwanted Male

BY JEREMY M. WILLIAMS

Sworn Officer, Montgomery County, VA Sheriff's office, Virginia Tech PD, retired after fifteen years.

In my fifteen years in law enforcement, I had several interesting things happen to me. The one that has always stuck in my mind as being the most unusual is this one.

It was spring of 1995 and I was working eight-hour days on a seven-day rotation, and it was my first day of days (eight A.M.–four P.M.). I was working as a deputy sheriff for the Montgomery County Sheriff's Office in Montgomery County, Virginia.

I pulled into the parking lot at the Sheriff's Office toward the end of my shift and, man, I was ready to head home and crawl into bed—I was beat. Just as I was getting out of the car, the radio cracked, "Montgomery to 24, we need you to respond to Arsenal Circle for an unwanted male at that residence." I flipped on the sparkling blue lights and wailing siren, threw the car into reverse, and screeched out of the parking space. I knew where I was going and that it was about twelve or so miles away. Not only was it Saturday, but I would have to pass the mall, and the road was a two-laner, one of the busiest and most dangerous in the county. I made it past the mall, and the traffic wasn't bad, but the dispatcher radioed me again, "Montgomery to 24." (Cops amaze me by driving eighty miles an hour, talking on the radio, and waving cars out of the way all at the same time.)

I answered, "Go ahead."

"Two-four, the caller just hung up."

Damn! I thought, now what is happening? Is he still there? Is he hurting her? Did he hang the phone up or pull it out of the wall? Just another thing to add to the eighty-mile-an-hour scenario. I put a little more foot on the pedal.

The dispatcher radioed again. "We got her back on the line, and all we can get out of her is, 'unwanted male, unwanted male.'" Now I knew this woman must be fighting for her life. She certainly sounded scared out of her wits. I hoped I would be able to get some backup.

I worked the siren and hit the horn and I could hear the dispatcher sending another unit my way. I knew he wasn't even close and wouldn't be able to help me for more than ten minutes. Again the dispatcher called my number, this time to advise me that an off-duty unit had checked out of his house and was headed my way. Another deputy from the adjacent county was headed to the house, but he was at least five minutes behind me. I was glad to have the help because this call had all the earmarks of serious trouble. A good dispatcher is a godsend.

Siren blaring, lights whirling, I screamed to a stop in front of the address. I threw open the door, pulled my gun, and started running. I saw a petite, brown-haired young lady standing in the glass of the storm door.

There were no cars in the driveway, just my patrol unit. She didn't look like she was hurt—or even attacked. She waved me in, and I thought to myself, the guy must have left the area. I must have passed him.

I spoke to her and asked if she was okay, and she said in a mumbly voice, "Unwanted male, unwanted male!" I asked her where he was. She shook her head and mumbled, "No, no," and pointed to the kitchen table, again mumbling "Unwanted male!"

And there it was, lying on the kitchen table. Three pieces of "unwanted *mail*." It was "junk mail." What the hell! I just about wore out a set of brakes, burnt a tank of gas, and scared the hell out of who knows how many people just because she was accosted by a Wal-Mart sales promotion, local grocery coupons, and, I believe, a CD club wanting her to join.

After seeing the "mail" I *still* checked the residence for anyone else. I guess I was still nervous from the drive and a little confused. I used it also to calm down because I was so pissed. After walking around, I sat down at the kitchen table, and she was still very upset and still shouting about the "unwanted mail." I was so darn mad, all I could do was glare at her.

I contacted the dispatcher and explained that everyone else could disregard the call, that the there was no male, just some "unwanted mail."

As I began to explain, I thought I had lost my dispatcher, but I hadn't. She just couldn't catch her breath from laughing. The young lady handed me a pad of paper. She had written me a note while I was on the phone with dispatch. The note said, "I do not have the money for the male and you take it with you," still misspelling it. I'm sure I about broke down laughing. As I was trying to write her back and explain the mail was free and not any type of bill, the young lady's mom showed up and explained to me that she was almost deaf and had just moved into the basement apartment that week and had never lived by herself.

When I first got dispatched, the dispatcher did tell me the call had been received by the TDD (telecommunications device for the deaf) system and all the caller would type was "unwanted male, unwanted male." Knowing this, the thought never crossed any of our minds that all it was, was "unwanted mail."

Mystery solved. I got a good story. And *finally* I got to go home and get some sleep.

Walking Among the Dead

LINE OF DUTY

BY MICHAEL J. EAST

Sworn Officer, Saginaw PD, Michigan, fourteen years.

It's just after eight A.M. on a deep-blue August morning in Saginaw, Michigan, when the early morning air is light and full of life.

My shoulders slump slightly under the weight of two five-gallon water containers as I pass small plots filled with animal-shaped crafts, family themes, and flowers of all colors. One garden is decorated with the names and handprints of children set in plaster. Another screams neglect, its flowers wilting and nearly dead.

Beneath the partial shade of a nearby tree, I set down the containers, wipe the sweat from my forehead with the front of my shirt, and begin my near-daily personal time with the deceased officers of the Saginaw Police Department in this garden, the Garden of Dead Heroes.

It was two years ago that my wife, Deanna, was selected from a list of "adopt-a-garden" wannabes. Her reward was about eighty square feet of earth near the chick hatchery at the Saginaw Children's Zoo. We knew immediately we would turn our garden into a memorial for local police officers killed in the line of duty.

Using large rocks bearing officers' names, ages, and dates of death, we set off now each spring to shape a new garden. Flowers fill our plot, set in the predetermined patterns my wife arranges. The crest of the Fraternal Order of Police Lodge No. 105 sits near the center. The Policeman's Prayer is positioned in the forefront. An American flag stands sentinel in the rear. In a front corner also stands a statue of a small child my wife recently added. He is dressed in an oversized policeman's uniform, a cop's hat drooping down over his forehead. My wife says the figure adds a sense of hope to the garden. I study it again briefly this morning, but I'm unable to see the hope of which she speaks.

My attention turns toward the dead as I water the flowers placed near the names on each stone. I always water these flowers first, while brushing sticks, leaves, and dirt from each stone, so the names—Charles Ring, John Schmiegel, Zigmund Ozerajtys, Roy McKee, Daniel Waters, Clarence Dietzel, Leon Scott, Gary Mc-Cullen, David Hubbard, and Kevin Sherwood—can be read easily by passersby. Someone must see these officers are not forgotten. To-morrow I will repeat this task.

Ring, Schmiegel, Ozerajtys, McKee, Waters, Dietzel, Scott, and Mc-Cullen were Saginaw police officers killed in the line of duty. Trooper Hubbard was assigned to a local post of the Michigan State Police. Deputy Kevin Sherwood was from a county not far from Saginaw. Al-though the garden was meant to honor officers killed locally, Kevin Sherwood was added at the request of his widow, who had seen the garden during a visit. His mother later sent me a message of thanks for adding her son's name to this garden. Her words left me in tears.

I knew none of these men personally. But as I gather two more containers of water—the scorching August heat plays havoc with our garden—I am at peace with being a cop. I feel an odd sense of purpose, if only for an hour. After fourteen years of working the streets of Saginaw, that sense of purpose is hard to come by.

My career as a cop began in a usual way. I was drawn to the ca-maraderie that policemen share. I loved the uniform, the cop car, and the thought of being in control. And then there was the adren-aline, that addictive rush of energy I got by responding to a shoot-ing, running down a bad guy, or sitting behind the wheel in a hundred-mile-an-hour, engine-rattling, tire-squealing chase. Saginaw was a great place to be a cop then, but those days are long gone, faded away like the faces of officers who used to stand by my side.

It was sometime in 2000 that I first heard rumors of police layoffs and budget deficits. Eight years later the decimation of my department continues unabated. Our officer count has dropped from 165 to 94, counting the six laid-off cops who were temporarily called back to work. The SPD has none of those youthful, enthusiastic rookies who complement a department's savvy veterans so well. The last cop to receive his pink slip had seven years' experience.

A former automotive boomtown, Saginaw, with a population of about 58,000, is now a violent, decaying city dying a slow rust-belt death. The city's high poverty and unemployment rates, combined with a poorly educated populace, allow thugs, dope dealers, and street gangs to thrive. And while citizens weep as their children die in the streets, tax requests to return our police department to workable staffing levels have been turned down time and again.

Crime statistics show Saginaw is one of the most violent cities in the country, per capita, with one of the lowest police-officer-to-citizen ratios. It is not unusual to have two or three shootings per shift. A double homicide no longer raises eyebrows. Many shots-fired calls go unchecked for hours. Yet the layoffs continue.

If you are a cop in Saginaw, the job is no longer about duty, honor, and courage. It's about survival. More than a hundred officers have come and gone during my fourteen years. Some retired, many laid off, and others transferred to less volatile surroundings. One former coworker killed himself after leaving the SPD.

Year after year the killing continues unchallenged. At times crime waves and shootings hit unimaginable highs, even by Saginaw's standards. Community leaders bellow for action. They hold prayer vigils, parades for peace, and crime prevention summits. Yet when even more cops lose their jobs, there is no public outrage. And those who remain, like me, will face another year of trying to survive on the streets of a town that refuses to help itself.

A couple of years ago, I stood alone in a garbage-strewn backyard, holding five reportedly armed men at gunpoint. During those tense moments while I waited for backup, my finger itchy near the trigger, sweat dripping from my forehead, a woman in her forties stood on a nearby porch, screaming repeatedly that I was mistreating the suspects by pointing a gun at them. Moments later, with backup on the scene and the bad guys secured, I scolded the woman for distracting me during such a tense situation.

"You know, next time, why don't you shut the hell up until the situation is under control," I yelled, my face flushed with anger. "I would rather not die in this shitty backyard because you can't keep your mouth shut."

Her response has stuck with me to this day: "You're a cop. It's your job to get killed." She walked back into her house and slammed the door.

So goes a cop's life in Saginaw, Michigan.

Like many of my coworkers, I have cried at the funerals of slain officers, comforted women as their sons lay dead in the street, and witnessed firsthand the destruction from drugs and gang warfare. I have faced the walking, breathing human nightmares who prowl our streets and prey upon the innocent. I've seen more death, hatred, and violence than I care to remember. Nothing, however, has scarred me more than a community that will not stand up for those who are asked to defend it.

In recent years citizens and city leaders have repeatedly funneled precious dollars away from the police department to fund social and recreational programs. And as our officers literally fight for their very survival, budgetary cuts have been justified by those who wield the knife. "How will the kids stay out of trouble without recreation programs?" and "Who will watch over the children and keep them from gangs and drugs?" are words heard far too often. The role of the parent appears lost in my community.

I find myself now a forty-three-year-old cop too close to a pension to quit, and too disillusioned to put it all on the line every day for a city that has turned its back on its police force. My department's collective pleas for help from those we serve have gone unanswered. Yet the calls still flood Central Dispatch day after day, hour after hour; calls from those who refused our cries for help, now screaming for our assistance. More often than not, I find myself unenthused about risking my life in such surreal surroundings. Many coworkers confide that they share the same dilemma. Yet we continue to answer the calls as best we can, wading waist-deep through the human carnage that pollutes our city.

As I water the last of the flowers planted in a garden for these cops who gave their lives, I wonder if they ever shared the doubts and frustrations I feel every day. And as I walk toward my car, and think about the workday ahead, I feel my sense of purpose fading.

Editor's Note: Shortly after this story was written, the city of Saginaw, citing severe budget shortages, announced nearly fifty more police officers and firefighters were scheduled for layoff. Members of the Saginaw police and fire departments helped raise tens of thousands of dollars for a public-awareness campaign aimed at passing a public safety millage initiative. Officers went door to door for weeks in Saginaw, literally begging taxpayers to support this initiative. Many city leaders, previously silent regarding public safety layoffs, finally joined in the fight, as rejection of this tax would have rendered the Saginaw Police Department useless for all practical purposes.

The months prior to this crucial vote were marred by some of the worst violence Saginaw has ever witnessed. Ironically, the murders and bloodshed Saginaw police officers fight so hard to prevent were thought to have greatly swayed public opinion in their favor. When voting results were tallied, Saginaw's citizens overwhelmingly passed a five-year millage to support the city's police and fire departments and avert planned layoffs.

On April 23, 2007, at a public ceremony at Saginaw's city hall, three new police officers were sworn in to service—the first new hires at the Saginaw Police Department in nearly ten years. Fueled by the positive response of Saginaw's voters, Officer East has since abandoned plans to leave police work and go into private business. He continues to spend his days patrolling Saginaw's streets, answering calls for help from those who finally answered his.

Wayne

THE FALLEN

BY KEVIN WHITE

Sworn Officer, Pocahontas County Sheriff's Department, West Virginia, twenty-three years.

I was working the dispatch on the eighteenth of January 1999. It had been a fairly quiet shift, with only one complaint and one accident. As a large county in West Virginia with a small number of officers, including the city officers and troopers, we usually had only one or two officers working at a time, as we did on this day.

I took a call of a minor, two-vehicle crash, no injuries and no damage to anything other than the vehicles. Our only county officer had stopped at his house for supper, so the call went to Senior Trooper Wayne Bland, and he said that he would run out to the scene and take care of it.

About thirty minutes after I took the call and dispatched it, the tow truck driver called and asked where the officer was who was coming to the wreck. I told him that he should be getting there anytime. I attempted to contact Trooper Bland on the radio but couldn't get him. I called the State Police detachment and had the radio operator there attempt to contact him, and he got no answer.

After a few more minutes the tow truck driver called back and told me that the officer had not yet arrived and that's when I started getting worried. Something was wrong, very wrong.

I contacted our county officer at his residence, and he said that he would head for the wreck to handle it. I contacted the city officer, and he also started looking for Wayne while I kept trying to contact him on the radio. I called the State Police radio operator again, and they were also attempting to contact him, but with no success. I knew Wayne's sergeant was at home, so I called him and told him what was going on. He left immediately to look for Wayne. I heard the worry in his voice. We were all worried . . . and getting more worried every minute.

While we were looking for Wayne and calling him on the radio, many people called the radio room volunteering to join the search, including off-duty officers, wrecker service owners—even members of the general public. We are a close-knit community, and when something like this happens we all pull together. Wayne was well liked by everyone.

Our civil process server, Frank Closter, and his wife, Mary, came out and were looking also. They met the first tow truck as it was heading back to the garage towing a vehicle from the initial call. Right after meeting the tow truck, Frank noticed a car part lying on a bridge. At first they thought it dropped when the tow truck went by, but they got out of their car and, using flashlights, began looking from the bridge into the woods and into the river below. As he was looking into the woods, Frank heard his wife scream. He ran over to her as she pointed down into the water. "Oh, no, Wayne!" he yelled, when he saw the rear wheels of an upside-down car sticking out of the water.

Eight years have passed since that night and I remember, still hear, that radio call as if it happened five minutes ago. Frank, his voice full of panic, was calling for Wayne's sergeant and our deputy to return to the bridge. I asked what he had, but inside I already knew. He said, "There's a car in the water . . . and I think it's Wayne's."

Did he want the ambulance? "It won't do any good," he replied.

I dispatched every unit I could think of—ambulances, fire trucks, on-duty and off-duty officers. Two wrecker services showed up on scene. One tow truck driver jumped from the bank onto the rear of the car and hooked the tow cable as the other tow truck driver winched it back to the bank. As the car neared the bank our sheriff and Wayne's sergeant entered the rising, freezing water and removed Wayne from the car and started CPR. They kept at it until the rescue squad arrived.

Wayne had been under water for more than an hour and twenty minutes.

His body was loaded into the ambulance and carried to the hospital where the fight for his life was ultimately lost. They did everything they could, but he'd been in the water too long . . . far too long. Senior Trooper Wayne Bland was pronounced dead a little after midnight.

During the rest of the shift, as officers filed into the office, we realized that ambulances, fire trucks, tow trucks, and officers had passed over that bridge while Wayne was in the river. One officer had even turned around on the bridge and noticed no signs of a wreck. Wayne was there all the time, desperately needing our help. Though none of us realized it, we all had passed him by. It made the tragedy all the worse knowing we could have saved him.

Wayne had lost control of his car—we'll never know why—and hit the guardrail, snapping it off its post and sending the car flipping end over end into the freezing water. The guardrail then snapped back into place showing no signs of ever having been broken. A freak accident cost the life of a fine man and a fine police officer.

One of the worst memories of this tragedy is a telephone call I received after I dispatched fire and rescue to the scene. The phone rang. I answered, figuring it was a squad member wanting directions. It wasn't. Wayne's wife happily asked if Wayne was there with me. I couldn't think of what to say. All I could say was that he was on a wreck call. I just couldn't tell her what I suspected. I was too scared and too sorrowful to deliver to her such horrible news.

Two days later I found out that on Sunday, January 17, Wayne and his wife had found that she was going to have a baby. They celebrated quietly, joyfully that night. The next day, January 18, 1999, Wayne died responding to a simple accident call.

Now, eight years later, his little girl is happy and healthy. She knows who her daddy was and, most important, what he was. She is proud of him and looks at every law enforcement officer with respect.

I am sure she sees her daddy in each one.

What the Public Doesn't See

LINE OF DUTY

BY BRYAN MUTH

Sworn Officer, Kalamazoo, MI PD; Phoenix, AZ PD; retired after twenty-four years.

Kindness and compassion are as much a part of a police officer's days as anything else.

When I was on the job, I tried to do at least one good deed every shift, something that didn't involve putting someone in jail. Whether it was helping change a tire or assisting a burglary victim to reach their family or insurance company, I had to go home thinking I made a difference and possibly changed someone's mind about what we do and what we stand for.

Some people might argue that we're too busy chasing the bad guys and answering calls, and they're probably right to a certain extent. But isn't squeezing in a little kindness also part of our job?

There are plenty of officers who feel the way I do. My department had to switch from carrying wool or cotton blankets in the patrol cars to disposables. Why? Because it still gets cold in Phoenix in the winter, and officers were constantly stopping to give a shivering homeless person the blanket from the patrol car.

Two officers in our department would stop occasionally, especially on holidays, to make sure the local transients on their beat had something to eat. One Thanksgiving morning they worked out a deal with a local McDonald's to run a tab for an hour for the homeless to have a hot breakfast. Other officers in the precinct bought into the program and between calls would drop off the homeless folks from their beats at the restaurant.

After the hour was up, the officers came in and settled up the tab. This paid surprising dividends when one of the same officers found himself in a wrestling match with a drug-crazed suspect. A couple of the folks who had benefited from the holiday breakfast came to the officer's assistance. The officer was afraid that they might do a little too much damage to the resisting suspect, but it was clear that they respected the officer enough to get involved.

One of the most memorable incidents for me happened when I was working patrol on a Christmas Eve. I have worked during many Christmas holidays and have too often encountered children who received nothing from Santa. I always made sure I had gifts in the trunk of the patrol car for that reason. In the Phoenix area, law enforcement is blessed with a volunteer named W. Steven Martin, a former local radio personality who established a program to provide a warehouse full of new toys for officers to give away. Mr. Martin's theory was that officers would know the kids and families in need during the holidays since they had likely visited their home. This program helped weed out some of the abuses that have occurred with other charities. It also allowed kids to see the police officer a little differently than just the one who hauls a family member off to jail. In 2007 the program will celebrate its twentieth year in service to law enforcement.

On this particular Christmas Eve I had loaded up the trunk with gifts for both boys and girls. One of the department chaplains had asked to ride the shift with me so I was pretty well set for whatever I might encounter. It was shortly after midnight when we received a "check welfare call" of a young boy and an intoxicated person staggering along a busy street. We located the pair minutes later, and the caller was correct. It was pitiful to see the boy, nine years old, guiding the obviously intoxicated man by the arm.

When we contacted the boy, we learned that his mother had gone to a party at a bar and had left him with a family friend who later became so intoxicated he could barely stand. The man set out for a walk, and the young boy tried to lead him back to the house, but he got lost. While we were awaiting the "drunkmobile" to take the adult to a facility to sober up, I asked the boy what Santa was going to bring him. His response broke my heart. He replied, "Santa doesn't come to my house. We move around too much."

I quickly walked to the trunk of my car, not only to work on some gifts but also to compose myself. I couldn't let the boy see my tears. I managed to get the chaplain to learn the young man's name without him hearing us, and I quickly began writing the name of Christopher on packages for him.

When I returned to the car, I said to the chaplain, "I'm afraid Santa is going to be mad at me."

"Why?" the chaplain replied.

"I'm making some deliveries for him tonight, but I can't seem to find this nine-year-old kid named Christopher. Santa's counting on me to find him."

The little boy quickly threw up his hand. "My name is Christopher," he said, starting to become excited. "Could those be for me?"

I looked at the chaplain, "Hey, I'm in luck! I found him!" When we gave the young man his new helicopter and action figures, even the chaplain had to step out for a walk.

Later we were able to find a family that had actually been the foster parents to Christopher's mother years ago. They were willing to take him for the weekend to avoid getting the Children Protection Services involved especially on Christmas Eve. The foster father himself was a retired highway patrol officer.

The next time you hear that a police officer is just out to put people in jail or to write tickets, try to remember a couple of these incidents. There are plenty more just like these.

What's in the Shop Above the Garage?

LINE OF DUTY

BY PAMELA MONSON

Corporal, Boise PD, Idaho, twenty-nine years.

The city's pulse was throbbing, edgy, on a hot, festering afternoon, and as the beer and heat took hold, the swing shift promised to turn from a steady stream of assorted calls for service straight into Code 3 runs. Assigned to the Bench Division, I got a missing persons call in the Boise Valley and U-turned my cruiser.

Upon arrival, I met with the caller, Sandra, a thirty-something, petite, fit, and striking. This girl knew how to dress. The few lines of age that the antiwrinkle cream couldn't conceal were enhanced with worry. Her husband, Eric, Sandra stated, was missing. She showed me a photo of an older man, very handsome, with a full head of hair. He was a little overweight but still appeared athletic and powerful.

"He's never done anything like this, never!" Sandra assured me. She introduced her two daughters, ages nine and thirteen, from a previous marriage, and their concern appeared genuine. She and Eric had been married for ten months, this being his fourth marriage.

Rapid-fire information included that her soul mate Eric had gotten up at 0430 hours to run his paper route. Even though there was absolutely no response from me, Sandra was quick to defend her husband's choice of jobs. She assured me this was just temporary, to get them through until he secured other employment. Eric was skilled with his hands and could repair anything from lawn mowers to guns.

Around 0830 hours that morning, Sandra had received a phone call from Eric's boss asking if she knew where her husband was. The morning newspaper bundles had been picked up but never delivered.

After that call, Sandra and her daughters went looking for Eric, certain they would find him broken down by the side of the road somewhere, smiling, with a wrench in his hands. But it now seemed as though Eric had vanished without any logical explanation.

Gently, I asked Sandra about any troubles and explored the financial problems she had hinted at earlier. Hesitation and uncertainty crossed Sandra's face, and she seemed to shrink into herself. Patiently, I waited while Sandra collected her thoughts. She knew that Eric had been a bit down lately and had been to a doctor, but she didn't know the doctor's name or even what the appointment was for. Sandra showed me sample medication for depression that had been given to her newlywed husband, but there was no name of a doctor or actual prescription. Also, no pills were missing from the bubble pack. There were no other medications in the home for Eric. Not one single bottle of anything.

It appeared that Sandra's husband could be hiding something. I tried questioning her again, asking if there were any weapons in the home that she knew of. With a bit of a laugh, Sandra stated that there were lots of guns in the home. The garage was full of them. Eric had been a gunsmith before his third divorce forced him to shut down his business and move into their home. Various gunsmithing tools and numerous guns had all been stored in disorganized piles in the junked-up garage. The door was never locked, but no one but Eric ever ventured into that area of the home.

It was time to ask the wild-card question. "Has there been any kind of weird stuff, you know, surprising things that maybe have scared or frightened you since you married Eric?"

Immediately and firmly, Sandra answered. Her response raised my alarm and I felt chilly psychic waters begin to part. Eric would sometimes retreat into himself; he could be in the same room and might as well be a thousand miles away. He seemed not to be able to hear, respond, or even comprehend that his wife and stepdaughters were there, asking if he would come to the dinner table. At other times, this mystery man would go into the garage and, as if by stepping across the threshold, he seemed to pass into another world. Eric would stand still, seemingly unaware of the passage of time, unmoving. If Sandra or, heaven forbid, the girls, dared to intrude into this area of his life, they would be firmly rebuked and ordered to leave. Sometimes he even physically removed them. There were things about Eric he carefully guarded.

Furthermore, there was an incident that had occurred approximately two months prior. While coming home from church, she and Eric had begun to argue over something stupid. Eric, against all reason, became belligerent. Punctuating his talk with profanity, Eric began to drive recklessly, swerving wildly, driving onto the sidewalk and through parking lost, while degrading her with sexually graphic and crude statements.

The girls were crying and Sandra begged Eric to stop. No man she had ever known had been this dangerous and threatening. Most unsettling was the fact that the behavior had no reasonable explanation or trigger that should have caused such a reaction.

When Eric slid to a stop for a red light, Sandra and both girls simultaneously bolted from the car, literally running for their lives. Then it was over. Eric did not try to follow them as he spun the tires. They were alone in their Sunday school clothes on the street. Just like that, from rage to solitude. As best she could, Sandra tried to reassure her daughters. Holding onto one another, they walked home, each seeking comfort in their mutual misery and uncertain of what had just happened.

The traumatized trio heard Eric and his car before they saw him.

"He had a gun," Sandra said. "A little black gun with a really short barrel. I had never seen that one before. I didn't know he had it. Eric held it out the car window and *stuck it right in my face!* I just stood there. I didn't know what to do. I kept thinking that if he looked at me, if he would just see it was me, he would snap out of it. He was talking crazy stuff, calm and quiet like. Spooky. It wasn't his voice . . . The girls . . . the girls were so scared, they were crying and begging for him to just leave me alone."

"I'll . . . see . . . you . . . in . . . hell!" Eric deliberately spoke in staccato as he rhythmically pulled the trigger on empty chambers with each word. He slammed the accelerator to the floor and the car leaped forward, screeching, smoking, and fishtailing.

"I've never seen that gun again. I don't know where it is and I don't know where he put it or where he keeps it," Sandra stated flatly. "It—," her voice broke. "It . . . was . . . like nothing had ever happened when we got home. Nothing. I mean it was like *absolutely nothing at all had happened!* He was smiling and happy. Eric was singing and grilling hamburgers for our Sunday dinner. It was never mentioned or talked about again. I never told anyone else about it. The girls—the girls and I don't talk about it. I don't know who that man with the gun was, but he is not my Eric. *He is not* the man I married."

After making absolutely sure that Eric wasn't lying dead in the garage, bathtub, crawl space, or someplace else, I gave Sandra instructions that she was to contact me ASAP if she learned anything more or actually heard from Eric. I secured family information and left.

At the station, I placed a call to Troy, Eric's younger brother. I did not want to speak in front of Sandra, as I needed Eric's sibling to be completely honest and candid. My trepidation increased as Troy filled in blanks that Sandra appeared to know nothing about. There were five kids in Eric's family, Eric being the oldest. Depression, with a fifty-year history, ran in both sides of the family and affected both their mother and father.

Their father was the worst of the two parents. He had eventually committed suicide with a gun. Troy revealed that three out of the five brothers and sisters had attempted suicide, while never admitting or denying which group he held membership in. Further, Troy had spoken to Eric's three ex-wives and learned that depression was a constant factor with him.

Troy believed that his brother deliberately hid his depression and dysfunction from the rest of the family. It had fallen upon Eric, as the oldest of the kids, right or wrong, to hold the family together. Eric's lot in life was to keep his brothers, sisters, and mother safe after their dad was gone. It was a burden that no sixteen-year-old boy should ever bear.

I began to probe for the details of the father's suicide. "What kind of gun was it? What did your dad . . . the gun, Troy, what was it? What happened?"

Their dad had a shop that was built on top of a detached garage. It was there that he would spend his time, sometimes building things or repairing guns as a part-time job to bring in extra cash. Other times their father remained secluded and alone, escaping his demons in his own way. It was in this shop that he had taken a two-inch 38-caliber blued revolver, placed it in his mouth, and pulled the trigger. No one heard the shot, and it was Eric who eventually found their dad when he was late for dinner.

"Where's the gun now? Do you know?" Sandra's description of the revolver and the suicide-shop pistol were too similar not to ask the question.

"Yeah, I know, Eric had to have it. The son of a bitch was obsessed with getting that gun back. He kept at it until he was eighteen, and the police eventually gave him the damn thing. He just wouldn't give it up. None of the rest of us wanted it around, but he had to have it.

"Where would he go? Troy, where would he go?"

Keenly aware of exactly what I was asking, Troy answered quickly and decisively. "One of two places. The first I would try is a little campground where we went as kids. It was the only time we really could just be kids, playing and having fun. It was good times for all of us when we went camping there. The second place would be that house we grew up in, not the house, but the shop, the shop built above the garage. If I was you, and I'm not, that's where I would be looking. The shop."

"Give me a call if you hear from him, night or day. Call me, call the police, and I will call you when I know anything."

After arranging for the County Sheriff to do a security check for my suicidal missing person, I put myself on the road to Eric's childhood home. Upon arrival there, where this tormented and tragic family once lived, I spoke with the current owner, a friendly sort who told me he had a little jewelry shop in the upstairs of the garage. "Really a nice little place. You can see out. The trees cool it down and it is quite relaxing. Go on and have yourself a look around. It's not locked up, I haven't been there in about a week. You'll find the stairs alright."

As I entered the dusty garage, the heat of the day seemed to double. Sweat beaded on my temples and ran down my collar. My ballistics vest was stuck to my T-shirt, soaked with sweat that ran in droplets down the center of my spine and soaked the back of my gun belt. The stairs were surprisingly steep. The wooden handrail was worn perfectly smooth, polished by many hands over the decades. As I ascended, the heat increased proportionally and the air became suffocating.

With each step I wondered how many times members of Eric's family had walked these stairs, holding this same rail. In the dim light I grasped the antique doorknob and flashed on the legacy of depression, suicide, fixation, hidden lies, a family's failure, and a bullet from a snub-nosed 38-caliber revolver. I wondered if the crippling bouts of twisted despair this room had borne witness to would continue to carve out its wretched path of self-destruction and misery, just another chapter, another secret sealed in blood. I could nearly smell the fear and horror of a boy, now a missing suicidal man, bolting down the stairs, his life forever altered by what had occurred in this shop I was about to enter.

Uncertain if danger had been silenced by deliberate choice, I stepped out of the funnel of the doorway and announced, "Police officer!" Silence. I entered the shop, built so many years ago, above the garage.

What was behind the door? The monstrous depression that is passed from generation to generation, father to son, and sucks everything human from a man, will not be ignored. Perhaps it is just enough to know that there is always on officer, 24/7/365, who is on duty, in harm's way, standing ready to open the door to the shop above the garage, just as I did on that hot, festering afternoon on a swing shift.

You Don't Understand!
You're the Enemy!

THE BEAT

BY ROCKY WARREN

Sergeant, Placer County Sheriff's Department, California, twenty-eight years.

I sat in a lounge chair looking around at my family, both immediate and extended, a noisy and loud group even under the best of circumstances. I'd grown up with them, but I know their chatter makes my wife nervous. We all sit and argue over religion, politics, and world affairs, but no one takes the arguments too seriously. Usually nobody steps on anyone too hard, but I'd missed too many of these get-togethers in the past few years. Uniformed patrol duty as a police officer on nights, weekends, and holidays had often kept me away from these family or holiday gatherings.

I sat and looked at the face of my smug, condescending uncle, Bobby. A product of the 1960s, he'd stuck several needles into me about my job over the last hour. I'd had about enough of him and his garbage. When Bobby turned to me and said, "You don't understand, man. You're the enemy! The cops are the enemy." I turned back and replied, "Bobby, I know you've never been in the military nor been a cop. You've never protected anything in your whole life, so I'm going to tell you what being a cop is all about. Why people do it and why they risk their lives for it."

I leaned forward, "A partner and I saved six people from drowning in the rising tide and surf. I've placed two tiny, lost children, back in the arms of their parents. If we hadn't found them, they'd be dead. A partner and I stopped and arrested a guy who had a loaded shotgun in his car. He was less than fifty yards away from killing his stepfather and candidly admitted it. I kept a crazy woman from running out into freeway traffic. I've walked four people off the Foresthill Bridge and saved them from taking a 720-foot leap into oblivion. A man walked toward me with a knife and I let him get way too close. By all rights, experience, and my training, I should have shot him. Instead, I got an inspiration and lit up my gun with a flashlight. I backed the guy down and disarmed him. He went to a mental health facility instead of a hospital or morgue."

I sat back and lowered my voice. The entire room had gone quiet. "You've never protected anything Bobby. Not ever. You won't ever know what it feels like to save more lives than there are in this room. You just want to degrade those who do protect. That makes you poor in spirit, and I'm sorry for you. I'm not the enemy, Bobby. Cops aren't the enemy. Your selfishness, blindness, and malice are the enemy."

I got up and walked through the silence into the kitchen, to make myself another drink. From there I walked out on to the deck. I figured my family had probably heard quite enough from me over the last few minutes. My wife walked with me. Having her at my side was extremely comforting. I wasn't happy with myself. I should never have let him get to me like that.

Bobby wouldn't ever be able to understand why men and women risk their lives in the police or military. What I had told him were the successes in a warrior's life. I couldn't even begin to explain the feelings of the occasional no-win situation or the outright failure. And yet. I go on. It's a job that has to be done, or else others suffer.

I was astonished to have my family filter onto the deck, coming out with smiles and hugs. The good news is this: Most people do understand that we are the good guys. The police and most ordinary citizens—we, together, are the good guys. And we all need the love, comfort, and support of our families and friends to do what we do.

A Dark, Cold Night

BY SCOTT BARTHELMASS

Corporal, Overland PD, Missouri, thirteen years.

Tuesday, January 11, 2005, was a cold night, and I was feeling a little worn down. I lead what some would call a rather hectic and often stressful life—often juggling a constantly changing duty schedule, court, off-duty employment, and outside activities. Life can get stressful, but it's never boring. Sometimes, though, I'd give anything for "boring."

I had worked that day, but I didn't have any meetings or activities that night, so I crawled into bed early. I had drifted off to sleep when my phone rang. I could see from the caller ID that it was my good friend Scott Armstrong. He's a good man, I thought, but frankly I've had enough for today. I can always call him back tomorrow. I rolled over and went back to blissful sleep.

At four in the morning my sleep was interrupted by the ringing phone. I answered, and it was my dad. He was panicked and obviously disturbed. In all my life, I had never heard my dad so upset. He has always been a hardworking man who cared deeply about his family, but he never really showed a lot of emotion. "Is this Scott?" he asked. Yes, I said, of course.

Just minutes earlier Larry Armstrong, Scott's father, had called my father and told him: "Scott is dead. Scott is dead." My father, sound asleep when he received the frantic call, had not been able to make the connection that it was Scott *Armstrong* who had been killed. Now, although my father was relieved to hear the sound of my voice, another reality quickly set in: A close friend of our family had just been killed.

While I was dreaming of sugar plums, in the early morning hours of January 12, Scott was killed, while on duty, by a drunk driver going the wrong way on Missouri Highway 370.

I had lost my last chance to speak to him.

I jumped out of bed and ran across the street, without my shoes or coat, to my youngest brother's house. My brother Matt is married to Scott's younger sister, April. When I arrived at their house, Matt was pacing the dining room and April was crying. My heart sank.

April just sat there and cried while I hugged her. She and Scott had been so close. And April is such a precious, outstanding young woman. I knew she was going through hell.

My family has strong ties with Scott's family. Obviously, my youngest brother was close to him. My sister had been close friends with Scott, and Scott and I had planned on boxing in the annual Guns 'N Hoses charity event. Our families had spent a lot of time together. We had a whole future of things to do. Not any more.

My family has also become a police family. I entered the police academy in 1994. Todd, my other brother, became a Missouri State Trooper in 1996. My youngest brother, Matt, had been a police officer for a couple years.

As I sat there and held April, she asked for my sister. I rushed off to her house. When I showed up at just after five, from my knocking on the door she knew something was wrong. "Scott Armstrong is dead, isn't he?" She said she'd just seen that a Bridgeton Police car, the municipality where Scott worked, had been struck head-on on the Interstate. They were saying the officer was seriously injured, and the pictures she saw on TV were bad. I told her, and she began to cry.

I rushed Carrie to April's side. We spent the next twenty-four hours with Scott's mom and dad. It was tough. Larry asked my brother Todd and me to start to work out the funeral arrangements. It was very tough.

Everywhere I looked, every channel I turned to featured Scott's death. I saw the gruesome scene over and over. The story unfolded, and we learned that Scott probably never knew what hit him. It is estimated that at the time Scott was hit, dispatchers were putting out a broadcast warning about a wrong-way driver on Highway 370. The whole day was filled with the death of a dear friend and the tears of mourning from those who loved him. We couldn't believe it.

It was like being drunk on grief, like the cold, gray morning of loss after a dark, cold night of death.

January 13, 2005, was one of the worst days of my life. Scott's young son, Tyler, lived in Washington State with Scott's ex-wife. My brother Todd, sister Carrie, and I had the task of picking him up at the airport as he arrived that morning.

We had a marked patrol car from my department and were met by uniform officers who even in this supercautious post-9/11 era took us right to the gate to meet Tyler. They then made sure he got his luggage promptly, and provided multiple patrol cars to escort Tyler on his journey to his grandparents'.

That afternoon we escorted Tyler to the funeral home, and I watched a nine-year-old boy quietly walk up to the coffin that held the remains of the father he loved so much. He stood for just a moment and I realized he was just a little boy, that he shouldn't have to go through something like this. I knew he was going to have to grow up and face this terrible thing, make it a part of his life, and still he was just a little boy.

Tyler began to cry when he saw his father lying there in the coffin. He reached up and put his hand on his father's chest. He bent over his dad and just cried. That image will forever be etched in my mind.

Friday, January 14, we buried Scott—my brother in blue, my good friend, my boxing buddy, my fellow jokester. There are so many things I could say about him. He was a good cop and a good man. My brothers and sister, April, and Scott Armstrong—we were an inseparable group of six. Now we are five.

It has been hard on his family and our family since Scott was killed. There have been struggles, and I know our hearts were broken, our dreams tattered and torn. The journey has been full of many obstacles.

In May 2006, we all journeyed to Washington, D.C., and were there when Scott's name was officially added to the National Law Enforcement Memorial's walls in Justice Square. We listened as his name, and the names of many other officers who lost their lives in the line of duty, were read and echoed throughout the capital. We got up early each morning to race to the wall to make sure that the mementoes and pictures were still sitting there as perfectly as they were when we left them. I escorted Scott's mom and dad—Karen and Larry—during many of the events. It was a hard week.

Things continue to be hard at times. It's a struggle to drive down Highway 370 and pass the cross that marks that tragic location. Every event that honors Scott brings up the memories of a good friend who was lost.

Scott's life, like that of too many other police officers, was cut short. He died protecting his hometown, protecting his family and friends, and even strangers he never knew.

Each day police officers across the country do just that. Each year about 150 of our nation's officers die in the line of duty.

Some good has come out of it all. There has been a substantial amount of attention given to the drunk-driving problem here in the St. Louis area. The story further strengthened efforts nationwide to protect our officers on the roadways, for nearly 50 percent of policemen's deaths are the result of crashes on our roadways.

And now there is a little bundle of joy named Morgan Rose

Barthelmass—my niece. April, my sister-in-law, gave birth in June 2006 to a beautiful girl. This little girl would have also been Scott's niece. That little girl is named in memory and honor of Scott *Morgan* Armstrong.

In a way, life has come full circle.

A Katrina Story

BY STACEY PEARSON

Sergeant, Louisiana State Police, eight years.

I work in Lafayette. It's a close-knit, well-run community of strong, old traditions. I was called, along with many other Louisiana State Troopers, to join the rapid response teams sent to the city of New Orleans. We had no idea what we were getting into.

I first arrived in New Orleans the evening of August 31, two days after Katrina made landfall. Though the hurricane had passed, there were terrible thunderstorms. We thought that was bad. Later on, after living through day after tropical day with no rain, we would pray for the return of thunder and lightning.

A small group of ten officers from the Lafayette Troop were briefed at Troop B in Kenner. We were told we were going to I-10 at Causeway Boulevard to an evacuation staging area. Our mission was to load as many people as possible on buses for transport to shelters. At our briefing, they did try to give us an idea of what it was like. We were to learn—the hard way—that mere words were not enough.

We traveled a few miles east in complete darkness and parked behind concrete barriers that normally divided east- and westbound traffic. We came out into the storm and I thought I had stepped into a war zone. The sky was filled with Coast Guard and Army helicopters landing one right after another, providing a steady stream of exhausted, bewildered, and traumatized people rescued from rooftops or out of hospitals. And that was the beginning of our time in what I believe to be one of the worst embarrassments this country has ever inflicted upon itself.

We had to carefully navigate through a makeshift medical facility set up in the westbound lanes of I-10 directly under the overpass—the only cover from the searing Louisiana sun. We weaved in and out of critical patients lying on cots or on the ground. I looked at them as I passed, and their eyes held that blank, thousand-yard stare. Some looked like they were hovering between life and death. Some had open wounds, and I'm ashamed to say that I couldn't bear to look at some of them. Doctors and medics worked frantically in an environment that was clearly not sterile to save as many as possible.

A concrete median ran between the medical area and the thousands of evacuees waiting for buses. In the evacuee area, metal barricades typically used to separate crowds from Mardi Gras floats divided the noncritical but relatively immobile people from the relatively healthy. Behind the metal barricades we met up with a young trooper who filled us in on the procedure for loading the buses. He told us to never go in the crowd alone, to always load women, children, and the elderly first, and to not allow pushing. I later found out that the young trooper's house in New Orleans East had been destroyed when the levees broke, and his wife and two small children were staying with relatives in another state.

Loading the buses proved difficult. Young men unencumbered by family tried to push their way onto the bus, while women with babies fought to maintain their position in line. Families were separated. The clothing of many people had been soiled with urine and feces and, for some, menstrual flow. They waited for hours, even days, in filth and litter, only to miss the bus and find out there would be no more buses that evening. A man walked up to me and handed me a loaded ammo magazine, and I wondered who had the weapon and if they would use it against me. I saw women carrying babies limp from dehydration, and I saw a boy vomit continuously. I saw a girl of about ten go into seizures. There were no portable toilets; we walked in human waste. It was so hot that our boots began to slowly melt.

A bus driver told a young man whose only possession was a dappled dachshund, "No dogs allowed." I hoped he would wait for another bus and hide the small dog under his shirt, but he made the heartbreaking and tearful decision to let the dog loose and get on the bus. The frightened dog narrowly avoided being run over and ran off through the crowd. Since rescuers had told victims they could bring their pets, most bus drivers were more sympathetic and chose not to further traumatize these people and so allowed the pets on board.

As I write this, I realize it's impossible to describe the chaos. There were so many people—thousands. Helicopters were bringing in more than we could get out. The medical personnel eventually pulled out, and we were left in a disaster zone with no medics and no medical equipment—nothing but sick, injured, traumatized people who believed they would go home in a couple of days. We watched a chemical plant explode in the distance.

My second day on the Causeway, I helped load special-needs patients on buses. These were not specially equipped buses with electric lifts. Makeshift stretchers wouldn't fit. If the person could not walk or be carried, they had to wait. One man sticks out in my memory. His mother weighed well over three hundred pounds and was confined to a wheelchair. We asked him if she could walk at all, and he said she could not. He was adamant when he said he was going to carry her onto the bus, and I thought to myself, "No way." But he did it. He hooked his arms under her armpits and locked his hands in front of her chest and literally dragged her onto the bus and into a seat. Then he gave his seat to a crippled woman. I watched tears well up in his eyes and run down his cheeks as he tried to maintain eye contact with his mother through the bus windshield.

I have to stop here because I can't put into words all that happened.

But throughout my initial month-long deployment, I witnessed many incredible feats of emotional and physical strength, and incredible human weakness. I heard racial comments directed toward me. I saw people sleeping and eating in indescribable, deplorable conditions. I saw body bags containing those who didn't survive. I learned I couldn't help everyone; I could only help individuals or small groups of people.

It was an impossible situation. There was, and is, no training for this, no tactics to follow. This comes from your heart and you just have to do the best you can.

You have to forgive yourself for what you cannot do, and I'm still working on that.

A Lasting Impression

BY KEVIN J. BYRNE

Police Officer, Nassau County PD, New York, thirty-six years.

In the early 1970s, I was sitting in my patrol car in Westbury, Long Island, New York, watching for stop sign violations when two little boys approached shyly and said hello. Curious as cats, they wanted to see everything in the car. Demetri, the more vocal of the two, was about ten years old; his brother Nicholas was backward and shy for his eight years. I showed them the usual things: lights, radio, and other equipment. I had to explain everything—and every time I told them something, or explained how something worked, Demetri asked, "Why?" At the time, I remember feeling, at first, a bit impatient. As time went by I became really impatient. Who was I, their teacher? I held my temper, however, because they were *so* cute and so innocent. They were just wide-eyed and so in awe of everything. Demetri was very talkative and animated and Nicholas just had a big smile on his face the whole time. So, though I knew I had better things to do than babysit two kids for nearly an hour, I went along. It *was* kinda fun.

When I told them—finally—that I had to go, they asked me for my autograph! I was taken aback and gave them some official sounding mumbo jumbo, but they wouldn't take no for an answer. So, I reluctantly—at first—wrote my name on a scrap of paper and gave it to them. It took about six seconds for the experience to grow on me. They actually wanted my autograph, like I was somebody important, someone to be admired. I thought about that for a minute and realized that it was a good thing that kids should admire policemen, firemen, teachers, emergency service personnel, and their parents, just as much as they admire sports heroes and actors and pop singers.

Patrolling that post for sixteen years, I would see the boys from time to time, and they would always wave to me. Sometimes I'd stop and we'd talk for a bit. I knew they were into mischief, though never anything too bad. As they got older, however, other officers and I would get called to their house by their father, Nicholas Sr. The boys would fight and he couldn't stop them, because they had gotten so big and a little out of control. Every time I entered the house, Nicholas Sr. would yell up the stairs, "Officer Byrne is here!" The boys would creep down the stairs with their heads hung down, apologizing all the way. It was lucky for me that I had this mysterious power over them, because they were both bigger than me.

I took a desk position in 1990, so I didn't see the boys on the street anymore. In 1991, while I was preparing for a softball game, I was approached by PO Al Barnych, who asked me if I had heard the whole story of what happened at my old beat. He received a radio call to the boys' home. Nicholas shot his mother as she sat in the living room; and he shot Nicholas Sr., as he came downstairs. Nicholas had problems, very deep, hidden problems. For reasons that no one will ever know, he snapped that day. He did something terrible and violent and unthinkable.

I was appalled. Little Nicholas, the boy with the face-wide grin had killed his parents. PO Barnych said that when he confronted Nicholas, he wasn't sure what Nicholas would do. The boy stood there with a loaded gun in his hand and his parents' bodies at his feet. Barnych told him, in a quiet voice, to put the gun down, slowly, and to put his hands behind his head. For a moment, he was sure, Nicholas was going to try to shoot him, but all the rage seemed to flush out of him at once. Suddenly, Nicholas surrendered and said: "I will respect you, because I have always had respect for Officer Kevin Byrne and because he has always treated me with respect."

As amazing as this sounds, I was reminiscing with my desk lieutenant Robert Nash recently, and he told me that he not only remembered the incident, but he received the call and was the supervising officer on the scene. Lieutenant Nash recalls the shooting like it was yesterday.

On the job, they always tell you to treat people the right way, because your contact with them may be their only contact with the police and create a lasting good or bad impression. One day I gave two young boys a little bit of my time, and I always wonder what would have happened between Officer Barnych and Nicholas if I hadn't.

Nicholas was sentenced to sixteen to forty years for manslaughter. I still see Demetri occasionally. He says that he can finally forgive his brother. As for me, I can't forget Nicholas's smiling face on that sunny day in the early seventies; and I don't think I ever will.

Angel on the Table

LINE OF DUTY

BY DON WHITEHEAD

Lieutenant, Major Investigations, Kokomo PD, Indiana, twenty-three years.

In February 1999 I was working as a detective sergeant on the afternoon shift as I had for about five years. A bunch of us had been complaining about getting extra on-call duty because our chief had recently decided that we no longer needed an accident investigation unit. Apparently he thought people would no longer die in traffic accidents in our city. When it became clear that some people were going to die in accidents despite what our chief thought, he did just what we expected and dumped that responsibility on us, the detectives.

Since some of us had prior training and had worked in Traffic, naturally we had to be on call in the event of a fatal accident, thus doubling our on-call to about two weeks out of the month. Needless to say, we were pissed, and we weren't gonna take this without a fight. I told my detectives, "If they call me at home for an accident, I'm not coming." I figured if a fatal accident came in and nobody was on duty working, they couldn't force us to come in. They would *have* to take care of the problem, right?

Well, it sounded good, but the truth was that we all cared too much about what we do and who we do it for to not answer "the call" whenever it came, or whoever it came from. So, a few days later, when my captain called me at 9:00 A.M. to tell me we had just had an officer-involved shooting and a child killed by a school bus at the same time, I replied, "I'm on my way."

It's funny, that Monday morning call changed my life forever, yet I don't have any idea what the weather was like that day or what I had been doing before the phone rang. All I remember is what happened after I answered the call.

A short time later, when I arrived at the office, the captain told me that two of our midnight patrol officers had chased a thief and had shot him after the guy pointed a gun at them. The cops weren't hurt; the suspect was seriously injured, but was going to live. Now, you have to understand that this might be an everyday thing in many departments, but in our department this was the first officer-involved shooting in several years. So we were all pretty worked up.

Then he told me that a five-year-old girl had been crossing in front of her school bus and was run over and killed by the driver. He assigned the accident to me since I had worked in Traffic before and had experience in fatal accident investigation. This, just after the shooting, was a little overwhelming—to say the least. To make matters worse, the bus driver didn't know she had struck the child and continued driving her route until contacted by radio telling her to stop and wait for the police.

I've investigated countless deaths. You just can't be a cop for very long without seeing this kind of stuff. Over the past twenty-two years on the job, I have seen just about every imaginable way you can die or be killed. Old people, young people, children, and babies, I've been there. Some tragic, some sad, some even funny. You just go and do what you have to do. After all, somebody has to, right?

So I gathered some equipment and met the patrol lieutenant at the scene. Several years prior I had worked for him in Traffic, so he and I had done all this before many times. He briefed me on what he knew. There was the usual crowd of people standing around. I saw some blood in the street where the child had been lying, a shoe, and a book bag. I took some pictures, gathered up the shoe and book bag and went to the hospital to photograph the body and talk to family members. Again, I had done this a thousand times before, and this was just another death investigation to me, or so I thought.

When I arrived at the hospital, I photographed the body, documented the injuries that I saw, and talked with the coroner covering the case. Through all that I never really *looked* at the girl on the table. I was totally wrapped up in what had to be done. A nurse came in and told us the parents were waiting outside. Telling a family member that a loved one is dead is one of the most difficult parts of the job. Whether it's a child or an adult, old or young, sudden or expected, it doesn't matter. But I have learned that what I say and how I say it will be remembered by that family member forever. It has always been very important to me to do it compassionately, properly, and professionally. I've done it more than most because I know how important it is and how it needs to be done.

They had already been told their daughter was dead, so I knew I wasn't going to be delivering *that* news. Somehow, in my mind, that made me less apprehensive about meeting them. When I was satisfied I had gathered the evidence I needed for my investigation, I asked the nurse to prepare the child for the parents to view. This was pretty standard and involved wiping blood and dirt from the body and covering it to the shoulders with a blanket. There's nothing you can really do to prepare someone for the moment when they see their loved one dead for the first time. All you can do is try to prepare them for what they will soon see and comfort them as much as possible. You have to be a professional.

Just before I left the room to talk to the parents and bring them in to see their child, I turned and really saw (as if for the first time) the beautiful little girl lying on the table. She looked like an angel, as if she were asleep. I paused for what seemed like an eternity. *How can this be? What kind of world is this?* I thought. My mind and heart and spirit reeled from the shock. I composed myself, then went outside and met the parents. They were young and, judging from the depressed area where the accident happened, didn't have much. I told them what I knew, and what I was going to be doing to investigate the accident. I prepared them as much as I could and led them into the room. Part of the anxiety of delivering death notifications and dealing with families is that you never know how people will react. Some cry, some yell and scream, some will even attack you.

I don't remember what they looked like, and wouldn't know them if I saw them today, but I will never forget what I saw and felt when the father sat down beside his little girl.

For some reason I wasn't prepared for this one. This man, with tears running down his face, simply leaned over his daughter, put his arms around her, and asked her to wake up. He held her in his arms and kept repeating over and over, "Wake up, Angel, wake up. Everything will be OK. Just wake up. Please." His wife stood behind him, sobbing. He just kept begging his little angel to just wake up over and over.

I know that denial is part of the process, but it just caught me by surprise. I don't know if all the other emotions I had been feeling that day caught up with me, or if it was because I had a wife and three daughters at home. It doesn't matter, does it? I had just realized that the life of a beautiful child had been snatched from her parents for no apparent reason, and I couldn't maintain my composure any longer. Tears flowed down my face as if it were *my* child lying on that table. I didn't know what to say or do for them. I had felt sadness for victims and their families many times before on the job, but never like this. I just couldn't handle it. I simply stood behind them as they held their child, and I cried. No one noticed that I had fallen apart, which was important to me, because I was the one who was supposed to be in charge. I was the one with the answers. I was responsible for taking care of everything for this family.

Before, God forbid, anyone *did* notice, I left the room, got into my car, and drove away. I didn't share my feelings with anyone except my wife. I don't think I would have ever been able to do this job without her strength, wisdom, and understanding. Not that I necessarily hid my emotions; I just didn't talk to anyone else about it. Although it affected me profoundly, and forever, it was my personal experience and I chose not to share it with anyone else . . . until now.

Over the next few days, I continued the investigation into the death of this child. I found that the school bus was equipped with a video camera that clearly showed the children on the bus bounce when it passed over her body first with the front tire, then with the rear. I interviewed several children who, when they felt the bus run over her, looked out the windows and saw her lying on the street. Some told me they tried to tell the driver, without success. When I completed the investigation, I recommended that charges be filed against the bus driver. I admit it: I was angry and wanted someone held responsible.

When it was all said and done, no charges were filed. The prosecutor felt the woman driving the bus had suffered enough, and he was probably right. She hadn't been irresponsible in the past, and it *was* an accident. I was told she quit her job as the result of the accident. Safety equipment has since been added to all of the buses to help protect children walking in front of them.

I've not spoken to the woman who was driving that bus or anyone from the family of the little girl since then. I wish them all well. I wish them peace and understanding. I hope none of them have to go through anything like this again.

I, on the other hand, will continue to deal with death as part of my job for as long as I choose to be a police officer, and I will be professional, proper, and competent.

But I will never forget that little angel.

God willing, I will continue to learn, feel, and be a better person for it.

Another Beautiful Day

DEADLY FORCE

BY GREG BROWN

Senior Officer, Rocky Mount PD, North Carolina, retired after eleven years.

September 9, 2005, was another beautiful day in Rocky Mount, North Carolina. I was working the north end of town, which was known as Beat 16. I had been transferred to the day shift only a couple of months before and the city seemed so different during daylight hours. After working nine years on night shift with the narcotics unit, it was a pleasure. I had answered several calls that day, but nothing could have prepared me for what was going to be the most eventful day of my life.

I was working traffic at the charter school when dispatch gave me a BOLO (Be On the Look Out) for a burgundy car driven by a Hispanic male who was running people off the road and pointing a gun at them. I was in the area and decided to see if I could locate the car and the driver.

I was near the trailer park where the car was last seen. As I drove down Instrument Drive, which dead-ended at the back of the mobile home park, I didn't see a vehicle fitting the description. As I started back toward the charter school, I passed a burgundy car matching the BOLO description. I pulled the vehicle over in front of a residence in the mobile home park, after calling the traffic stop in to dispatch.

The driver, a Hispanic male, exited the vehicle and I asked him if he had a weapon. He shook his head, no, and even pulled up his shirt to prove it. I spoke with him a few more minutes, and his wife and small child came out of the residence. I asked for consent to search the vehicle and he said okay. When I found a box of ammunition under the seat I could see my suspect begin to get uncomfortable. He shrugged his shoulders as if to say he didn't know they were there. I called him over and told him to put his hands on the hood of his car. I then began to call for another unit on my radio. Out of the corner of my eye I saw the muzzle flash from a gun and by instinct I turned sideways to make a smaller target. I should have frisked him; I knew I should have frisked him, damn it. I threw the box of shells down and tried to take cover on the passenger side of my vehicle, but as I ran to the side of my car I felt the impact of the second shot.

I dropped like a ton of bricks.

The pain was unreal.

As I fell, I drew my weapon to return fire, but the shooter was running down the side of the trailer. I couldn't get a good shot without possibly striking another home or person.

As I lay there, I asked to be forgiven for all my sins, and I asked the Lord to watch over my family if it was my time to go. Then, all of a sudden, I got pissed off and told myself, *Greg, you are not going out like this.*

I got my bearings and found my radio mike and called for assistance. My exact words were: "116 to Central. Shots fired, officer down. I have been shot." Dispatch acknowledged, and I gave them the description of the suspect and his last known direction of travel. I knew in my mind I had to keep talking to keep calm and get through this ordeal.

It was a blessing to see a red Ford truck pull up behind my patrol car. It was the citizen who had originally called the police about the car and driver. I asked him to help me, and without hesitation he came over. I gave him my service weapon and told him, "If the suspect comes back, shoot him." He said that he would, and I believed him. Even though he stood there, head swiveling without stop, gun in his shaking hand, I knew he'd rise to the moment if he had to. Luckily, he didn't. The man stayed with me until the cavalry arrived. The first unit on the scene was a plainclothes officer named Phillip Gardner in the Community Resource Officer Unit. He had stopped a block away from where I lay. I saw him get out of his car and run toward me. He was so nervous he didn't look where he was going and fell into a mud-filled ditch. I began to laugh, I just couldn't stop. The man staying with me couldn't believe I was lying in the street bleeding from a gunshot wound, laughing.

I guess some people just don't understand cop humor.

As I waited for the ambulance to arrive, all I could think about was my wife and kids. I had some part-time work lined up so we could pay off some bills, and I thought to myself, "My wife is going to kill me because I can't work tonight."

My good friend Chris Williams was the second officer on the scene, and he held my hand until the ambulance arrived and rode with me to the hospital. It was a long ride and I was sure glad to finally get there. When I arrived I asked for my wife, Shannon. She came back to the emergency room, and I reassured her I was going to be alright and we were going to get through this.

I stayed at Nash General until I was flown by heliocopter to Pitt Memorial. That was the quickest trip to Greenville I ever made. When we arrived, they wheeled me in and people were asking me two hundred questions at once. All I wanted was some pain medication because the wound hurt bad.

They operated to remove the bullet, but I didn't know if I was going to be paralyzed or not. After the surgery I was in the recovery room and Shannon came in. She was a beautiful sight to see. She was crying and so was I.

I was just glad to be alive.

I spent ten long days in the hospital and just about every officer around came to see me. I couldn't believe the number of friends I had. It's a grand feeling to have real comrades.

I was unable to move my left leg, but I walked out of the hospital on the tenth day with the help of a walker. I had to wear a brace from my knee down under my shoe for support.

I spent eleven months doing rehab, but I was unable to return to work. I retired on August 1, 2006. The suspect, Luis Ramirez was captured in Mexico, where he fled after the shooting. He was extradited back the United States and then to Nash County in December 2006.

I have found a new meaning to life and I am Mr. Mom now. I was also elected state trustee of our local Fraternal Order of Police, Lodge No. 46 Rocky Mount, North Carolina. My wife was my rock during this trying time. She told me only a few months ago that the doctors did not expect me to walk again, but I did. I have to use a cane and still wear the brace, but it sure beats being six feet under.

I tell people that my story is not a big deal, but let's be honest: Some days are really hard. I lost my career, my vocation, because of that asshole. I had to find a whole new way of life. I was a damned good police officer. Still, my story is a testimony to being able to survive a line-of-duty shooting. Even though I don't do police work now, I still respect the job and the badge. I pray every day for my fellow officers everywhere.

Brown Eyes

LINE OF DUTY

BY J. R. DAVIS
Sergeant, Winter Park PD, Florida, thirty years.

Sergeant Will MacPherson I crept up the stairs toward the apartment door, our leather gear squeaking with every step. Even these small sounds echoed loudly in the stairwell. Funny, movie cops never seem to make a sound. We had already turned our radios down to minimum volume after requesting emergency traffic on Channel One, but we still prayed that no one would blunder onto the air before we had a chance to assess the situation. I could hear my heartbeat as we covered the last few feet to the landing. I forced myself to take three deep breaths to slow down.

We were there to check on the well-being of the resident, Dianne Marcus. Her boyfriend told dispatch that she had been terribly depressed lately. Three days earlier she had asked him where she could buy a gun. She told him she wanted it for protection at the apartment, but it had been twenty-four hours since he had spoken to her. She had not shown up for work that afternoon.

When we reached the landing Will took a position on the opposite side of the apartment door. The apartment was the first one at the top of the stairs, so I was forced to stand slightly below the door on the first step. The doorknob was on my side, so I reached up, grasped it slowly, and tried turning it. Locked. I looked over at Will and shook my head.

By watching the crack under that door I could see a shadow pass back and forth. I could hear someone moving inside the apartment. Will reached up and knocked on the door. "Ms. Marcus! I'm Sergeant Will MacPherson with the Winter Park Police. I need to talk to you, please."

No response. Just more movement within the apartment, a little more hurried, I thought.

"Dianne," Will continued, "please, we need to talk to you. Please open the door. We just need to make sure—"

Bam! The muffled shot caught us by surprise. Automatically, we drew our service weapons and were now crouched, assessing ourselves and each other. No pain, no blood anywhere. I gave Will a thumbs-up. He nodded he was also okay.

Will had already stepped back from the apartment door in readiness to kick it in. I nodded and positioned myself to cover him as he stomped forward behind the doorknob. Nothing. He kicked again, and we heard splintering, but the door remained shut.

I stepped up beside the sergeant. "Will, on three. One! Two! Three!" Both of our feet hit the door together and it swung in, slamming against the wall. Wood splinters scattered on the beige carpet.

As the door flew open, the sergeant and I shifted to either side of the opening, surveying what we could of the inside of the apartment before entering. I saw no movement. Will indicated there was nothing where he was looking either.

He then signaled that he would enter first. With a nod Will ran through the doorway, with me on his heels. He peeled to the right and I went immediately to the left.

That phenomenon of everything going to slow motion during a traumatic or stress event is common, and this one was no exception. From the instant the shot was fired time had slowed. What seemed to take long moments was actually occurring in just seconds.

I scanned what must have been the living room of the apartment, my service weapon covering what my eyes were seeing. As I swept the far side of the room I took in a surreal, slow-motion scene.

A beautiful young woman casually leaned back in a gray La-Z-Boy chair. The chair gently inched back into its fully reclined position, and a snub-nosed .38 revolver dropped from the girl's right hand to the soft carpet. It seemed like I was moving through mud as I covered those last few steps to Dianne Marcus. Her beautiful brown eyes bored into mine as I walked up to the recliner. There was a small hole in her yellow T-shirt. The center of her chest. Damn it! Oddly, there was no blood. I heard Dianne moan slightly. Her eyes never left mine, and I had a hard time looking away.

"Roll rescue! I have a white female with a gunshot wound to the chest. Slow all other responding backup units. 305 and 306 are 10-4 at this time." I spoke the words into my shoulder mike, but my voice sounded distant.

Will had finished clearing the rest of the small apartment and hurried over to me. "Let's get her on the floor," he said. Carefully, Will and I lowered Dianne to the carpet. My hands came away from her back red and wet. The bullet had passed through her petite, delicate body.

I knelt beside Dianne and held her hand. Her eyes were trying to tell me something, I knew it, but what was so important? What did she want me to know? "Stay with me, Dianne! Rescue will be here in a minute!" Her breathing was labored, shallow, punctuated by an occasional deep gasp. Her dark brown eyes, flecked with red, speckled with shards of black, wide with surprise, were locked onto mine. "Stay with me, dammit!" I said. I squeezed her hand tighter. I couldn't look away and felt myself drawn deeper into her gaze.

Dianne's eyes never left mine even as that last breath left her. I honestly believe I felt a gentle squeeze from her soft hands as her body completely relaxed and death shaded her eyes. Almost as if to let me know "It's okay."

"J. R." I felt Will's hand on my shoulder. "Hey! J. R., c'mon, man, let the paramedics work." I stood up and stepped away from Dianne as the paramedics went through the motions of resuscitating her. Time had resumed its normal speed.

"J. R., come over here. You've got to see this." I followed the sergeant over to the small table beside the La-Z-Boy. Laid out neatly on the table was an open photo album. Photos of Dianne and a little girl with Mickey and Minnie. Carefully, folded beside the album was an elegant black dress with a note pinned to it. "I'm so sorry. But I cannot go on, knowing I was responsible for my baby's death. Please bury me in this dress beside my daughter, Cari." Underneath the dress were the funeral arrangements Dianne had recently made. There was also a newspaper clipping. Will read it.

"It's about that car accident in Altamonte Springs a month ago. Remember? The one involving the waitress and her four-year-old daughter. She was drunk, ran off the road, and hit a pole. The little girl was killed. This is her, Dianne Marcus. No wonder she ended it. Hey, J. R., you all right?"

"Yeah. Yeah, Will, I'm fine. I'll go get my paperwork and get started on the incident report. You already notify the detectives?"

"Yeah," Will replied, "Franklin's on the way. I'll let him make the call to the Medical Examiner. And I'll see if I can find any next-of-kin info around the apartment."

I walked to the apartment door and looked back to where Dianne lay. The paramedics were packing up their gear. Somehow she looked smaller now, empty. I glanced down at the dried blood on my hands as I walked down the stairs to my patrol car. The sun was just setting. I stood a few moments in the waning sun, bloody hands held in front of me, thinking about the last thirty days of Dianne Marcus's life.

Five more hours till the end of my shift.

I thought of other suicides I had worked. After a while you get a little numb. Your mind begins to close up, trying to protect itself from too much tragedy, too much pain. Each of those deaths had become just another body. Just another incident report. Another tragic story.

Not this one. And maybe not ever again. Walking back to the apartment I knew this would be one funeral I needed to attend.

Dianne Marcus had brought me directly into her tragedy.

Pulled me in with those brown eyes.

A Christmas Story

THE BEAT

BY PONZIO OLIVERIO

Deputy Sheriff, San Diego County, California, twenty-two years.

It was Christmas Eve. Soon the young deputy sheriff would be off to spend the holidays at his parents' cabin in the mountains near a ski resort. He'd been waiting for this trip for months and he'd earned every minute of the R&R.

The rest of his family had been there for a week already, but he couldn't get the time off. Fortunately, Christmas Day fell on his scheduled day off, and he was able to take a few days of vacation after that. He was going to drive straight up after work. It would make for a long day. The drive was about eight hours, but he couldn't wait to start the vacation. Only a couple of hours to go.

He was roused from his reverie when he recognized the man driving by his position. It was a man he'd been looking for, a criminal with an outstanding warrant. "Well, this should be easy," he thought. "There's just enough time to process the warrant arrest, and then I can forget all this on the ski slopes."

He pulled the man over and verified his identify and the warrant. It turned out the vehicle had not been registered for over a year and therefore had to be towed. The man pleaded with the deputy not to tow the car, to allow his wife to come pick it up. "It's our only transportation," he said. "I was just on my way to buy the kids Christmas presents."

"Look, that's not my fault," the deputy said. "It was *your* business to clear up the warrant and get the car registered. You'll be a little more responsible in the future."

"You're right, sir. I know you're just doing your duty."

At the station, while I was processing the arrest, the prisoner continued pleading with the deputy to let him go. He promised to take care of the warrant after Christmas. He explained he was trying to get his life back together and had just gotten a job. The deputy was not moved; he'd heard it all before. All he wanted was to get to the ski slopes. He'd earned this vacation and time with his family; he was not going to let this guy get in his way. He did allow the prisoner to phone his wife to tell her what had happened. The deputy began to feel a little sympathy as he heard the man apologize to his wife for ruining the family's Christmas.

"I guess even bad guys love their kids," he thought. But he had his own worries, like holiday traffic on the way to the mountains.

"Deputy, could you allow my wife to come here and pick up the cash I was going to use to buy gifts? Please, I'd really appreciate it. I only live ten minutes' walk from here." The deputy checked his watch. The sooner he got out, the sooner his Christmas would begin. "Okay, but she's gotta get here before we transport you to jail. I'm not waiting around." The woman made it to the station in the allotted time and the deputy gave her the cash her husband had. The couple's two small children were with her, and the deputy thought it was really sweet the way they ran up to their father and hugged him. They were pretty cute, and just looking at his face, it was obvious how he felt about them. They looked a little scared, though. It was a tough way for them to spend Christmas, but it didn't have anything to do with him. He watched them walk out of the station and out of his life.

Back inside, the deputy's prisoner was readied to be taken to the jail by a transporting officer. The deputy's shift was finally finished. He hurriedly got dressed, then ran out to his car. It was a cold night, just above freezing. The deputy was overjoyed. The snow conditions up in the mountains would be perfect. It was going to be a grand

Christmas. It was just after 6:00 P.M., and the deputy calculated he would be in the cabin by around 2:00 A.M. With a few hours of sleep, he would be ready to hit the slopes in the morning.

As he drove out of the station, he saw the woman and her two kids at the bus stop. They weren't dressed for the weather, and the kids were shivering. The bus would be there in a few minutes, he was sure. He drove on. He had to get going or he'd lose a whole day trying to catch up on sleep.

"What the heck," he thought. "I can give them a quick ride home, and then be on my way and still make good time. It won't kill me to be a little generous at Christmas. They look like they could use a little help." He turned around, went back and asked the woman if they needed a ride home. The woman explained that she had to do the Christmas shopping her husband was unable to do. They were going to take the bus to the mall. The deputy checked his watch and thought about how much time he would lose. But he looked at the wife and the kids and changed his mind. "The mall is on my way. I can at least drop you off." The woman said, "That's alright deputy. You don't have to. We'll be fine."

"No, really, it's not out of my way at all."

"You're sure?"

"Yeah, I'm sure."

So the woman and her kids piled in for the fifteen-minute drive to the shopping mall. The deputy did not want to get into a conversation. He had nothing in common with these people, he wasn't going to waste his time, but the kids were so full of happy Christmas spirit, and the woman began talking.

"He's not a bad man, you know. He's had a drug problem for years, but he's working really hard to overcome it. I have to say, though, that he was gentle with the kids, and even went out of his way to show them how much he loved them—even when he was at his worst. And he's a *good* man. The drugs just overpowered him."

"Well, I'm sure there's good in everybody. We'll be at the mall in a minute," he mumbled. The deputy just wanted to get this over with. He'd done his good deed, and it was time to think about himself for a change.

She looked over at him for a moment, "I know it's hard for you to really understand what I'm talking about—you have a good family and a good life. You're a smart man, a strong man—"

"Whoa, hold on there, ma'am. I'm not perfect," the deputy said. "Your man made his choices. Now he's got to live by them."

"Yes, and so do we. But he loves us. We know that. He loves us more than drugs. And we love him and we're going to help him." There was no doubt in her voice, the deputy thought as he turned into the mall. In the rearview mirror, he could see the kids—they were so little!—nodding their heads. They'd listened to every word of the conversation.

He pulled in front of the mall entrance. He leaned over to the woman and said, "How are you gonna shop for the kids if they're with you?"

She whispered back, "Well, it won't be a surprise, I guess, and I don't see how I can tell them Santa brought the presents, but it sure does beat no presents at all."

By the time the deputy pulled into his parents' cabin, the sun was up; everybody was gone, skiing already. He would miss that early-morning ski run, and he was totally beat, but he didn't mind at all. He would remember sitting with those two kids in the food court, doing silly magic tricks while their mother shopped for them. He insisted she have their presents wrapped, and he paid for that himself. They left the mall as it was closing, and he drove the family home. As she got out of the car, the woman had squeezed his hand and said, "Thank you, deputy."

Surprisingly, he was not tired on the drive up to the cabin, despite being hours behind schedule. Once inside the warmth of his family's cabin, however, he slept deep, and sound, truly contented for eight straight hours, with a big grin on his face.

Close Encounters of the "Cop" Kind

BY RON CORBIN

Police Pilot, Los Angeles PD, retired after nineteen years.

Since the beginning of time, man has been obsessed with solving the mysteries of the universe. Hundreds of sightings and reports of personal abductions by little green men in saucer-shaped flying craft are collected each year by various private and governmental agencies. Cults are known to worship the existence of alien beings. Top secret military programs like Area 51, Project Blue, and Roswell, New Mexico, have become household words.

And then, there's the following incident, one that played out during the morning watch in the early 1970s over the sunny skies of West Los Angeles.

To set the scene, imagine a front-page photo on the *Los Angeles Times* of two LAPD officers. One officer had taken a picture of his partner pointing into the western sky toward Santa Monica and the Pacific Ocean. These were accident investigation (AI) officers; a camera was part of the standard investigation equipment stored in the trunk of their vehicle.

Looking closely at the photo, you could see the object of the officer's attention: a fuzzy white, cigar-shaped image. The headlines screamed that these officers were witnesses to a UFO. Of course, police officers are generally considered trained, professional observers, right? So there'd be no better source to validate this unexplained sighting.

This was not some isolated stretch of a lonely road in Kansas, or the desolate, icy expanses of Siberia. This was Los Angeles, and after reading this top news story, the citizens of the City of Angels would spend the next several weeks gazing at the stars . . . and not just the Hollywood celebrity types either. But the UFO sighting of this night would never be repeated. Why? Because it was all a hoax, one that was inadvertently created by a police helicopter from LAPD's Air Support Division.

Cops are notorious practical jokers, usually playing their ludicrous or grotesque gags on their fellow officers rather than the general public. But on this night, what started out as an experiment, an exercise in curiosity, backfired wildly and turned into a citywide prank.

So, I have to tell you that the names of the two air crewmembers—who both have long since retired—will remain forever a secret, just in case the statute of limitations on practical jokes has not yet expired.

Before getting into how all this took place, I would like to quote *Dragnet's* Jack Webb. "Ladies and gentlemen, the story you are about to hear is true. The names have been changed to protect the innocent." (Or in this case, the guilty. Any resemblance is unintentional and purely coincidental.)

Police pilot Rob Cochran that day was flying a Bell Jet Ranger helicopter with Observer Lance Clarion. Assigned to "Air-80," their primary area of patrol took them from downtown LA to Harbor Division, and from the eastern boundary of Watts to Venice Division and the Pacific Ocean on the west. Since the city was basically asleep and all the bars had closed at 2:00 A.M., the police radio was quiet and void of major calls for police service.

It was about 3:00 A.M., and in an effort to keep their minds occupied, Air-80 was slowly "boring holes in the sky" over Wilshire Division. One of seventeen patrol divisions for LAPD, this area was geographically situated north of the I-10 Freeway and west of downtown.

During this quiet time, a discussion arose between Cochran and Clarion as to the limits of the Nightsun. This is the powerful, 30 million candlepower searchlight used on the helicopter for lighting up the ground. Along with the *whop-whop* noise of the rotor blades, it's the annoying device that flashes through your bedroom window at night while you're sleeping. Both officers wanted to satisfy their curiosity as to the range of rotation that the Nightsun would travel on its mounting brackets.

To answer this burning question, Cochran, for some unknown reason, turned off the navigation lights (the red and green lights) and strobe beacon. Clarion then turned on the Nightsun light and rotated it forward and upward. The beam of light just barely hit the tip of the rotor blades as they traveled around the path in front of the helicopter. This provided an oval-shaped projection of silvery-colored light, intensely bright, and one that flickered as each blade passed through the beam.

Are you starting to solve the cause of the UFO sighting yet? These few seconds of a flickering, oval beam of bright light, seemingly just hovering or moving very slowly across the black sky, triggered many, many calls to the police communications center as well as to the FAA (Federal Aviation Administration) at Los Angeles International Airport. The police radio crackled alive when the LAPD communication's dispatcher contacted Cochran and reported the citizen calls of a UFO sighting. Cochran immediately turned all the aircraft lights back on and Clarion switched off the Nightsun so they could scan the skies for other traffic flying in their area. Of course, they didn't see anything else. They didn't realize that they were the cause of the citizens' reports on the ground.

After searching for a few minutes, Cochran even contacted LAX Control (air traffic radar) and inquired if they had anyone else on the scope in the vicinity of the reports. LAX replied with a negative; Air-80 was the only aircraft up in that region at that time of the night. Of course, this made Cochran and Clarion even more concerned: Maybe they weren't flying alone in the "friendly skies."

About a half hour of searching for the reported UFO and seeing nothing, Cochran and Clarion decided to continue their discussion on the Nightsun. By this time, they had traveled several miles over the city to another general location. After again switching lights on and off, they were immediately contacted by the two AI officers mentioned before. These officers stated that they had just taken a picture of the UFO, and asked if Air-80 could see it.

It was about this moment that Cochran and Clarion put two and two together and realized that *they* were the UFO. Knowing that citizens had made numerous inquiries, even reporting the incident to radio and TV stations, both crew members of Air-80 decided now was the time to disappear. So all the helicopter's identifying lights were turned off and they rapidly flew away from the scene. At the same time they were making their hasty and covert retreat they radioed back to the AI officers saying that they didn't see anything.

By this time, Air-80 was scheduled to return to the heliport in Glendale for refueling. On the flight back, a "to-our-deaths" pact of secrecy was made between Cochran and Clarion. But sometimes even cops can't keep secrets. There was a lot of "hangar talk," and soon the cat was out of the bag—to other pilots and observers in the unit, not supervisory personnel, of course.

This story was passed along for many years after as new pilots came aboard. Each time it was told, it became like the fisherman's tale of the "one that got away." As far as I know, the truth was never known beyond a few insiders. And now I'll swear that it is just one of those myths and urban legends.

But I wonder: Could a crop circle be made by a police helicopter?

Heaven's Little Policeman

THE BEAT

BY KEITH BETTINGER
Sworn Officer, Suffolk County PD, New York, twenty-two years.

I am a proud member of the Shields of Long Island. The Shields is a fraternal group of police officers who live on Long Island and work for many different police departments. At each of the six yearly meetings there is an officer-of-the-month award as well as a guest speaker.

As the guest speaker chairperson, I had to find someone special every month. I was fortunate to find John Carlsen; for through John I met his son, Danny.

At that time, John Carlsen was a deputy inspector with the Nassau County, New York, Police Department. He was the deputy commanding officer of the Marine/Aviation Bureau. He and his wife, Kathleen, had a son named Danny. Danny was a unique child. I don't like to say he was handicapped, because what others considered handicapped never stopped Danny.

John came to the Shields meeting because he had a story to tell, a story about Danny.

Before Danny was born, doctors told his parents there were problems. Ultrasound showed a condition named hydrocephalus, more commonly referred to as "water on the brain." There were suggestions made to terminate the pregnancy. After a great deal of discussion, prayer, and tears, Kathleen and John decided they would have their child and love him no matter what.

On June 6, 1983, Danny was born. Not only did he have hydrocephalus, but he also had spina bifida and other complications. Within an hour of his birth, Danny underwent dangerous, but necessary surgery. Danny wasn't expected to survive the surgery or to live long afterward, but he did. Again, doctors told Kathleen and John that if Danny lived, he would never walk or talk. Kathleen and John never gave up hope and never stopped praying. Someone was listening.

He grew up to be a loving, wonderful child. Danny went to school and had many friends. None of his friends looked at Danny as being handicapped; he just used special equipment to get around, and get around he did. Danny was always in the center of what was going on in the neighborhood. He competed in the New York State Games for the Physically Challenged for six years and won more than twenty gold medals. His friends from school and the neighborhood came to the games to cheer him on. Thanks to Danny, they learned to see what a person could do, not what a person couldn't do.

Danny also became a Youth Ambassador for the March of Dimes and held the position for a number of years. He was a natural for the job. He had a warm smile and the gift of gab, a born politician. When introduced to Michael Crawford, the star of *Phantom of the Opera* in New York City, Danny introduced himself as the March of Dimes Youth Ambassador, and then asked Crawford, "What do you do around here?" Crawford looked dumbfounded, a Broadway star upstaged by a five-year-old.

Helping the March of Dimes was important to Danny. He met many celebrities while doing it. Every time his photo appeared in the paper, he called his father at work and said, "Hey, Dad, I'm famous again!"

Having something that made him different from other children never stopped Danny or his family. He and his parents did everything other families do, maybe even more. They did the big things:

baseball games, Disneyworld, and the Smoky Mountains by helicopter. They also did the little things that are important for all families: They went out to dinner, to the movies, had family birthdays, entertained family and friends. Danny was so well known and liked, that in 1994, his community invited him to be the official lighter of the village Christmas tree.

Danny endured many surgeries during his childhood and always persevered. He seemed to give strength to the people around him and had an amazing sense of humor and a quick wit. At the same time, he was sensitive. He wasn't embarrassed when he was hugged and kissed in front of his friends.

Danny was one of a kind.

For a while, John was the commanding officer of Emergency Service Bureau of the Nassau County Police Department. Danny loved to be around police officers, and the officers loved his visits. Like many kids, Danny wanted to be a cop. He would write his own police reports about the activities in the neighborhood. He told his parents that he was going to be a police officer, just like his dad.

This left John and Kathleen with a problem. As Danny was growing up, they always encouraged him to do his best. They told him he could be anything he wanted to be. He was a wonderful son with tremendous strengths. After all the encouragement they had given their son, how could they tell him that the one thing he really wanted was beyond his reach?

Then one day in August 1995, Danny collapsed. He stopped breathing. He had developed a heart infection, myocarditis. His parents called 911, and Danny's heroes—the police—responded. They came with their patrol cars and ambulances. John gave his son CPR. All the officers helped, doing whatever they could. They rushed their friend, the child who wanted to be just like them, to the hospital. Doctors did their best, but to no avail. There had been no heartbeat for forty minutes. John was in the room with Danny, holding his hand and telling him to keep fighting. The monitor gave a few beats, and then it was over.

Few people know the agony of trying to save their own child and losing. As devastated as they were, John and Kathleen decided to let Danny give the gift of sight to people in need. Doctors harvested his corneas and sent them to other hospitals. Danny, who never stopped doing nice things for other people, would now let two other people see the world through his unjaded eyes.

John and Kathleen were amazed when more than one thousand people attended Danny's wake. It seemed as if everyone came to pay their respects. His friends and relatives, the school bus drivers, his teachers from school, and of course his special friends—his police officers—all came to say goodbye to their friend.

The day of Danny's funeral was a typical, hot summer day on Long Island. Danny received full police honors. Members of the Emergency Service Bureau were his pallbearers. Rows of police officers stood at attention and saluted while the bagpipes played. School crossing guards stood in formation at the entrance to the church. A police motorcycle escort led the procession to the cemetery. When the cortege entered the cemetery, a special honor guard of mounted officers, and an honor guard of his friends from Emergency Services met him. All the officers were saluting and crying at the same time.

Heaven's police department had just appointed a special little police officer.

A few months after the funeral, Kathleen and John wanted to share Danny with the people who received his eyes. They contacted the eye bank and asked if a meeting could be arranged. It is a complicated task, and it takes time. It is also the recipient's decision whether or not to meet the family. After a while, a letter arrived. A young man, one of the recipients, wanted to meet Kathleen and John. He wanted to thank them for allowing Danny's cornea to be donated, and for giving him the gift of sight. Kathleen and John wanted to let this young man know what a wonderful child Danny had been. When they met this man, Ray, they realized once again that God and Danny work in mysterious ways. Ray was about to lose the sight in one eye due to an infection. Danny's cornea saved not only Ray's sight, but his job as well.

Ray is a New York City police officer.

Kathleen and John looked at one another and knew Danny, their special child, finally got the job he always wanted. In his own unique way, Danny is working the streets as a police officer, just as he always wanted.

The Enemy Among Us

BY JOHN MILOTZKY

Sworn Officer, Wauwatosa PD, Wisconsin, eight years.

Everyone knows where they were on September 11, 2001. Every American remembers that day. It was the beginning of a war with a very mysterious, nebulous enemy. However, I know of a few people who will not only remember this as the day of a very tragic event, but may also recall the battle between a group of neighbors, an out-of-town guest, a police officer, and a raccoon.

I was working the swing shift, 3:00 P.M. to 11:00 P.M. The mood was somber during roll call, and we were all instructed to be on heightened alert due to the increased threat level warning that the government had issued. Following roll call, I grabbed my squad bag, a radio, and a Benelli shotgun, and headed out to my squad car. It seemed warm for mid-September, and the sun was intense on my navy-blue polyester uniform. Strange, it was a warm day for such a cold-blooded act. I began to sweat as I locked the shotgun in the rack, checked the lights and sirens, and called 10-41, letting dispatch know that I was in service and available for calls.

I drove north toward my assigned squad area, wondering about the future, and observed that there was much less traffic than usual for that time of day. The squad radio was unusually silent. Most people were glued to their televisions watching the events at the

Twin Towers unfold on TV. The silence was eventually broken by the voice of the dispatcher.

"Squad 205."

"Go ahead," I replied.

"Respond to the 3100 block of North 104th Street for report of a sick or injured raccoon."

It took a minute for my brain to register, but finally I said, "10-4."

I sighed as I hung up the mike. I thought that at least this would give me something to do. I arrived at my destination, and was greeted by a gentleman in his early forties. Unshaven, he was dressed casually in shorts and a T-shirt. I wondered why he wasn't at work or inside watching CNN. He quickly explained that he was visiting relatives, and pointed to a house a few doors down. He went on to tell me that he had noticed a raccoon in the area earlier in the day, and he believed the animal must be sick. He based his diagnosis on the fact that it was the middle of the day, the raccoon stumbled as it walked, and it appeared to be foaming at the mouth. He then pointed to the raccoon, which was perched on the branch of a tree, approximately twenty-five feet up.

I saw that the raccoon was drooling, and I guessed that it was likely rabid, which is fairly common in this area. I explained to the gentleman that I could not shoot the raccoon while it was in the tree. Unlike the bullets on TV, real bullets actually do pass through things. I told the gentleman to call when the raccoon came out of the tree, and I would respond. His face fell, and he asked me to take care of the problem now. He was afraid that little children might try to pet the sickly beast or that family pets could be infected. I thought about it a moment, and knowing that there was not much else happening in the city, I agreed. But I insisted that we must get the raccoon out of the tree before I could take any action.

By now, several of the neighbors had come out to see what was going on. Surprisingly, most of them stayed outside, and I suspected they were looking for a break from the news. The news programs were filled with images too horrible to bear, images we could do nothing to stop. We were fighting an enemy that had no substance and was damn near impossible to locate. We all wanted to get "them," bring "them" to justice, but who were they, where were they? There didn't seem to be anything we could do but suffer in silence.

The attempts to get the raccoon out of the tree began with a garden hose. The raccoon turned away and hissed, and its claws gripped the branch even tighter. This wasn't working, even though the drenched raccoon looked sicker than ever.

But in a small way this was an enemy we could fight, a problem we could solve together. Collectively, we attempted to plan our next action. As we pondered how to defeat our foe, a frail old lady with white hair slowly came out her front door. She was wearing some type of nightgown with a floral pattern, and was carrying a softball that looked as old as she was.

She'd had the ball for a long time, and had not known what to do with it. She gave it to me, and in a frail voice, stated, "You can throw this at the raccoon." Then she returned to her front step to watch the show. I'm no baseball player, and after numerous misses, I was drenched with sweat. I had about given up, but just as I suggested that I leave, another neighbor suddenly appeared, carrying a pole saw designed to trim branches at high levels from the ground. I could have sworn the raccoon was mocking us.

This man explained that the tree was scheduled to be cut down by the city. He offered to cut down the racoon's branch so the raccoon would fall to the ground. I could then put an end to the suffering of the rabid animal. I realized that I had now been there almost an hour and a half. This was far too long to be out of service at a "sick or injured raccoon" call. I hesitantly agreed to the plan but insisted that *he* cut the branches and deal with the property owner if he was mistaken about what the city had planned for the tree.

I ushered the onlookers back across the street, worked the slide of the Benelli to bring a shell from the carrier into the chamber, and took up my position. The crowd grew silent, and the only sound was that of the saw cutting through the branch. The silence was broken by the sound of the branch cracking as it broke free from the tree. The limb fell in what seemed to be slow motion, bouncing off other branches. However, I saw that the will to survive had set in, and the raccoon, with a burst of adrenaline, made an acrobatic leap to another branch. It had earned itself a few more minutes of life. I heard a groan from the spectators, almost as if they had been holding their breath, and they exhaled collectively when they realized that this battle was not over.

The neighbor quickly went to work on the next branch, vigorously cutting away with his saw. The branch tumbled to the ground, and the raccoon struggled to grab onto anything in its reach. Its attempts were unsuccessful, and it struck the ground with a thud. It began to stagger in a westerly direction toward the backyard. I immediately took off in foot pursuit, drenched with sweat, my blue polyester pants stuck to my legs. The soaking-wet raccoon was also not moving very quickly, and we were both exhausted from the fight. As we made our way toward the backyard, I knew I had to act quickly. As I was gaining ground, I switched the safety of my weapon off and nestled the shotgun into the pocket of my shoulder and collarbone. I gently squeezed the trigger, and fired two shots in quick succession. The beast that had terrorized this neighborhood lay beneath me, twitching in its last seconds of life. I cleared the shotgun, put the safety on, and slung the weapon. Grabbing a pair of surgical gloves from my belt, I slid them over my sweaty hands. After picking up the lifeless raccoon by the tail, I turned to carry it to the curb, where the street department would eventually pick it up.

As I turned, I was surprised by the reaction of the onlookers. I received a round of applause. Many people thanked me for sparing their children and themselves from this "monster" that would have kept them trapped inside their homes. There was little we could do right now about the almost unimaginable terror in New York City, but working together, we were able to deal with this.

As I made it to the street, my new friend—the neighbor—handed a camera to one of the spectators and insisted that his picture be taken with me and the corpse of our enemy. No one at home would believe how he had spent the afternoon, he said, and he needed a photo to prove it. We all had a good laugh, and I obliged.

I thought of how I had spent the last two hours with these citizens I didn't know, and a smile crept across my face. It was the first time that I had smiled that whole day.

Final Goodbye

THE FALLEN

BY PAUL NANFITO

Captain, Red Bluff PD, California, twenty years.

November 19, 2002, will always stand out in my mind. It's a date I will never forget.

It is the day Officer David Mobilio was murdered as he fueled his patrol car. We learned that Dave had been killed by a former army Ranger who wanted to make a political statement by killing a police officer. He chose Dave at random. He killed a fine human being, a fine man, a good friend, a wonderful police officer—to make a political statement.

At about 0204 hours that day, I was awakened from a sound sleep by the ringing phone. It was Dispatcher Sue Myers, "Dave Mobilio was shot and killed."

All I could say was "Holy shit." I immediately showered and suited up to go to work.

As I turned onto Main Street from Walton Avenue, near my house, I saw all the police vehicles near Tops and Warner's fueling station. I could see Dave's black and white police vehicle still parked at the gas station. The scene was taped off with yellow police tape.

I could see a covered body lying near the gas pumps. While I had been to many death scenes in my career, it was horrifying, and surreal, to think that it was Dave Mobilio under the tarp. I couldn't think of it as Dave. It was too much to bear.

I began driving to the home of each officer in our department to let them know that Dave had been killed. At first it didn't seem real. Then I drove to the scene and looked across the street at Dave's body. I could see his gun lying on the pavement just a few feet from his body. I was told that he'd been shot three times—twice in the chest and once in the head.

Then it was real. I couldn't deny it any longer. It was Dave.

I returned to the business of notifying department members of Dave's death. Each time I knocked on someone's door, it became more and more difficult to say the words, "Dave Mobilio has been shot and killed." Not only was it difficult to say this to fellow officers, but their wives were usually present. Most of the wives did not react well.

At about 0800 hours, I had finished the detail and was free to return home to my family. Connie and the kids were up. My daughter Lexi had stayed home from school. Lexi knew Dave worked with me, but she also knew Dave because he was a DARE officer and came to her school. Lexi loved Dave and she was trying so hard to be brave in her own little-girl way, but tears kept leaking out of her eyes. It darn near killed me to see her so hurt—and to think that Dave was gone.

My son, Anthony, chose to go ahead and attend school, which surprised me, since Dave had been his DARE officer. It was just his way of dealing with things. He had to keep to his schedule; it was what he held on to to stay together.

First, Connie and I drove to her workplace to make arrangements for her to take the day off. As we were leaving her office, I could see that Lexi was very upset. I went to hug her and she burst into tears. When this happened Connie lost it, too. This was the beginning of a long, long week for our family and for my "family" at work.

I returned to work the next night for my first graveyard shift since Dave was killed. There had been a command post set up in the council chambers for the task force that had been set up to investigate Dave's murder. It was staffed twenty-four hours a day, and there were investigators from the California Department of Justice working there all the time. They had come up from Sacramento. Since I was the graveyard sergeant I was placed in charge of the command post.

Several times during the night I left the command post, as I needed to get away. I drove to the scene where Dave had been killed. I stood at pump number 4 and looked at all directions trying to figure out from what direction his attacker had come from. The first night I was immediately met by my coworkers, who were concerned about my safety since the suspect was still outstanding. I did this several nights in a row and was met at this location by my coworkers each time.

As the days went by we began preparing for Dave's funeral. I say we, but in reality it was many other departments and organizations that prepared for this funeral. Chico PD took the lead and made almost all the arrangements. We received food from people throughout our town and help from almost every nearby police department. The day of the funeral our department was completely staffed by officers and the dispatcher from Redding PD, Chico PD, Orland PD, and other departments. For twenty-four hours all Red Bluff police personnel were relieved of their assignments. It was a tremendous contribution on the part of those agencies.

As a member of the honor guard I attended the viewing, followed by a Catholic ceremony, then a public ceremony held at the fairgrounds and the burial service held in Chico, California.

At these four events, I and the other honor guard members carried Dave's coffin eight times. The first was the viewing held at the Catholic church the night before the Catholic ceremony. I and my fellow honor guard members drove to the mortuary to pick up Dave. We loaded the coffin into the hearse and then drove to the Catholic church. We brought the coffin up the steps into the church and up to the altar.

We were the only people inside the church at this point, when without warning, the mortician suddenly opened the coffin. I had seen many dead people in my life but nothing had prepared me to see Dave lying there wearing his police uniform. I still vividly remember the reaction of some of the honor guard members. I remember one who burst into tears and ran to the back of the church. I went to comfort him because I, too, could not look at Dave for very long. I returned to the front and saw another honor guard member touching Dave's hands in a gesture of goodbye. I also wanted to touch him and say goodbye but just couldn't get myself to do it. I looked back at the pews and saw yet another honor guard member sitting in one of the pews just rocking back and forth, becoming angrier every minute.

Once we regained our composure we went out to the church steps to await the evening's guests. I remember greeting Dave's wife, Linda, embracing her, and being unable to say anything but "I'm so sorry."

I remember her sobbing, telling us that it "hurt so bad." I can only imagine.

I can recall seeing Dave's parents kneeling in front of the coffin trying to maintain their composure. Dave's dad was very upset and I couldn't help but wonder how my father would be reacting if it were me. People began to filter into the church, including many Red Bluff police personnel who were in uniform.

The honor guard waited around until the end of the viewing. We were to return Dave to the mortuary until the following day for the Catholic ceremony. But we did one last thing before we left. Linda wanted to keep Dave's badge (no. 7). I returned to the office and took a reserve officer badge from the commander's office and brought it back to the Church. One of our detectives removed Dave's badge and replaced it with the reserve officer badge. This was difficult as he had to stick his hand underneath Dave's shirt in order to unclasp the badge and remove it from the shirt.

The following day the honor guard returned to the mortuary and brought Dave back to the church. After the service we brought the coffin back to the mortuary. The next day we returned to the mortuary to pick up Dave again. This time a flag was draped over the coffin. Red Bluff police vehicles then escorted Dave and his family to the fairgrounds. Each Red Bluff police car was paired with an officer and his wife.

Dave's coffin was brought into the fairgrounds by a horse-drawn caisson followed by the eight members of the honor guard team. This was the beginning of a very long and emotional service.

After the ceremony we escorted Dave on his final trip to Chico, for the graveside service. Our honor guard team folded the flag draped over Dave's coffin and the chief of police presented the flag to Linda Mobilio. Chico PD's honor guard team fired a twenty-one-gun salute.

After the graveside service we attended a reception held by Chico Police Department. We returned home at around 2200 hours. After that, Red Bluff PD personnel had their own little wake at one of the officer's homes, since we still had some free time until Red Bluff Police personnel would once again take over the city of Red Bluff.

The Ranger killer was arrested in New Hampshire on the day of Dave's funeral. He's now on Death Row in San Quentin.

Since 2002 I have been promoted a couple of times. It is part of my job now to take phone calls in the middle of the night when my staff have questions. There is rarely a night that I don't go to bed wondering whether, when I pick up the phone, I'll receive another phone call just like the one that came on November 19, 2002, and hoping I won't.

For, when the phone does ring in the middle of the night, I immediately expect the worst.

Happy Thanksgiving

LINE OF DUTY

BY RANDY SUTTON

Lieutenant, Las Vegas Metropolitan PD, twenty-two years; Princeton Borough PD, New Jersey, ten years.

The screeching of the alarm clock pierced my brain like an ice pick. Nine P.M. A graveyard cop's morning wake-up. I had to get my ass in gear if I was going to make it to a ten P.M. briefing. I hurried through the rituals of shaving and a hot shower, threw on some jeans, stuck my pistol into the leather holster at my waist, and grabbed my jacket as I jogged down the stairs. I heard my mother rustling around in her room getting ready for bed and stopped at her doorway to say good night. "I'm headed off to work, Mom," I said as I popped my head into her room. She was turning down the bedcovers and dropped them as I spoke. She shook her head and got a look on her face that might as well have been in screaming neon, "Why can't you work *normal* hours!" but she said softly, "I left a plate for you since you missed the meal." It was then that her words mixed with the aroma of roast turkey that lingered in the kitchen, reminding me that I had missed yet another holiday dinner. For an instant I tried to remember the last holiday meal I had actually sat down to, but gave up as I walked into the kitchen and grabbed a drumstick sticking out from under a foil-covered plate. My mother was standing in her doorway watching, and I turned toward her, brought the turkey leg up to my forehead in mock salute, and mumbled yet another apology. She got that funny smile and said, "Be careful tonight, Randy." I hesitated for a moment. She didn't usually say that, and I wondered briefly if she sensed something. But, in truth, I really didn't want to know. I glanced at her one more time as I opened the door to the biting November wind. She was staring at me sadly as I stepped into the wind's blast to begin another shift.

2300 Hours: On Duty. The officer didn't realize that the searing pain he felt in his thigh was caused by a knife that had just been plunged into him. He thought that perhaps he had pulled a muscle as he rolled around on the frozen dirt fighting off the man who had, moments ago, been just someone he had approached to ask if he had heard gunshots in the area. The officer was responding to a call that had come in to 911, a routine call for a graveyard patrol cop humping a "black and white" in the Vegas barrio. The young cop had no way of knowing that the man standing in the littered yard had minutes before filled his lungs with PCP-laden marijuana and that the sight of the officer's uniform would ignite his addled rage. Backup arrived as he managed to thrust his attacker away for a moment and the backup cop's taser prongs, carrying 50,000 volts of stunning electricity, short-circuited the doped-up gang punk long enough to get him cuffed.

I knelt down by the ashen-faced young man as he sat shivering on the crumbling cement curb, his disbelieving eyes staring at the slash in his thigh that was oozing rivulets of rose-colored blood, his blood. I wrapped a blanket around the trembling cop's shoulders while the paramedic cut open the pants to expose the wound and slapped a bandage against it. As the cop gathered the blanket tighter around himself, his eyes took in the gleaming bars on my collar and I saw his sudden recognition that the watch commander was squatting next to him. He had probably never even spoken to a lieutenant before now.

"A few stitches, a few beers, and you'll be good as new," I told him, trying to make myself smile.

"I never even saw the knife," he mumbled, as much to himself as to me. His eyes blinked back tears and he turned his head.

I glanced up as his sergeant strode up to us. We'd known each other for years, more as colleagues than friends, but he wore his stripes well. His face showed concern for his young trooper. He squatted down by the young man. "You did just fine," he told him. "This asshole was born with a blade in his hand and, hell, now you've got a damn good war story to tell the girls at the pool when they ask about your scar." He grinned at the young cop, who did his best to smile back through the pain that was ratcheting up as the shock wore off.

The medical crew helped him up and eased him onto the bright yellow stretcher. They wheeled him over to the waiting ambulance, and as they lifted him into the rig, I couldn't help but wonder if he would survive. Not physically, his injury wasn't life threatening, but emotionally. Coming to terms with your own mortality and second-guessing your combat responses is part of the seasoning of a cop. But if he stopped believing in his own abilities, the cost could be staggering, ranging from withering courage to turning in his badge. During the last thirty years I had watched many a badge get pushed across the desk, and I felt another surge of sadness well up within me. Their frequency was disturbing and had me questioning my own continuing tenure in a job that served up tragedy like a diner's soup du jour. The ability to retire was rocketing toward me. In a few short months the brass ring would be within reach and decisions would need to be made, because I knew I would not remain if I could not believe in my effectiveness as a cop and a leader.

"Coffee, Lieutenant?" The sergeant's words brought my eyes around and I saw him extending a dimpled Styrofoam cup with steam rising into the winter air, whipping away with the icy winds. He'd been a cop for many years and a sergeant for a few, choosing to spend a lot of his time working criminal investigations. He'd been around, and the lines carved into his craggy face were exaggerated in the dim glow of the few streetlights that survived the nightly drug-fueled gangster target practice. I gratefully accepted the carry-out cup and felt the warmth seep into my hand. We each took a sip and mumbled our approval and watched in silence as the ambulance drove away.

"The kid's freaking lucky," he told me. "Another inch or so and the knife could have hit the femoral artery and we would be going to another freaking funeral."

I heard the anger edge into his voice and knew we both had the images of the all-too-recent burial of Sergeant Henry Prendes flashing around inside our memories. "I don't know if I can stand another one," I murmured, and realized he was staring at me.

He quickly glanced away. "Does it seem to you like this shit is getting worse every day?" he said. "When we were young cops we had our share of fights, I know, but the assholes aren't afraid of us anymore. Pulling a knife on a cop used to mean an instant death sentence. Now, I bet you the DA pleads this down to a goddamn misdemeanor." He spat the words as he looked at me and fired out, "Why do we do this shit anymore, Randy? Why do any of us do it?"

There was a silence broken only by the angry desert winds. I wished I had the answer, but in truth, I had the same questions. "I don't know, Gary," I said impotently. "I really don't." I raised my cup to him in silent goodbye. He raised his and said, "Happy freaking Thanksgiving," sarcasm dripping from the phrase. I walked slowly back to my patrol car to call the sheriff and let him know another one of our guys was on his way to the trauma center.

The long night's parade of mayhem continued into the early morning hours. A domestic violence call where a thirteen-year-old had beaten his mother with a tire iron. An armed robbery of a convenience store that left the sixty-three-year-old clerk with multiple gunshot wounds. The two punks were heard laughing as they ran away with the $60 that was in the cash register. And the sexual assault of an eleven-year-old girl by the mother's live-in boyfriend. By 3:00 A.M. I felt the fatigue creep its way not just into my body, but into my heart as well. The sergeant's words echoed around in my brain. "Yeah," I said out loud. "Happy freaking Thanksgiving." I had completely forgotten it was Thanksgiving night, but the holiday spirit, had it ever been present, wafted away the instant I had put my uniform on.

I aimed the patrol car toward my area command headquarters. It was time to take care of the mountain of paperwork that went along with the lieutenant bars. I figured that I had seen my daily recommended dose of misery, and the paperwork I usually dreaded seemed somehow appealing. I had just punched in the code to the electronic security gate guarding the parking lot when the emergency tone alert blasted out of the radio. "All units, 911 emergency reports a medical emergency. Ann Road and Rampart Boulevard. A woman reportedly having a baby on the side of the road. Any unit in the area that can respond. Medical units are en route."

The gate opened, but I slammed the car into reverse, reached down to activate my overhead lights and siren, and punched the gas. I was only a couple of miles from this call and had quite a bit of medical training and experience. "What the hell," I thought. Paramedics will probably already be there, but this was unusual enough to have piqued my interest. The paperwork would still be there waiting for me. A couple of patrol units covering that sector radioed that they were on the way. I yanked my mike out of its bracket and told dispatch that I was also en route. I felt the almost comforting drip of adrenaline begin its flow as I rocketed my police interceptor into the frozen night.

The dispatcher, whose voice usually never deviated from a professional monotone, seemed animated as she radioed that the woman was parked on the side of the road; her water had broken, and the contractions were increasing. I pushed the black and white even harder and felt a sudden need to be a part of this, even if it meant just playing witness to the paramedics taking care of business. My searchlight captured the woman's SUV parked on the side of the road, a rumpled and frantic young man and an older woman danced in the harsh light, waving their arms and motioning me to hurry. Two other units, their red and blue lights cutting through the darkness, were arriving from the other direction. I radioed, "Unit 360 arrived," and threw the mike down as I jumped out of the car. The rear passenger door of the SUV was open, and I could hear the agonized screams as I jogged up to it.

The young man was screaming, "It's okay now, Baby! They're here!" The relief he evidently felt was quite the opposite of what ran through my mind as I got to the open door and saw the sweating woman writhing in pain, screaming, "Oh God, Oh God, Oh God!" One of the young patrolmen ran up at the same time, and he turned a bloodless face toward me. "This baby ain't waitin', Lieutenant." Sure enough, the crown was already visible.

"You ever done this before?" I asked him.

"Well, I was in the room when mine was born," he said sheepishly.

Another scream ripped out of the woman, spurring us into action. "Glove up," I told the young cop. "You're catching." He turned a bit pale, as he slipped on surgical gloves that are part of every cop's uniform nowadays. I grabbed on to the woman's hands and looked into her face. Despite the freezing winds, her long brown hair was dripping with sweat, and strands of it draped themselves around her forehead and cheeks. She was a plump and pretty girl, maybe twenty-five years old, with pale blue eyes that searched mine frantically for some sign of . . . what? Experience in childbirth? Confidence? I had neither. But she would never know that. And the words of an old academy instructor came ringing back, "Whatever you do, do it with authority and nobody will ever know you're full of shit."

I took hold of both of her hands and looked into her eyes. "It's okay now. We're going to get you through this. What's your name?" I asked.

She grimaced and through clenched teeth whispered, "Darcy. It's Darcy. Oh my god, it hurts!"

"I know it does, Darcy, but the baby is almost here. You're doing just fine. We're going to get through this together, okay?"

She nodded her head, the fear and pain evident on her face. "Please," she whispered. "Please make my baby be okay." Her eyes locked onto mine and in that moment, streaks of emotions welled up in silent conflict. I was afraid that something would go bad, that

I would let this woman and her unborn child down. Yet I felt an amazing sense of excitement. The pumping adrenaline that I thought had become rare after thirty years peaked and spread through me, isolating me in the moment and locking me into a bond with this woman, this stranger.

"Here it comes, Lieutenant I've got the head!" the young cop yelled. "Just guide it out and support the head and neck," I told him. And then to Darcy, "Another push, Darcy, just another push." Her face was flame red and drenched as she gave one final bellow. "I've got it, Lieutenant I've got it!" my cop excitedly announced. "It's a boy!" I heard a whoop of glee from the father and looked down into Darcy's sweat-soaked face. "You've got yourself a son, Darcy," I told her softly. Her tears began to flow in earnest, this time from relief and joy. She squeezed my hands and whispered, "Thank you."

"Where the hell are those paramedics," I wondered. Donnie, my young cop, was holding the wailing infant, who was slick with blood and fluid and attached to the twisted umbilical cord. He looked up at me with a quizzical expression on his face. "Should we do something with the cord, Lieutenant?" I didn't want to push our luck and knew that the pros would soon arrive.

"No, let's wait for the paramedics, but we need a blanket for the baby. It's freezing out here." The other cop, who was on the scene, ran to the patrol cars, but came back in moments empty-handed. "They're covered in grease and dirt, Lieutenant. We can't use them." I looked into the SUV and asked the frantic father if they had a blanket or a jacket, but he told me that they had just run out to the car when the baby was coming. I looked at the baby, who was making little squeaking cries as his miniature arms and legs pumped in the frigid air. I knew what had to be done and quickly stripped off my uniform shirt and carefully wrapped it around the infant. The bundle squirmed beneath the rough fabric. Seeing his little face surrounded by the badge and insignia of a Metro cop caused me to smile broadly as I placed him in his mother's arms. She clutched him to her, and her husband stroked her hair and murmured how beautiful she and the baby were. We heard the siren of the approaching ambulance in the distance, but for a moment this image was frozen in time, and I knew I would carry it with me forever. The other two cops stood shoulder to shoulder with me, gazing down at the mother and father and a baby swaddled in Metro green.

"That is the coolest thing I ever saw," Donnie said softly. The other cop nodded his head silently in agreement. The ambulance crew poured out of the rig and the paramedics came running up. "All done, fellows," Donnie told them, and we all stepped back to give them room.

Among them was a crusty veteran fireman I had seen at many incidents of violence and accidents. He smiled wryly as he looked at me standing there in nothing but uniform pants and gun belt. "Is that the new Metro uniform?" he asked innocently. He and the two cops started chuckling, which grew into laughter as I joined them. One of the paramedics handed me a blanket and I wrapped it around myself just as I had done for the injured cop a lifetime ago on the dirty barrio street. The incredible contrast of those moments washed over me. As Darcy and her family welcomed a new life into the world, the bitter question that the sergeant asked earlier came flooding back. "Why do we do this, Randy? Why do any of us do it?" As I studied the faced of my two young cops with their broad smiles etched on their faces, I knew the answer. "Happy Thanksgiving," I said to myself, and headed back to my patrol car.

Terry

THE FALLEN

BY RICH FORSEY

Sworn Officer, San Diego PD, California, six years.

At about 1221 hours, Motorcycle Officer Terry Bennett radioed that he had just seen a utility truck go off the freeway and down an embankment. At first, he thought it had been involved in a collision. When he attempted to contact the driver, however, the truck sped away. He pursued it and attempted to make a traffic stop. The truck driver ignored Terry's emergency lights and siren and fled at high speed.

Being only two years on the job, I was pretty much new to everything, but I could tell it was a wild pursuit. Even so, I figured I would get to the area and make an attempt to set up the spike strips to try and slow down the truck by flattening its tires. Terry needed backup and I wanted to be there for him.

Terry was doing an excellent job giving the directions for the pursuit. From my experience I have found it difficult to give directions while driving a car in a pursuit; I couldn't imagine doing this on a motorcycle.

I hit my lights and siren and tried to predict where the pursued and the pursuer would end up. I was planning on setting up the spikes, but was wondering whether that was such a good idea since Terry was behind the truck on his motorcycle.

About a minute and a half later, the radio suddenly went quiet. The dispatcher diligently tried getting an update from Terry but at the same time was obviously trying to be patient, knowing the stress he was under. The seconds ticked on and still no response. I continued driving to the last location that Terry put out, but figured he would be long past by the time I arrived there.

When the dispatcher clicked the microphone for the next transmission, I got that gut-wrenching feeling that something was not right. The next words on the radio were "All units . . . 11-99. We have an officer down . . . 11-99."

They tell you in the academy that you only put out 11–99 if you are fighting for your life, or if the sun falls out of the sky. When I heard those chilling words, my pulse shot up and my heart sank. I knew that Terry was in serious trouble. Terry was famous for always being there for brother officers. When a cop was in trouble, Terry always seemed to the first one there.

The dispatcher got back on the radio and told us that a citizen called in and said they saw a motor officer down in the street.

I shut down my air-conditioning and pushed my accelerator so hard to the floor that I could have sheered it off. As I got close to the freeway, I got stuck in gridlock traffic. As usual, the blare of my siren and flashing of my lights had no effect on the people in front of me.

I wasn't going to let traffic or any other obstruction get in my way. I cranked the wheel left, climbed the curb and plowed through the bushes in the center divide. I didn't care what I had to drive through; I was going to help an officer I admired, a man who I knew would move heaven and earth to help any fellow officer out.

As I wound out my car on the on-ramp to the freeway, I just couldn't get the car going fast enough. I wanted to click my fingers and be at the scene to help, but I also knew that I had to get there in one piece.

I watched 90 mph come and go as I jammed the brakes getting off the freeway. I got my first look at what I was dealing with as I started racing down Euclid Avenue. I could see car parts left in the roadway after the suspect crashed into other cars. It was like I was following a crumb trail of broken plastic and metal. The only good thing I saw was red and blue lights from every direction heading the same way.

Before I arrived on the scene where Terry was down, the officers who arrived before me made a horrifying plea for the dispatcher to expedite paramedics. Another officer on the scene advised that they were starting CPR and again begged for medics and Life Flight.

I pulled up to where Terry's motorcycle was crushed in the roadway. Several officers yelled for me to go after the suspect, who was now getting away. I closed my door knowing that these officers were doing everything they could for a brother officer. It was now determined the truck Terry was chasing was a stolen vehicle. I wasn't going to let this driver slip through my hands.

I raced my car over to 69th Street, where someone had spotted the truck going south. I was unfamiliar with this area and had a stream of black and whites behind me who I imagined also shared my determination to get this guy.

The unit that spotted the truck yelled on the radio that they were now in foot pursuit with the driver and a few seconds later advised they had him in custody and were Code Four.

I wanted to get to the suspect, but since he was now in custody my greater concern was finding out how Terry was. Back at the scene there was now a sea of patrol cars from every agency and every division of the San Diego PD. A lieutenant asked me to shut down one of the streets leading to the scene.

As I stood at the blocked street entrance I saw patrol cars getting towed away from the scene. I later learned that other officers had pushed their cars so hard trying to get to Terry that they had blown the radiators.

I held the traffic post for three hours and watched as cops, medics, and media came and went. They all had that pale look on their face.

Later I heard that Terry died.

The stolen truck Terry was chasing had made a U-turn in front of him. The driver charged Terry as he tried to get out of the way. Terry ditched his motorcycle and attempted to get on the sidewalk. The truck drove up on the sidewalk and ran him down.

Terry never had a chance.

The driver later claimed to be so strung out on drugs that he didn't know what he was doing. I believe he was sentenced to a mental institution.

Terry was a great police officer, a man we could depend on. He was an example for all of us, especially the rookies. He was a first-class SDPD motor officer and a first-class human being. He was rated number one in his motorcycle skills and was well liked by everyone who worked with him. He never let his buddies down, but on that day we all felt like we let him down. It was a sad, sad day. Terry left behind a loving family who misses him every day.

Everyone wishes they could have helped him that day, but we failed. I failed. We were helpless in the face of the terrible fate that threatens us all.

"Terry, I'm sorry."

Thank You

THE BEAT

BY NATHAN JACOBS

Sworn Officer, Ponca City PD, Oklahoma, seventeen years.

One Friday evening I was patrolling in my beat area. It was still light out, and the weather was just right. I was enjoying the warmth of the setting sun, the heat of the day beginning to dissipate. The shadows were just starting to grow, making everything seem quiet, calm.

Unfortunately, I was driving residential streets in an area that is rougher than most. It *was* beautiful . . . if you could ignore the junk in the front yards, the garbage, the unpainted houses, the rough and noisy people. This evening looked like a fair number of people had a good start on getting high.

In other, more well-to-do areas, that would mean that people were relaxing, enjoying a nice summer night, getting ready for a weekend spent with their family. Here it meant I was going to have a busy night. People were going to get in my face. I was going to get in people's faces.

As I drove the streets, I began to forget the rays of the setting sun, the feeling of the cool breeze on my face. I began to become more alert, literally looking for trouble. Many of the people I saw pretended that I wasn't there. Some were way too busy to even notice me. Others yelled insults.

As I passed one house, I noticed an elderly lady sitting in a chair on her porch. My glance passed over her, until I saw she was waving. Sensing trouble, I swerved over to the curb, quickly jumped out of the car, and started to run toward the porch. I swiveled my head looking for what could be wrong, my hand on my gun.

I stopped short when she waved me back and yelled, "Just wait there! Stay there!" Then she started the difficult task of standing up and walking toward me.

This was obviously no easy task. She had to use a walker to stand up and to walk. As she started across the lawn in a painfully slow way, I tried to meet her in the yard. Again, she waved me back and told me to stay where I was. I was really confused now. My first instincts seemed to have been wrong. I couldn't see anything dangerous or illegal going on. What *was* going on? It took her several minutes to cross the lawn—it seemed like hours. Each time I tried to meet her, she told me to stay put. Finally, I just did what she said and leaned against my patrol car, waiting for her.

When she finally got to the curb where I was parked, she stopped and took a breath. I asked her what the problem was. She said there was no problem. She had no complaint. Then she said, "I think you guys do a great job and I want to thank you. I don't think you should have to come to me for that." Then she turned around and walked back to her chair on the porch.

While I waited to make sure she got back alright, I thought about what had just happened. A lot of people tell me thank you, but this lady *meant it*.

It did, indeed, turn out to be a rough night. But it was a good one.

Thank You for Protecting Me

THE BEAT

BY SCOTT WALKER

Sworn Officer, Grosse Pointe Woods Public Safety, Michigan, three years.

When I was little I remember knowing that, no matter what, I could always count on police officers and firefighters to help. So when I grew up, it was no surprise that I wanted to work in public safety. I began my career with a small volunteer fire department when I was only nineteen years old, just twenty days before 9/11. Like the rest of the country, I watched the events of that day unfold on television. I spent the entire day at the firehouse, and from that moment I knew I had made the right career choice.

Early in my career, we arrived at the scene of a car accident where an elderly woman was trapped in her car. While we were removing the door from the car, I could hear the woman crying and screaming from inside. No one else heard it, but I did. After a lot of hard work we finally did get her out of the car and to the hospital where she died hours later. This was my first dealing with death. It was hard, but I knew that the woman was grateful that she did not die alone in her car that day.

After three years with the fire department I joined the Grosse Pointe Woods Public Safety Department. We are a small suburb east of Detroit. We are by no means busy, but we do get a steady stream of calls. Most of our numbers come from traffic (traffic and warrant arrests). Becoming part of this department allowed me to see things from both sides: police and fire.

Right after I finished my field training, I worked midnights and had stand-by duties. Stand-by duties require an officer to remain inside the station for the entire shift and take desk reports, check prisoners, and drive and engineer the fire engine in case of a fire. During my shift, a woman came to the station at about three o'clock in the morning, stating that her husband had beaten her. For the next three hours, I talked to her and tried to help her deal with her abusive situation. Finally, she decided to leave her husband. Our officers had to take her home and act as peace officers while she collected her things and left. I could see in her eyes that she felt comforted after talking with me, and I knew that I had helped her.

Fast forward a couple years later. Honestly, by then I would have told the lady that we couldn't help her. I would have told her that if she wanted to leave her husband it was a civil matter and that I couldn't get involved. I was starting to feel burnt-out from work and beginning to lose my patience with the residents of the city. Nothing in particular triggered my change of heart, just normal things that can wear officers down: too many horrible sights, too many negative experiences. I felt like I was becoming one of the officers who didn't care anymore. The ones that give the public a bad perception of police. I didn't want to be one of those officers.

On April 29, 2007, I was working the day shift and things were not going well. I was moody and angry. During my shift I went to the local gas station to get a soda. When I got there I noticed a mother helping a young boy out of his car seat. I overheard him ask her something about the police. I didn't pay much attention to what was said because I just wanted to get a drink and go about my shift quietly. While I was inside the station I was dispatched to a burglary alarm on the other side of town, so I hurried and picked up my drink and started for the door. That is when the young boy approached me.

"Thank you for protecting us."

I was taken aback. He couldn't have been more than five years old, and he had just said the nicest thing I have ever been told. This little boy reminded me of myself when I was little. He saw the police and fire departments for what they are—everyday heroes.

"You're welcome," I told him.

Then the little boy said something else that shook me.

"Thank you and have a nice day."

I told the little boy also to have a nice day and explained that I had to go. I was then out the door and on my way to the alarm. The rest of the day, all I could think about was what that little boy had said. Such a simple thing, yet it completely changed my day and attitude. He reminded me of why I became a police officer and firefighter—to help people. I felt rejuvenated and wanted to do all I could to make a difference in each person's life that I came in contact with on duty. The look of innocence and of honesty in the little boy's eyes made me think of police officers and firefighters that I saw growing up. The people that made me want to be someone others could count on.

Thank you, little boy, for protecting *me*. Thank you for keeping me from becoming a cynical burnt-out police officer. Thank you.

The King of Heroes

BY MICHAEL SUMMERS

Lieutenant, Burbank PD, Illinois, retired after twenty-four years.

His name was Patrick Michael Righi-Barnard, "Pat" to his friends and coworkers. Pat was a thirty-year-old police officer with the Burbank, Illinois, Police Department.

It was Wednesday, November 24, 2004, the day before Thanksgiving. I was Pat's watch commander and we worked the afternoon shift together that day. It was toward the end of the shift when Pat came to me with what he described as a "small favor." He explained that he had an individual in custody for theft who worked as a delivery man for a furniture store in town. Pat told me that this individual had delivered a couch to his mother, who also lived in town, but he had stolen the couch from the store's warehouse to give it to his mother as an early Christmas present. The value of the couch made the crime a felony, and Pat came to me to discuss the arrest.

He told me that the individual had no prior arrest record, was pretty much down and out on his luck, and was remorseful—he just wanted to make his mother happy. Pat asked if I would allow him to charge this individual with a misdemeanor rather than the more serious felony charge. I trusted Pat's judgment completely and agreed, but he had to convince the store manager to go along with it. Pat had repeatedly referred to himself as a "silver-tongued devil," so schmoozing people was his specialty, and he had no problem with the store manager, who had already considered letting the mother of the arrestee keep the couch.

It was now the end of the shift and snowing like hell. Pat and I were cleaning the ice and snow off our cars in the parking lot when he told me that he was going to brave the storm and drive the 160 miles straight to his hometown in Tremont, Illinois, since this would be the first Thanksgiving he'd had off in more than seven years as a cop. He smiled from ear to ear and told me how great it felt to spend the holiday with his family and new fiancée.

As Pat pulled from his parking space we both exchanged Happy Thanksgiving goodbyes. I waved and yelled, "Be safe!"

It was 7:30 A.M. Thanksgiving morning when I was awakened by the ringing of the telephone perched on the nightstand next to my bed. I just had a gut feeling that something was wrong, so I reluctantly answered. I immediately recognized the voice of one of the day-watch sergeants. Now I knew for sure it was most likely going to be bad news, and a feeling of anxiety filled my body. In a shaky and crackling voice he told me that Pat was killed at 12:20 A.M. helping a motorist who had slid off the icy Interstate 55 into the grassy, snow-covered median.

Anxiety turned to anguish as the sergeant went on to tell me that Pat had apparently seen the vehicle in the median, and while other vehicles streamed by, he pulled over to the shoulder and rushed to offer assistance. As Pat made contact with the occupants of the vehicle, he ascertained that they were shaken but okay. He then escorted Mr. Fredrick Davis, one of the adult occupants of the vehicle, up the median incline toward his own vehicle to call for help. As the two approached Pat's vehicle, another vehicle veered off the roadway, killing Pat instantly and seriously injuring Mr. Davis. The driver of the vehicle continued back onto the roadway and fled the scene, only to be apprehended a short time later.

In a daze I hung up the phone and became overcome by emotions as I tried to explain to my wife what had happened. As I was choking out the story, my mind kept trying subconsciously to block out the news. In the twenty-three years that I've been a police officer I never met anyone quite like Pat. In this profession we deal mainly with the dark side of society, and most of what we encounter is negative. It doesn't take long for most of us to become cynical and jaded.

But Pat was different. He was like a breath of fresh air. His passion for his chosen profession was outweighed only by his regard for others. I don't think I ever saw him without a smile or a sincere look of concern on his face, whether in the station or out on a call. He possessed the quintessential ability to put others at ease. He was always upbeat and pleasant, had high moral standards, and rarely had a bad word to say about anybody.

Pat was the kind of person we all strive to be, and he was a natural police officer. He never knew the difference between "on duty" and "off duty" because in his mind there was no difference. He was a cop 24/7.

Thanksgiving will always be different now. It will be a day when I hold my head a little higher and feel a little prouder because I had the honor and pleasure of knowing and working with Pat. In a job where we receive little or no recognition for our efforts, Pat's dedication to duty on that fateful Thanksgiving morning put all of us in law enforcement in a bright and positive light.

Over the years, I've often wondered why Pat and the rest of us in law enforcement selflessly sacrifice our personal safety and our lives to protect people we don't even know. We receive training on how to be safe and protect ourselves, but I can't recall being trained on how to die, but yet it happens to us all the time.

So why do we do it? Why do we continually put ourselves in harm's way, or, like Pat, stop on a cold, snowy morning while off duty to help someone in need when nobody else will? To me the answer is crystal clear now. It's not training and it's certainly not the pay—it's honor, dignity, integrity, trust, impartiality, and loyalty. These are the words all police officers solemnly swear allegiance to—the common thread that binds us, our guiding light, our heart and soul—our *oath*.

In his years as a police officer, Pat took the oath twice. First with the Markham Police Department and most recently with the Burbank Police Department, both in Illinois. Pat lost his life upholding the oath of office because he, like all cops, understood that his duty to others is paramount, above all else, whether in uniform or not. He gave his life as he lived his life, helping and protecting others, deservingly earning him a space on the National Law Enforcement Memorial wall in Washington, D.C. A hero is defined by the author as somebody who is admired for outstanding qualities or achievements. Well, I guess that would certainly make Pat "the King of Heroes."

Rest in peace, brother.

Friday the Thirteenth

DEADLY FORCE

BY JOHN WILLS

Sworn Officer, Chicago PD, Illinois, twelve years; FBI twenty-one years.

Quite frankly, the shot surprised me. Seeing the muzzle flash, hearing the loud report, and feeling the incredible impact caused me to lose my bearings momentarily. I slumped against the wall and lowered myself to the floor. A few seconds later came the second shot.

I was a young Chicago cop, five years on the job, and working the six P.M.–two A.M. power shift on a warm summer night in the Englewood District, one of the highest crime areas on the South Side. I loved the work; my partner and I responded to high-risk felony calls—man with a gun, robbery in progress, and so on. In between calls we made street stops of suspected stolen vehicles, lined up gang members searching for guns and drugs—you know the routine. It was expected that each team make two or three felony arrests per shift. We were the Area 2 SOG (Special Operations Group), and we were routinely deployed in areas experiencing high crime, particularly involving guns and violence.

The night of Friday the thirteenth, we had a traffic stop going when the call blared over the radio: "Robbery in progress, 63rd and Ashland, Church's Fried Chicken." We looked at each other, recognizing that the location was only a few blocks away and said, "Let's go!" That night my regular partner had taken time off, and I was paired with another cop from my unit whose partner was also off. I had a hunch that this would be a bona fide robbery. I knew that at this time of night the store was closing; the bad guys would be looking to snatch the day's receipts.

We pulled up a bit away from the storefront so as not to alert anyone inside should the robber still be on the scene. No cars out front. Store doors locked. No sign of employees milling around inside. These are all signs that this was the "real deal." I silently went to the window out front where the paid-for items are given to the customer. In a high-crime area, the counters are protected with bulletproof glass. The pass-through food window ensures that the store isn't too easy a target.

I peered through that little opening and saw the bad guy holding a gun on two women employees. He was yelling at them to open the office door so that he could get to the safe. Apparently, the store manager had locked himself in his office when the robber announced the stickup. There was a hallway separating the front of the store from the rear, enough distance to allow me to crawl through the food window and creep down the hall. My plan was to surprise the robber when he escaped out the rear door, which was plainly in my sight.

As I was moving down the hall, another unit arrived on the scene. This turn was catastrophic for me. The assisting unit pulled right up to the front doors—lights and siren blaring. The bad guy heard the commotion, saw me, and fired. At the same instant, I pulled the trigger. I felt as if a hot sledgehammer had just hit me in the right side of my chest. The impact caused me to drop my weapon; I slid down along the wall to recoup and recovered my revolver with my left hand, not knowing whether the bad guy was still in the game or had a partner in crime.

Just as I raised my weapon, the second shot hit me. The pain registered in my right leg. More confusion: Where did this one come from? I was looking right at the bad guy, who I had instinctively shot, and knew that he had not fired at me again. Where did the shot come from? As I looked to my right, I saw my partner leaning through the food window with his gun sticking inside and the rest of him on the outside. I knew at once that *he* had shot me in the leg.

I looked back to the bad guy. He had finally dropped to the ground, succumbing to a .38 round in the solar plexus. My partner later explained that he was unable to get through the window because he was overweight. When he heard the shot and saw the bad guy with the gun and me on the floor, he took a shot while leaning in the window. Unfortunately for me, my partner's marksmanship rivaled his fitness program: Both were sorely lacking.

My "Friday the Thirteenth" journey was just beginning. When the smoke cleared, and it was finally determined that the gunman was alone, the three employees locked themselves in the manager's office and refused to come out. The problem was this: I could not walk, thanks to my partner, and all the doors to the business were locked—no one could come in. I yelled for the employees to unlock the doors so that my colleagues could get me to the hospital, but they ignored my pleas. As I compressed the wound with my left hand, and saw my once blue uniform shirt now turning crimson, I knew that I needed help. My leg felt worse than the chest wound. The bullet had nicked my shin bone as it passed through my leg. Remember how painful that accidental kick to the shin was? Although painful, I knew that it wasn't life threatening. But I was getting concerned about the loss of blood from the chest wound.

My frustrated colleagues finally attached a chain to the front doors and to a paddy wagon and came in to get me. You would think that would be the end of the story, short trip to the ER, and so on, but you would be wrong. En route to the hospital, the brakes gave out in the paddy wagon that was transporting me. We had to pull over and wait for another wagon to switch out. When I finally arrived at the ER, the journey continued. The doctor wanted an X-ray of the chest wound before he operated. As I lay on the table in the X-ray room, the technician expected me to change positions for a better picture.

Due to the pain, and the fact that I was doing my best to stay conscious, I was having difficulty complying with her requests. She became angry, telling me, "You cops are all alike. No wonder you get shot!" I had a great response ready, but held it in check. My life was in the hands of these folks; the last thing I wanted was to alienate them.

Some time later I was wheeled into the operating room. I was finally able to "rest" and not have to fight to stay awake. I had felt that if I allowed myself to "sleep," I would never awaken. As I was being given the sedative I asked the doctor, "Is it okay now? Can I go to sleep? Do you have me?" That survival instinct was still in gear.

I awoke to find myself in a semiprivate room, my wife at my bedside. She related to me that she had been in bed when there was a knock at our front door. She opened it to find two detectives. They told her that I had been involved in a fight and injured my hand, the result being that I was not able to sign the papers at the hospital. This seemed plausible to her. I had been to the ER on several occasions as a result of street altercations. However, when she arrived at the hospital in the back of that car, there were a dozen news trucks there. Her first instinct was to think that I was dead.

That experience for a spouse is as traumatic as the shooting is for the officer. My hat goes off to all police families that routinely are exposed to these moments and move forward. About five years later, it would happen again. This time my sister-in-law's brother, who was in my same unit, was shot and killed during a traffic stop.

As my wife and I tried to comfort each other in that hospital room, I found that my black Friday had still not ended. I answered the phone ringing at my bedside. On the other end was a thug threatening to come to the hospital and kill me and then go to my house to kill my wife and children. It seems that the cretin that I killed was a member of one of the most violent street gangs in Chicago—the Disciples. He had just been released from jail on another robbery, and was practicing his trade again when I put an end to his career. That phone call triggered a 24/7 protection detail on my hospital room and my home. Lord, would this ever end?

Eventually it did end. In fact, once I got home and was feeling strong again, my police protective detail and I played games of cat and mouse. When it was clear that the phone call was bravado and nothing more, my family and I routinely tried to lose our "tail." My wife and I would load up the kids in the station wagon to go shopping. On the way we would try to lose the cops. The kids got a big kick out of it all.

My Friday the Thirteenth proved to be an extraordinary lesson. It reinforced for me the fact that fitness plays a tremendous role in survival. I had always known that my job as a cop would put me in great danger. The possibility of a life-threatening injury was always present. To increase my chances of surviving such an event, I worked out every day. I felt that being fit was just as important as being proficient with my firearms and tactics. After the operation, my doctor told me that had I not been as fit as I was, I probably would have died. He went on to say that most cops die in shootings, not from the wound, but from the trauma associated with it, since they had not experienced stress from the challenge of tough workouts and other "stress inoculators." They also have an unreal expectation of what happens to them in a shooting, most of their information coming from Hollywood movies. I vowed from that moment on to continue my workout routine, and to proselytize as many of my colleagues as possible.

I eventually left the Chicago Police Department after twelve years, becoming an FBI special agent. I became a "street survival instructor," both domestically and internationally, continuing to pass on my message to as many of my law enforcement brothers and sisters as possible. I retired after twenty-one years of service in the FBI. That black Friday was a pivotal time in my life. As strange as it may sound, I am thankful for having had that experience. Because of that long journey, I just may have helped some of my fellow officers survive a life-threatening incident.

Friday, I Cried

LINE OF DUTY

BY STAN TALTON

Sworn Officer, Wilson PD, North Carolina, twenty years.

I became a police officer because I wanted to help others and serve my community. Like most officers, I have come to realize that it's often a thankless job. We are called upon day in and day out to help people solve their problems, and we do this because we chose to, or maybe we do it because the job has chosen us.

While I was on patrol Tuesday, September 11, 2001, our country was both shocked and horrified by the events that occurred in New York, Washington, D.C., and Pennsylvania. When I first heard the terrible news, I pulled the patrol car over, stunned. I sat there, wondering how this could have happened. As the day progressed, I became more and more emotional. As I sat at a stoplight in my patrol car, listening to the radio broadcasts, my heart became heavy with sorrow for the enormous loss of life and for the victims' families. Tears welled up, threatening to overflow. The death of so many brave policemen and firefighters, so many innocent citizens, was worthy of my tears. It would be unusual if one *didn't* cry under such circumstances. As I glanced to the left and right of me, I saw so many of my neighbors stunned and in tears. I realized I was not alone; other people were watching. I'm a cop. I cannot cry. I can show no signs of weakness. Especially at a time when I knew we all needed to be strong, we all needed strong signs of reassurance.

So I took a deep breath and held back the tears; thinking to myself, "When I get home I can let the tears flow." I worked the whole day with my heart in my throat, holding myself in tight control. It was a quiet day in Wilson; the people were stunned, glued to TV sets, trying to understand the minds of those who could harm innocent people. Like the other policemen, emergency personnel, and firemen of Wilson, I worked the day through, did my job with professional pride, telling myself, over and over, that when I got home I could let go, be scared and enraged, and let myself cry.

This was not to be the case.

When I got home, I was greeted at the door with hugs from my wife and our three young children. My wife looked at me and said, "This is going to be tough to explain to them." They had seen the news broadcasts of the plane crashes and heard the words "attacked," "hijacked," and "terror." How do you explain such tragic events to seven- and four-year-olds? So with the news broadcasts playing quietly in the background, we sat down and tried to explain that some "bad men" had caused the planes to crash and that a lot of people had died. I could feel the tears welling up again, but knew I could not cry. I am the Dad. I have to be strong. I cannot cry. Again, I took a deep breath and held back the tears.

As I finished my workweek, I listened to the news broadcasts with the realization that the tragic events on Tuesday had made a great impact on our country and would be the cause of many changes in our country. As a veteran, I also realized that the actions taken by the United States would more than likely bring about the loss of many more lives. Again, my heart became heavy with sorrow.

Friday, my first day off, I went to the gym to work out. The talk around the gym was about the tragedies that had befallen our great country. As I spoke with Tracy, a staff member of the gym, we talked about the hundreds of firemen, police officers, and rescue personnel who rushed into the first tower without a second thought. Their

focus was on doing their job to the best of their abilities. Their focus was on helping others who needed their strength and skills.
They expected no thanks. It was their job, what they had been
trained to do. They were men and women, husbands and wives, sons
and daughters. And in an instant they were gone. Tracy told me that
she and the staff felt helpless and just wanted to do something. With
the blood drives delayed until the following week, they decided to
provide lunches for the firemen of Station Five. Tracy told me the
lunches were simple, and as they were presented, several of the firemen began to cry. As she related this to me, she, too, began to cry.
With tears in her eyes and a slight smile, she looked at me and said,
"If no one else has told you this, then I will. I appreciate what you
all do for us. Thank you."

Thank *you*, Tracy.

And on that Friday, I cried.

Ride-Along

BY TIM DEES

Sergeant, Reno PD, twelve years.

I think the reason that I enjoy being a field training officer (FTO) is that I am fundamentally a ham, and when you're the senior officer and have a captive audience of one, you get to perform and direct, too.

FTOs who didn't have trainees were generally assigned the ride-alongs. Ride-alongs are citizens at large who want to get some insight into policing and ride shotgun for a shift. Most people find it to be a memorable experience. They ask a lot of questions, do what I ask them to do, and are generally pleasurable company.

And then there was Steve.

My Steve experience began unremarkably. The briefing sergeant told me to pick up a ride-along at the front desk. I was looking at a downtown graveyard shift, and it was nice to have someone with whom to pass the time.

Steve was waiting at the front desk, bearing the expression and body language of a golden retriever who has seen what he believes to be the last tennis ball in the universe. He had recently discovered that the local DMV office sold logo apparel bearing the emblem of the highway patrol troopers association, and I think he may have bought out their inventory. He was wearing a baseball cap, sweatshirt, and T-shirt bearing the association's logo. Since the logo was based on the same seven-point star that we wore as our badge, I was a little concerned that someone might assume that Steve was a police officer. Steve, on the other hand, was hoping desperately that someone might make that assumption.

Steve was bursting to tell me something, but I told him to first lose the sweatshirt, hat, and T-shirt, or at least put something over them so that he wouldn't be mistaken for a cop. He found something else to wear, and we walked out to the motor pool to get a car and hit the street.

As soon as we got into the car, Steve began a kind of stream-of-consciousness narrative about his ambitions, his perspectives on law enforcement, his hopes for the night's events, and no doubt some other topics that got lost in the mix.

Like this: "I'mreallygladIcouldridewithyoutonightOfficerDees-becauseeveryonetoldmethatyou'reareallygoodofficer . . ."

Get the idea?

It was a Friday night, and the teenage cruisers were downtown in force. People drove over a hundred miles to take part in "the cruise" down our main drag, an activity we did our best to discourage with draconian traffic enforcement and a generally surly attitude. Someone had the idea that having a supermarket downtown would be a great addition to the casinos and souvenir shops, so we had a market with a huge parking lot—just where no one would ever expect to find one. The lot was a popular place to let overheated engines cool, get girls' phone numbers, find out where the keggers were, and start and end fights. I tried to drive through the lot a couple of times an hour. I turned into the lot and was immediately flagged down by a group that had been involved in a fender-bender. I told dispatch that I would be out taking a report and got out of the car.

Walking up to one of the drivers, I asked him for his driver's license, registration, and proof of insurance. While he was retrieving the documents, I became aware that Steve had gotten out of the car and was approaching the other driver. "Driver's license, registration, and proof of insurance," he said in his most authoritarian tone.

"Get back in the car," I said. Steve started to protest, but then demonstrated he was smarter than he looked and did as he was told. From his expression, you would have thought I had taken away his next three Christmases.

While I was filling out the report form, dispatch called on my portable radio, asking me if I could secure for another call. They didn't generally do that unless the call was something fairly important.

"I'm kind of busy right now. What've you got?"

"We have a report of shots fired at the Dairy Queen at Sixth and Virginia." The Dairy Queen was one block away.

"Securing."

I gave the vehicle documents back to the injured parties and told them to go to the station to finish their report. I ran back to the car and flicked on the overhead lights and siren and headed down the street. It was maybe a fifteen-second trip.

Although I never fully understood the logic behind it (this was not uncommon), our departmental policy stated that our primary weapon was the shotgun. If you had access to your shotgun, you were supposed to use it before your sidearm in any situation where the introduction of police firearms was appropriate. Our shotguns were 12-gauge Remington 870 Wingmasters, loaded with 00 (always pronounced "double ought") Magnum buckshot shells. At close range, a barrage of 00 pellets could sever a major body part. From a short distance away, the effect was that of firing twelve .38 Special bullets simultaneously, making marksmanship, at best, a secondary consideration.

But the most often used feature of the shotgun, and probably the most practical, was its capacity for intimidation. The sound of a shotgun's action, pulling the forearm back toward the receiver and then forward again to chamber a shell, translates into almost every language and culture as "Immediately stop what you are doing unless you are bored with life." In my experience, "Halt, police!" had an efficacy of maybe 50 percent, but "Halt [*rack, rack*], police!" worked every time.

Our shotguns were carried in an upright rack bolted to the dash-board, with the shotgun barrel pointed up. A cast-iron shank sur-rounded the magazine tube between the forearm and receiver, so a shell couldn't be chambered while the weapon was in the rack. Doctrine was to clear the shotgun before replacing it in the rack, re-turning it to "car condition," with four shells in the tube magazine and none in the chamber.

From time to time, a shotgun would be replaced in the rack with a shell still chambered, and someone would pull the trigger acciden-tally . . . or on purpose. The effect was spectacular. Patrol cars where this had occurred could be identified by the jagged holes in their roofs, missing or extremely disfigured light bars, and the occupancy of officers who responded to any question with "What?"

The shank that held the shotgun in place was released by pushing a small white button on one side. When the button was pushed, the latch was released, and the shotgun would fall into your hand. This was augmented by a large keyed cylinder that projected out of the shank. If the cylinder was extended, the button would release the shotgun. Pushing the cylinder in would lock the shank, and a key was required to unlock it. My practice was to lock the rack only when I was out of sight of the car. When I came back to the car, I would first unlock the shotgun, then put the keys in the ignition. Since I had not gotten out of sight of the car since we left the sta-tion, the shotgun was unlocked, and I was anticipating putting it to immediate use on arrival at the Dairy Queen.

That was the plan, but as a wise man once said, "Man plans, God laughs." If God was in the mood for a practical joke that night, then Steve was his instrument. Halfway to the Dairy Queen, without say-ing a word and to my profound astonishment, Steve pushed in the cylinder of the shotgun lock, making it impossible for me to get to the shotgun without fumbling with keys.

My response, I am sad to say, was something less than professional. Had I been given a bit more time to prepare an interrogative statement, I might have said, "Steve, please be so kind as to inform me why you have chosen this moment to operate this item of city equipment, when you have not first secured my permission to do so, and when you have not been properly trained in its use?" In my defense, time for proper reflection was a commodity in short supply, and I was under stress, given that I had every reason to expect that I was running toward a man who was shooting a gun, when anyone with good sense would be going the other way. Thus, my question to Steve was more pithy and agitated. "WHAT THE [*colorful expletive*] DO YOU THINK YOU'RE DOING!"

Steve started babbling something, but I was distracted, as I had turned the corner onto Sixth Street and saw the malefactor standing in the small parking lot of the Dairy Queen, pointing a semiautomatic handgun into the air. Shell casings littered the ground around him. Had he decided to open up on me, I might not be writing this now. Instead, he took the opportunity to depart the area on foot, and with great haste. He got less than a block before running into one of my comrades, who was also responding to the scene, and who collected him without further incident. Somewhere between me and the other cops, he had ditched the gun.

It took a few minutes for enough officers to arrive to secure the perimeter and begin a search for the gun. This was fortunate for Steve, as my affections for him had turned from annoyed to homicidal. Before I joined the others to search for the gun, I went back to the car, killed the engine, and took the keys out of the ignition. I looked Steve in the eye and told him, with as much restraint as I could muster, "Sit here. Do not get out of the car. Do not talk to anyone. Do not touch anything. If you ignore any of the instructions, I will lock you in the trunk." Uncharacteristically silent, Steve nodded his assent.

I made a brief verbal report to my sergeant, whose immediate response was "What the [*same colorful expletive*] did he think he was doing?" I told him I had made a similar inquiry that had so far gone unanswered. I also told the sergeant that my intention was to deliver Steve back to the station as soon as we were finished with the task at hand, as killing him would involve too much paperwork. My sergeant voiced his enthusiastic support for this.

On the way back to the station, Steve again went into his stream-of-consciousness narrative, but I can't remember a thing he said. I parked the car, got out, walked around to his side, and opened the door. "Get out. Do not come back. Ever."

"ButOfficerDeesIwashopingthatIcouldridewithyouagainnextweek-because—"

"Steve, if you ever ride in my car again, you will be sitting in the prisoner cage, wearing handcuffs. Goodbye."

10–13 MOS

BY EDWARD V. BURMEISTER III

Sergeant, New York PD, twenty-two years.

It was March 23, 1986, and I was doing a four P.M. to twelve midnight in the 73rd Precinct, located in Brooklyn, New York. It's a rough section of a rough borough. I was a sergeant, and that night my assignment was patrol supervisor. I remember the radio giving jobs to the sectors when the call came over: 10–13, off-duty MOS (member of service, an off-duty policeman) shot with his own gun by the perp who tried to rob him.

My driver and I rushed to Brookdale Hospital where the wounded officer was being transported. I got there praying selfishly that it wasn't anyone I knew, hoping that it wasn't serious, knowing my prayers and hopes were in vain. I found the MOS in the Emergency Room. The doctors were working hard, doing everything possible.

From where I was standing I could see the powder burns on the officer's chest. I couldn't look at his face; I didn't want to know who it was. It seemed as if time stopped. Nothing seemed real. It could be anyone, but I couldn't look up to see *who* it was.

Just then the doctors stopped working; they began to collect their instruments and walk away. I had a clear view of the body and still couldn't look at the man's face. One of the doctors walked over to me and said, "I believe this belongs to you." He handed me the officer's shield and told me he was sorry; they had done everything humanly possible to save the officer.

I held the shield clenched at my side, my eyes shut tight. I kept repeating in a whisper, "It's all a dream. It. Is. Nothing. But. A. Dream." I don't know how long I stood there like that. Too long probably. I could no longer fool myself when everyone from the police commissioner to the mayor and all the high-ranking officers came in to the ER.

I stood there still holding the shield, everyone talking at once all around me, and then I heard, "Can I see my husband." I looked up and saw a woman holding a child across the room and I learned it was his family. I immediately thought, *Thank God, it isn't anyone I know.* I was relieved until I saw she was walking right toward me. I began to panic all over again. Now I was thinking, *What can I possibly say?* There were no words in my head, nothing.

Suddenly, a chaplin was next to me. He said, "Sergeant, I'll tell her." He took her by the arm and began to lead her and the child away. When he told her that her husband was dead, she let out a scream that I will never forget; it still haunts my dreams. She asked to see her husband and the chaplin took the sobbing wife and child into the room. He stood in the doorway with his head down and his hands clasped before him as they ran to the body that no longer held the soul of the one they loved. They threw themselves over the body, praying and shouting, "This isn't real! This can't be real!"

But it was.

We all felt helpless, unable to bring back our gallant brother officer, unable to bring a husband and father back to life.

I was still standing there, trembling, holding the dead policeman's shield.

Finally, a chief walked up to me and said, "Sergeant, I'll take his shield and guard it just as you did." He gently pried it from my hands and patted me on the shoulder.

It's almost twenty-one-years since I walked out of that hospital, but I still feel the shield burning in my palm. I look at my hand, sometimes, expecting to see it there still. I hear his wife and child crying. I feel that hole in my heart as if I'd been the one who was shot.

The shield belonged to PO James Holmes, Shield No. 2492, PSA 3. I had never met him, but I knew him as well as I knew myself. My brother in blue.

Rest in peace, my friend.

Suicide

THE BEAT

BY KEN RAMSEY

Sworn Officer, Cypress PD, California, eighteen years.

When dispatched along with a second officer to a 911 hang-up call in the south end of town, I canceled my back-up and advised dispatch that I would handle it on my own, violating my own safety rules and those taught to me by my training officers. It's something I never did until that night, and I've never done it since. I did it for reasons I still can't explain, even a decade later.

Besides, I wasn't alone, I thought. I had my K-9 partner with me. It would be "just another one of those routine calls" I'd clear after five minutes and head to get a bite to eat. I was hungry anyhow, and this was the first hour of a twelve-hour shift.

When I arrived at the modest one-story residence, I made a routine tactical approach and walked toward the front door, which I could see was open. As I peered through the black screen door I heard music playing and could make out the faint image of a police officer's picture on the entertainment unit in the living room.

From what I could see, the officer in the picture resembled the officer from an adjoining jurisdiction who committed suicide the year before. I was working narcotics at the time, but I'd heard the story. He had a questionable shooting followed by a lengthy investigation.

He couldn't (or wouldn't) take it anymore. So with a single blast of a 12-gauge shotgun he ended the process.

I was a little vague on the details, but I recalled that he had killed himself in the south end of town at his modest one-story residence. It was then that I asked dispatch to research any previous calls at the residence. The response confirmed what I was starting to piece together. "914-S the previous year." Suicide. It was then that I requested a supervisor. I had a feeling I wasn't going to be eating anytime soon.

As the sergeant arrived, so did another rookie officer. We knocked on the door, but received no response. A telephone call to the residence also went unanswered. Advising dispatch, we made entry. I wasn't much of a country music fan, so when I entered the house and heard Garth Brooks's "The Dance" playing from a stereo in the back of the house, I wasn't thrilled. I also noticed a strong odor of ammonia, as if the house had been scrubbed recently with an industrial-strength cleaner.

We made our typical coplike tactical search. Nothing in the living room, nothing in the bedroom, and nothing in the kitchen. Then I rounded the corner to the bathroom. She was lying in the bathtub with her feet pointing north. There wasn't much of her head left. What was blown away now painted the shower walls and ceiling. Crimson fluid and brain matter was everywhere. Her left hand still clutched the shotgun.

That damned song was on a loop. It played over and over again.

A second sweep of the kitchen revealed the note. And the coffee. "Sorry for the mess. I made coffee for you guys. Please notify my parents and arrange for my pictures to be picked up from the drugstore. Thanks!"

When the dust settled, I learned the dead woman was the widow of the officer who had committed suicide the previous year, nearly a year to the day. In the same bathtub. With the same shotgun.

It added to the mess when I learned that she was a dispatcher for a large metropolitan sheriff's department in an adjacent county. She knew exactly what it would take to have officers respond. An innocuous 911 hang-up and the cops will come.

"God damn it! This is the same shotgun I *just* released to her last week!" The coroner's investigator wasn't pleased. He mumbled something about liability, but I was more concerned about the two newly orphaned children whom mom strategically arranged to be out of the house. How could she do this to them?

When the body was removed, another officer and the supervisor began to clean the mess, something that made me quiver. I was pissed at the cowardly manner in which she chose to handle her issues, not to mention being pissed at the husband, who had done the same. How could they now be cleaning her blood and brain matter? Fuck her. I wanted no part of it.

When her sister happened to arrive for an unexpected visit, she saw the police cars and started running up the driveway, crying. It was clear she knew exactly what had happened before a word was exchanged between us.

Suicides and death notifications are still my least favorite calls to handle, and I was about to get the double whammy that night. I was assigned to drive to her parent's house and make the death notification. Her father was a high-ranking official in a large county fire department.

I had long lost my appetite by this time.

The long drive to the exclusive neighborhood went by too fast, as I was dreading the task ahead of me. When I arrived and pulled into the driveway, my K-9 partner started barking at a cat that had walked by. This caused the parents to awaken, and I saw the downstairs light turn on. No time to prepare a speech now.

When I was a brand-new cop, a salty veteran accompanied me to my first death notification—a teenager killed in a car wreck on her way to a concert. It has been nearly eighteen years, but I remember it like it happened this morning. I still remember her mom's smile when she opened the door, not knowing that information we had would shatter her world forever. "Never bullshit 'em . . . Give 'em the straight scoop" was his advice.

Maybe the fireman father had an inkling when he saw an out-of-county police car in his driveway. Maybe he had done this himself at his job. He knew exactly why I was there before I reached the door. There would be no scoop to give tonight.

My most traumatic stories in law enforcement continue to be the suicides. Not because they take the easy way out, but because of the incredible destruction they cause the survivors: the family, friends, and children. This case was compounded by the tragedy that not one, but two members of the law enforcement family, who should have known the effects, were now dead by their own hands.

I never drove down that street again without reliving that night. The house has since been sold, but I wonder whether the new owners knew what twice happened in their modest one-story home.

To this day I still worry about those two kids.

The smell of ammonia still takes me back to that day nearly a decade ago.

Anytime I hear that song, I turn it off. I hate it.

Talk to the Hand

BY JOHN W. HOWSDEN

Sergeant, Fremont PD, California, retired after thirty years.

I was working the day shift, cruising through a residential area when dispatch advised a 911 call was coming from a house in my vicinity. I volunteered to handle the call.

I parked a few houses down from the address, a normal procedure, so I didn't alert the suspect I'd arrived and make myself a juicy target. As I walked up to the house, I noticed a garden hose sprawled across the dried-up, weed-infested lawn, a broken tricycle on the walkway, and candy wrappers strewn about.

When I knocked on the door, a short, heavyset woman with a flustered expression cracked open the door and peeked out. Her short gray hair was only partially combed. Her face was grooved with wrinkles and void of makeup. Although it was late afternoon, she was still in her ankle-length robe and tattered green slippers.

I told her we had received a 911 call from the house and asked if anything was wrong. She shrugged her shoulders and said, "I don't think so. Let me check with my granddaughter." I heard teenage girls giggling in one of the bedrooms down the hallway of the house.

Many 911 calls are pranks, kids having fun at the expense of the police department, wasting countless dollars in resources and time.

Worse still, after going to hundreds of these prank calls, officers wrongly, but understandably, let their guards slip a little. Once this happens, they open themselves up to being hurt or killed. The giggling signaled that this was one of those prank calls. I made my mind up right then that if this was a phony call by a bunch of teenage girls with nothing better to do, I was going to hand out a first-class ass-chewing.

"Bring your granddaughter to the door," I demanded. In a few seconds she returned, without her granddaughter. "My granddaughter doesn't want to come to the door. She told me to tell you that everything is alright and for you to leave." That was the last thing I wanted to hear. There was no way she was going to dismiss me like that. The girl had a scolding coming, and I was just the person to do it.

Sensing that the grandmother was allowing the granddaughter to boss her around pushed a button for me. I have no patience for adults who shed their responsibilities and allow the children to run the show. However, choosing not to have children has left me unprepared to deal with conniving, rebellious teenagers, and somewhat unappreciative of how difficult it can be.

I looked the grandmother in the eye and said, "Go back and bring your granddaughter to the front door. Now!" She sighed, and with a sheepish look on her face disappeared back into the house. Several minutes passed, and she came back, "She told me to tell you she's in the bathroom." This lit my fuse. "Bring your granddaughter to the door now, or I'll arrest her for reporting a false emergency." I couldn't do that, of course, but my mouth was working faster than my brain.

The grandmother shut the door and her slow, heavy footsteps faded into the back of the house. More giggling came from down the hallway, soon followed by footsteps coming to the door. I figured they had laughed at the old woman and sent her back to me empty-handed, but I was wrong.

The door creaked open a few inches. A girl's arm slithered out of the crack of the door and the arm extended out to the elbow. The slender fingers curled into a tight fist until the delicate knuckles turned white. I didn't know what to think, so I stepped back. I expected her to flip me the bird, but she didn't. Instead, she rolled her fist to the side, so I could see her thumb and index finger. That's when I saw the red lipstick drawn on her fingers, forming a mouth. Drawn over the upper lip with eyeliner were two eyes, complete with eyelashes. As it dawned on me that I was facing a hand puppet, a little voice behind the door said, "Everything is fine officer. You can go now." This was followed by an outburst of giggling.

I felt a little dizzy as I realized I was standing on the front porch thinking how best to negotiate with a hand puppet. I had no intention of going away until I had some face time with this disrespectful girl, and it became apparent that she had no intention of opening the door to let me lecture her. The more I demanded that she open the door, the more the puppet assured me everything was fine and that I should leave.

Out of the corner of my eye I saw neighbors standing in their driveways watching me talk to the hand puppet. I don't have a poker face. When I get embarrassed or angry, my face lights up like a red beacon. I tried to keep my back to the neighbors so they wouldn't see how embarrassed I was. I could feel the heat coming off my face.

The police academy training had prepared me for many different scenarios, but this was a chapter that wasn't in the manual; I was breaking new ground. At first I wanted to scold this girl for playing with the 911 system. Now I just wanted to get off the porch before another cop drove up and caught me matching wits with a hand puppet—and losing.

Desperate, I said, "You open this door right now, or I'll wait for you to leave your house and give you a ticket." I knew this was a bluff and unprofessional, but when arguing with a puppet, one needs to be creative. Hearing my thinly veiled threat, the puppet's smile faded and the door opened ever so slowly. A cute teenage girl with shoulder-length brown hair and a pixie nose poked her face out and calmly asked, "Now, officer, was that a nice thing to say?"

Batting her big brown eyes and giving me an impish grin, she waited for my response. She reminded me of my niece, Emily. As an uncle, I was woefully unprepared to deal with a teenage girl. I knew I was on thin ice with my empty threats. Now that the door was open, I could at least salvage my self-esteem by speaking to her face-to-face. However, the sooner I got off the porch, the better. I leaned toward her and said, "I'm going to let you off with a warning this time, but don't do it again." She smiled sweetly and said, "Oh, thank you so much, officer." I might have snorted. I don't remember. I just remember stomping off the porch, almost tripping over the garden hose as I cut across the dried-up lawn.

While sitting in the report writing room, winding down after the shift, I made the mistake of telling some of the guys about talking to the hand puppet. They thought it was hilarious, especially the dads with teenage daughters.

The next morning I walked into the briefing room and took my seat in the rear of the room as usual. I should have known something was up when I saw all of the officers sitting quietly, staring at the briefing sergeant. Normally, they are so busy gossiping with each other, you have to shout out, "The briefing is starting." When the briefing sergeant saw me sit down in the back row, he closed his notebook, looked up, and said, "Before we get started, would anyone like to say good morning to Sergeant Howsden?" With that, fifteen officers turned around and raised their left fists into the air. Each fist was decked out with ruby red lips, tiny black paper hats and ties. In a chorus of high-pitched voices, they all said, "Good morning, Sergeant Howsden!" I just wished the chief hadn't picked that day to sit in on the briefing.

The Longest Day

THE BEAT

BY JOHN NORDMAN

Sworn Officer, Savannah Chatham Metropolitan PD, Georgia, seven years.

At the beginning of 2006 I was working for Savannah Chatham Metropolitan Police Department as an advanced police officer. I was assigned to SWAT and the patrol division. Our department does not have a full-time SWAT team, which means that I share regular patrol activities in conjunction with SWAT activities.

January 16, 2006, started out as any normal midnight shift in the Islands precinct. It was a wet, cold, and windy night that began with the normal alarm calls from residences and businesses. A call came in for a motor vehicle accident around one A.M. and I responded. Once I arrived on scene I attempted to get out of my patrol vehicle when I saw a gray pickup truck coming straight into the intersection. Three vehicles were already there, strewn about, the injured occupants still inside. The pickup crashed into the accident and then T-boned into my driver's side door. The impact sent my head into the doorjamb and pinned the door shut. Once I was able to realize who I was and what planet I inhabited, I radioed for assistance and crawled out of the passenger side. After the shift I returned home to find my seven-month pregnant wife preparing to go to work around nine A.M. We both watched the local news, which showed the five-vehicle crash and my totaled patrol unit. She wasn't, and still isn't, a big fan of my being a police officer.

At just about that same time, two local wackos, Brett and Linda White, armed with explosive devices and firearms, stormed a Statesboro, Georgia, attorney's office and took all three employees hostage. The attorney, Paul Costello, had represented Brett on some charges a few years before in Savannah, Georgia. Now White and his wife wanted a "new day in court." As I went to bed, the first responding officers were arriving on scene, forty-five minutes away.

When I awoke around five P.M. I went about my usual routine and then drove over to my in-laws' home for dinner. During dinner my pager went off to call my SWAT team leader. As with most SWAT functions, the details were sketchy, but I knew we were meeting at headquarters at ten P.M. When I asked what was up, Sergeant Gay told me to watch the news: We were going up against two nuts with explosives. My wife was even more thrilled.

I arrived early at headquarters and began to get all of my gear and weapons ready. Our SWAT commander, Lieutenant Shoop, briefed us. "We are going to Statesboro to relieve the Georgia State Patrol SWAT team. The two suspects have released two of the three hostages and also sent out one pipe bomb to show that they weren't kidding around." Officer Murphy and I were assigned to drive our tactical van in the convoy to Statesboro.

Once we arrived, we staged our vehicles and then broke down into our teams. We had two entry teams and one sniper element. Murphy and I were assigned less lethal support, and we readied out shotguns with "super sock" low lethality beanbag rounds and loaded up on pepper gas grenades and other chemical munitions. I would carry the shotgun loaded with super sock rounds while Murphy would be my lethal cover in case my rounds did not work or things escalated quickly. We also were assigned the job of keeping the suspects or hostage from reentering the building if they came out. Murphy and I had done this before on similar call-outs, so we made our plans to covertly move up to the front entrance of the building.

Around midnight we began to relieve the GSP SWAT team from their positions. Right off the bat we began to flatten all of the tires on any vehicle parked near the building. My first look at the building showed a three-story brick building with the suspects' vehicle parked haphazardly on the sidewalk in front of the door. I could also see that the trunk was popped slightly open. Team One set up on the corner of the building that the Whites occupied, which gave us the quickest avenue of approach into the building should we have to make entry in a hurry. Our responsibility was to be the contact and arrest team should the suspects decide to give up. We would also make entry if things went bad. Team Two was assigned to the rear entrance, which was blocked by a police vehicle, and the opposite side of the building. They would be our support. Our snipers were posted as follows: Corporal Abbott was posted on the roof directly beside us, Sergeant Cortes was on a roof opposite Team One's location, Corporal Hinson was posted on the rear door and Sergeant Rowse and Corporal Morin were posted three stories up, right in front of the main entrance.

Once everyone was in place, the waiting began. That's when I first felt the cold. All of us had warm clothing, but when you're just sitting out on blacktop and concrete, the cold will find a way to sink down into your bones. I was thankful that I was not on the sniper element sitting on a roof with the cold wind blowing on me.

The first couple of hours were very uneventful. Every now and then we would get an update on the situation. The negotiators were trying to get the wackos to set their hostage, Costello, free, but they weren't budging. They insisted on getting their new day in court. I'm not sure what TV shows or movies these nuts watched, but it had little to do with reality. I cannot think of any time when a gunman took someone hostage and actually got what he wanted—unless it was a jail sentence, a gunshot wound, or a good butt whomping.

Around four A.M. we received word that they were giving up. Team One prepared to take down the two suspects when they exited the building. We sat on ready for fifteen minutes before the word came back that they were not giving up. Not more than twenty minutes later we were back on high alert because the suspects were giving up. Again they changed their minds. Two good adrenaline dumps and I was really getting pissed off. All of Team One began to "plan" our own assault if these knuckleheads didn't come out—and come out now. We then got word that they were going to send out another pipe bomb to show everyone that they really did have explosives and that they were ready to use them. So again we went to high alert and prepared for an assault or arrest.

Murphy and I were the first two at the corner of the building. As I was awaiting our next move, I heard whining coming from the command post. As the noise got louder, I could see that the ATF was sending in their bomb robot. I looked back at the team and said, "Now this should be interesting." The robot made its way down the street and to the front door. Of course, I was hoping to see a bomb robot get blown up. Brett White placed a pipe bomb in a bag and then gave it to the robot. The robot then backed away and slowly made its way back toward the command post. Adrenaline dump number three.

Around five A.M. we again were told, "They're coming out." We sprang up, only to look down the desolate street at cold concrete for about twenty minutes before we found out that they were just kidding.

About six A.M. we were told that they are coming out. "We really mean it this time." Team One got into position and we waited. Just as before, we were all juiced up and ready to assault the building or take down the suspects, yet nothing was happening. Then, just like that, the front door swung open and out stepped two suspects and a hostage . . . or so we thought.

From the start, things were just a tad weird. The Whites had Costello in between them and all three of them were holding hands like they were in kindergarten on a field trip. Brett White was yelling, "We're coming out. Stay back. Here we come!" over and over.

Over my headset I heard one of the snipers say, "Looks like there is something in the male suspect's pocket, possibly an IED (improvised explosive device). Once the trio made it to the street, Murphy and I began to slowly and covertly move toward the front entrance using the cars as cover. We stopped once we reached the suspects' vehicle and I heard Team One's leader, Lieutenant Wilkins, order the suspects onto the ground. I looked over the hood of one car and could see the ATF robot sitting in the street and Team One moving in on the trio.

"This wasn't in our deal. This isn't the deal," Costello yelled back at Wilkins. "Get on the ground. Get down now," Wilkins replied. I could see the female suspect complying and saying, "Please, no, let's not do this please." Brett White yelled at his wife to get up, and as she did, all three began to walk backward. Costello was saying, "This isn't what I agreed to."

Brett White grabbed Costello by the neck and began to yell, "I'll kill this motherfucker. I'm not fucking around. Back off or I'll kill him!" Murphy and I popped up from our cover and began to move toward the suspects, only about ten feet away. As they turned toward us, I heard a loud boom and felt asphalt stinging my face and bouncing off my helmet and eyewear. I also noticed that the female fell limp onto the street.

"Get back, Murphy!" I yelled. The boom was one of our snipers taking a shot. "The female's down and the male's next. Get out of the line of fire!" I continued to yell as we moved back behind the car. I could now see Costello and Brett on the ground next to his wife. I then heard over my headset, "*No knife. No knife!* The suspect does not have a knife." I was cool with that, but what about the IED—and what knife? As I continued to watch, Brett was yelling at Team One, and me, "I'll kill this fucker. I'll break his goddamn neck!" Only about one minute had passed, but it felt like thirty. I finally raised my weapon and attempted to gain a head shot on Brett. As he bobbed about, I noticed the female moving.

"What the fuck?" I mumbled again. I could not believe what I was seeing. Linda, Brett, and Costello all stood up and began to move toward the front door of the attorney's office, using Costello as a shield. During this I could hear Costello say to Brett, "If we walk like this, they can't shoot us." Idiot lawyer screwing up his own rescue.

I told Murphy, "Let's go," and we began to move toward the door to cut off their escape route. As we rounded the front of the Whites' car, Lieutenant Wilkins came over the headset, "Get back. The car is rigged with explosives. Nordman and Murphy move back." I wasn't sure if they knew something that I didn't, but I damn sure wasn't taking any chances. As we moved, walking backward, toward the corner of the building, the trio came into my line of fire. I fired once as they dived back inside the office. I chambered another low lethality super sock round and attempted to fire again, but I had no targets.

When we made it back to the corner, I remember asking what in the hell just happened. Details were sketchy, but it seemed that Corporal Morin fired at Brett when he grabbed Costello, thinking that Brett had a knife. We weren't sure if he struck him, his wife, or both. Either way, we now had two suspects . . . and one dopey lawyer hostage who was siding with his captors. And they were back inside of a building that had more explosives in it.

It was now about 6:30 A.M. and I hoped that my wife was not tuning in to the news because she would have gone into labor right then and there on our living room floor. I was about to call her when Lieutenant Shoop told us to get ready to make entry.

As Team One lined up on the corner of the building, we got word that the negotiators were somehow making progress—the Whites and Costello were going to give up. This was a relief. It was about an hour later when I watched the ATF robot go to the front door with a bag. I later found out that they were bringing breakfast to the three inside. It was around nine A.M. when we got word that they were going to come out again and give up, this time for real. The only thing was that Team One and all other SWAT, police, robots, and any other person or equipment was to be out of sight. A friend of Costello, a fellow defense attorney, was talking all three back out.

I would later find out that Linda was through long before this. She wanted out, and her husband was not far behind. It was the *hostage* who would not come out. This attorney had to convince Costello to give up. (And the public just can't understand why the police do not like defense attorneys!)

We were told to stand down behind the building until the suspects were in custody and Costello was free. This made no sense, considering that Costello was the one who aborted his own freedom three hours earlier. By this time nobody cared whether it made sense or not: We just wanted to go home. So a lone defense attorney walked out into the street and then all three nuts came out. I was ready for yet more problems or for more shooting or shit blowing up, but the attorney handcuffed both Whites and set Costello "free." A storybook ending.

Once we secured most of our equipment and weapons, I called my wife, who had heard about the shooting earlier. I explained that all was well and that I hoped to be home by dinner, depending on which three-letter agency wanted to talk with me. When I entered the command post, it was a chaotic scene, with more people with small badges and suits than I would ever care to see again. I met with Stateboro's police chief, who was very, very happy that the ordeal was over and very thankful for our services. I was led away to a room where my interviews began.

During these interviews the Bureau of Alcohol Tobacco and Firearms and Georgia Bureau of Investigation were blowing up the leftover Improvised Explosive Devices and other explosives found in the Whites' car and inside the building. I would be talking and suddenly someone would yell, "Fire in the hole! Fire in the hole! Fire in the hole!" followed by an explosion that would stop the interview for a few moments. What I heard about two blocks away made me happy that we did not make entry.

After a couple of hours I rejoined my team. Lieutenant Shoop debriefed us on what took place, and we began to pick it all apart, as most cops will do after a hot call or SWAT call-out. We found out that Corporal Morin's .308 sniper round had struck a concrete ledge and did not strike anyone. After hitting the ledge it bounced off the road, went through the car I was standing next to, through a window of a museum, and into some art. My round still has a lot of controversy over it. I have been told it hit Linda White in the calf or leg, and hit Brett White in the ribs, and I have heard, of course, it didn't hit shit.

When I got home I went right to bed. When I finally woke up and returned to work, I caught the news. There was no mention of our SWAT team being deployed or who fired the rounds. There was no mention of Costello screwing up the first surrender and joining the other two wacko jobs. The whole incident was swept away. I was not about to complain, because I had already done enough talking and writing about the incident that day.

One thing is for sure—it was a long, long thirty-hour workday.

The Memorial

LINE OF DUTY

BY CHARLES R. MARTEL

Deputy Sheriff, Harris County Sheriff's Department, Houston, Texas, twenty-five years.

The sky above was a radiant blue. The sun shone brightly upon the landscape below. A woman and her son walked gingerly across the freshly cut grass. Flags were flapping in the wind.

As they approached the granite monument and ascended the steps, the woman handed the little boy a bouquet of flowers. He laid them down in front of the memorial that honored the fallen officers whose names were engraved thereon:

J. D. Tippit, Billy P. Speed, Edward M. Belcher, Roger E. Barrett, Ray E. Kover, Charles D. Heinrich, James D. Mitchell Jr., Jeffrey "Scott" Sanford, Troy A. Blando, Randall Vetter, Aubrey Hawkins, John "Rocky" Riojan . . .

There were eight hundred others: police, deputies, troopers, constables, sheriffs, and rangers—law enforcement officers killed in the line of duty in Dallas, Houston, Austin, Fort Worth, El Paso, Waco, San Antonio, Amarillo, and all across Texas.

Mother and child stepped back and solemnly bowed their heads in prayer. A minute later, when she looked up, the bereaved widow noticed an elderly man standing nearby. His face was drawn and tired. He looked about seventy years old. He was dressed in a white shirt, string tie, and ragged jeans. His dusty boots had seen much use and were worn down at heel and sole. The man glanced in her direction, took off his hat, and nodded gravely. She offered a weak smile.

"Do you come here often?" she asked politely.

"I'm here much of the time, Ma'am," he answered.

At a loss for words, she fell silent. The old man said, "Is this your son?"

"Yes," she replied. "His name is Joey."

"A fine-looking boy," said the man. "How old is he?"

"He just turned seven."

The man lowered his head and whispered, "I was about his age when I lost my papa . . . His name's here, too . . . and so am . . ." He stopped. His heartfelt pain was deep and evident in his voice.

"I'm sorry," said the woman. "It's been a year since my husband—" She stifled a sob.

"Don't worry," the man assured her. "They're still with you . . . watching over you . . . till you're with them again."

The woman looked up and managed a smile.

"God bless you," she said.

"And you, too," he replied.

She then reached down and patted her son on the head.

"C'mon, Honey, it's time to go. Tell Daddy goodbye."

The little boy came to attention, raised his right hand to his forehead, and saluted.

"Bye-bye, Daddy. See you next time."

The old man looked away so they couldn't see the tears in his eyes.

Dusk was now falling. As the sun dipped in the west, beneath the horizon, the clouds turned reddish purple. Hand in hand mother and child began the walk back to their car.

The little boy took a few steps, then turned and looked over his shoulder.

The old man was gone.

The Loss of Innocence

THE BEAT

BY JESSE ROYBAL

Sworn Officer, Las Vegas Metropolitan Police, Nevada, five years.

We in the police profession are so vulnerable, we can become calloused because of the many terrible things we encounter. Most people would stand in utter disbelief of the horrors and tragedies that we encounter on a daily basis. Unfortunately, this is one of those horrors.

This is not a story of heroism or laughter, but of the day I lost my innocence, the day that is probably one of the most memorable in all of my five short years with my agency.

The first two years I was a police cadet. I was hired right out of high school and went into the police academy when I turned twenty-one. During my time as a cadet, I drove an unmarked Crown Vic, took basic burglary and auto theft reports, and did another one of my favorite things—assisting on car accidents with traffic control.

August 16, 2002, started as any other typical day—at Starbucks with a friend. As a fresh cadet, I was at the halfway mark in my cadet career, about a year away from getting ready for the police academy. I was starting to do the things that would prepare me to become a police officer, like making sure I had coffee *and* breakfast, the most important meal of the day.

This Thursday was no different from any other. I had the pleasure of being on a day-shift squad, with Saturday, Sunday, and Monday off, in one of the most senior area commands. This was about my third month on this squad; I had come from a squad of newer officers, who all said that I needed to be careful because all of these salty officers would abuse the hell out of me. Boy, were they wrong. I had never been better taken care of in my time in the department. True, I was working with a bunch of senior officers who weren't easy to change, but I learned a lot from them, besides just where to go for coffee.

I was leaving a local high school parking lot, where I was running license plates on my computer, when a message popped up on my screen. It read "401B ANN/95, POSSIBLE 419 BABY. Nevada Highway Patrol will be handling." The number 401B is our code for accident with injuries, and 419 means dead body. To break it down even more: It was a vehicle accident at Ann and U.S. 95, with injuries and a possible dead baby.

As soon as the message came out, I knew I wasn't far away. Not having any sirens or emergency equipment on my car, I put the pedal to the floor. I heard officers getting on the radio asking if Nevada Highway Patrol needed our assistance. Then these old, seasoned officers did what any of us would do. Just knowing that a baby, an innocent being, could be hurt or killed, they went to assist, jurisdiction or not. I could hear officers getting on the radio now, their sirens in the background. I really couldn't do much when I got there, but I just knew I had to get there and help.

As I drove, all I could think of was getting there, not what I might witness. You see, before I was a cadet, I was an Explorer and did many ride-alongs. Before today, I had seen dead bodies, but nothing too earth-shattering, nothing so horrible that I couldn't find the words to describe it—that is, until that morning.

I pulled up as the fire department and ambulance were arriving. As I was getting out of my car, I saw it—the carnage, the wreckage, the shock and disbelief on the faces of the people. I saw paramedics running to an ambulance and leaving just as I was arriving. In the middle of a sea of debris, I saw a baby blanket, lying on top of a pile of metal. I started doing all that I could to try and help clear the scene. I saw the body parts, skull, brain, all over this normally busy freeway. Off about a hundred yards from the accident was a gravel truck, with the trailer's back wheels missing.

As I looked closely at the wreckage, I saw a green minivan. The passenger's side of the vehicle was completely intact, but the driver's side was brutally smashed, the metal twisted and torn and smeared with blood and pieces of human flesh. It was a horrific scene. I had to work hard to keep my composure. I could not allow myself to think too hard about what had been done to fragile human beings in that terrible accident.

Yet every time I looked back at the crash site—and I found it hard *not* to keep coming back to it—I saw more and more to upset me: a stroller, children's clothes and toys. Talking with a witness, he pointed out brain chunks and other human remains, which I had just recently trampled through, trying to secure the scene. I learned that the ambulance, which left upon my arrival, carried a baby, still in a car seat. We learned later that the baby only had a minor cut. More and more officers from my agency and Nevada Highway Patrol came flying up, all trying to see if there was anything they could do. I sat in disbelief, not understanding how this could happen. As I was just a rookie, there was nothing I could do to help. This was the worst thing I had ever seen. I felt like I needed someone to help *me*.

Then the bad news came. The driver, a twenty-four-year-old mother, and her four-year-old son, were now an unrecognizable combination of body parts in the backseat area. I'm glad I didn't go with the investigators and lift up the sheet to see the bodies. Everyone who had a family said that they saw their own child in that accident. I didn't have to see it to have it hit home.

I left that accident scene reeling and in disbelief. I had to go handle another call; we can't stop because of a tragedy—we still have others to serve. I got to this call, took the information that we needed, then went back to my car for something. As I sat down I looked at the bottom of my boot and saw a small piece of brain and hair on the bottom of my shoe.

I suddenly felt as if my breath was taken away. It happened so quickly that all I could do was sit back in my seat and try not to break down. Just when I thought that I was over it, boom, there it was. The emotion of seeing the mother and child dead in the car was enough, but now having to live that over again was probably one of the hardest times in my life.

On August 15, I lost my innocence. I saw what no person should ever have to see. Unfortunately for us, in our work, we see it too often. Since that day I've been on many terrible calls, the ones where people are dead or dying, adults, children, even a baby girl who died at her grandparents' house.

I know that in my career I sometimes will see such things, but I also know I have emotional outlets—friends, family, churchgoers, and coworkers. It may still be hard, but I would rather let myself feel than not. I want to be one of those officers who keep their feelings, not one who gets rid of them. I don't mind if I have to get sick at heart from time to time. I would rather do that than become a hard, emotionless officer. Those old salty officers I was telling you about taught me one thing from that day. They didn't have to say anything, but just being able to see the emotion in their eyes made me realize I don't need to be a hard, calloused person to be a good officer.

I may have lost my innocence by seeing that horrible event that morning, but I try every day to hang on to my compassion.

This was, not the last tragic scene I witnessed. The very next night after I originally wrote this story, I was the first to arrive at another accident in which four children and a mother were killed in a fiery crash. Two children died in the burnt car, with the firefighters and everyone trying desperately to help. It was probably the worst scene I have ever been on—all caused by a nineteen-year-old drunk teenager who ran a stop sign. From the hurting witnesses to the awestruck fire captain to myself and coworkers, once again I was reminded of my duty.

This was not the way I originally planned on ending this, with another story of tragedy, but it served as goad, to cause me to remember that there are going to be other horrors I cannot avoid. Through those tragedies, it is my duty to be strong, for my partners, as they were strong for me. Even though this car accident brought back all those painful memories of that initial crash, it made me that much better able to handle the scene in the midst of the horror.

It all boils down to this: We must feel, and we must hurt. We must do everything we can to remain human, vulnerable to our honest feelings. I may have lost my innocence, but I know I must fight to preserve my humanity.

The Man in White

WAR STORY

BY DAN SIMON

Sworn Officer, Adams County Sheriff's Department, Wisconsin, five years.

I was only a summer police officer for a resort area in Wisconsin, but with resort areas come very interesting people and very interesting calls. In the middle of summer, at about five P.M. dispatch contacted me: "One-two-three Sauk, we have a report of a suspicious black male wearing white near the florist shop at 134 West Monroe Avenue. Wants to speak to an officer."

"Ten-four Sauk, 10-76."

While on my way, I wasn't thinking much about the call. It's a resort town, and everyone could look out of place or suspicious. I also thought it could be a person who might be prejudiced and just trying to get someone in trouble. The village's resident population is only 2,000 people, but in the summer the population of the village and the bordering town, another tourist trap, can rise to about 50,000 to 100,000. There are the quiet days, but it can get busy fast.

I arrived at the florist and didn't see anyone matching that description. I went in and found a hysterical female in her mid-twenties. She told me, in between crying fits, that a male black wearing all white had scared the crap out of her. She had been out watering her flowers in the front of her store when she saw the man walking by. She said he kept looking at her and wouldn't stop. She

ran back into the store to get away from him, but he kept staring at
her from outside. He wouldn't go away, and at that point she called
the police.

I asked her if he said anything to her or did anything to her, and
she said he hadn't. I asked her if she knew where he was or the last
direction he was seen going. She said she had last seen him near the
Laundromat across the street. I asked for more information about his
physical description and she told me, "He's a black guy wearing all
white. You can't miss him." Well, I thought, the usual harmless
kook. Still, I'd like to get a look at this person.

I drove across the street and checked out the parking lot, but still
no suspicious person wearing all white. I entered the Laundromat
and looked around inside really quickly from the doorway. Still no
suspicious person. As I was looking around, I heard something behind me and whirled around quickly. Lo and behold, I spotted him,
hiding in the bathroom. I chuckled and thought, that's original. The
second he saw me, his eyes went wide and he shut the door.

I knocked on the door and he knocked back. I knocked again and
announced myself. I informed him I needed to speak with him.

Then a voice came from behind the door, "I can't come out."

"Why not?"

"Because I'm hiding."

I had to stop myself from laughing out loud. This guy was a riot.
"Who are you hiding from?"

"You."

By this time, I was holding my sides and my hand was over my
mouth so he couldn't hear me laughing. I managed to get out, in
an even voice, "Well, will you please come out now that I've found
you?"

There were a few moments of complete silence, and then I got
a mumbled response that he was going to be right out. After a few
seconds of fumbling around and then a flush, he came out. And sure
enough, he was a mid-forties black male wearing all white. He was
wearing a white suit jacket, white pants, and white shoes—tennis

shoes with all other colors scratched off or painted over. He was also wearing a pillowcase folded small enough to be used as a bandana on his head and had painted his fingernails white using Wite-Out. He was also carrying a white pillowcase. Why do I get all the fruit-cakes?

I asked the man to come out of the bathroom and step outside so we could talk. He came outside without any resistance and at this point another officer arrived. He took one look at the man in white, leaned against his patrol car, and said, "You go right ahead. I wouldn't *think* of interfering."

I gave him the look I usually reserve for kids when they're being wise and turned back to the desperate criminal. I asked him if he had any guns, knives, bazookas, or similar weapons on him and if I could have permission to look inside the pillowcase for my safety. He said he had no weapons and that he had a law degree (they always do) and to search him was illegal.

"Let me see your degree," I said.

My partner piped up behind me, "*Good* question, Dan."

I ignored him and told Mr. White that I only wanted to look in the pillowcase for my own safety and to make sure that we would all be safe. After a few seconds of thinking and persuading, he finally gave consent and said I could search the pillowcase. When I looked inside, I found that he had a bunch of other pillowcases in it and about thirty white BIC disposable razors with the razor blades taken out.

He said he was just traveling. I asked him why he was bothering the woman across the street, and he said he wanted to ask her for directions, but she just kept getting away from him. I asked him why he had so many razors, and he told me that he collected them. I was able to get a Wisconsin ID off of him and ran him through dispatch. He came back clean, and I asked him if he had family in the area. He said he didn't. His ID said he was from Milwaukee, and I asked if he had any family there. He said he did, but they didn't talk to him.

I asked him if he would like for me to contact them so they could pick him up. He didn't want me to.

In our area we sometimes offer transients or homeless people a bus ticket from the local shelters so they can go to Minnesota or Chicago to get them on their way. I offered him a bus ticket, but he turned it down and told me he'd find his own way.

My partner and I agreed that we didn't have enough for any criminal charges and, as odd as he was, we didn't have enough to take him to the hospital for a mental commitment. We were worried that he might have been a patient at a state mental facility but that would have come up when we ran him through dispatch. My radar was tweaking just a bit—the guy was strange, no doubt about that, and almost certainly harmless, and just too much of a hoot. But there was just a teeny little bell going off in the back of my head. We just didn't have anything on him, so I decided to ignore it. Besides, we were having such a laugh.

We informed him that as long as he didn't harass anyone else, we would just cut him loose but put an advisory within our department and neighboring agencies for other officers to keep an eye out for him in case he was up to something.

After he left, my partner and I laughed till we cried and I went back to the florist again to talk to the female Reporting Person to reassure her we had handled it and he was on his way. I told her that we cut him loose and that he shouldn't be a problem anymore. She thanked me and I left the florist. I forgot about the little warning bell in the back of my head and the man in white.

I left the florist thinking that would be the end of my suspicious black male wearing all white. And for me it was. But two days later one of the female officers in my department came up to me and said, "My husband arrested your guy wearing white." For a second I was confused about what she was talking about, and then it dawned on me. Apparently the man in white had gone to that city and exposed himself to a woman in public. Of course he was an easy person to describe and was easily arrested by my coworker's husband. I just stood there with my mouth open. My instincts were right.

So the moral of the story is this: This job is *serious*. Sometimes it's funny as hell, but it's *always* serious. You just never know what kind of people you will run into.

The Mild Spring Morn

BY ANGELO L. FLORIO

Detective, New York PD, seven years.

My life changed forever on a sunny spring morning in Brooklyn. As I parked my car on a tree-lined street in the Bedford-Stuyvesant section, I had no idea what was awaiting me.

What cop does when he begins a tour of duty?

I joined the New York Police Department as a police trainee about a year and a half out of high school. I graduated from Erasmus Hall High School in Brooklyn, and was appointed a police officer on my twenty-first birthday.

Fast forward to the morning of April 4, 1974. My assignment since 1972 was the undercover unit of the Narcotics Division, Brooklyn South. Although this was not a routine drug buy because of its size—a half kilo of cocaine at $13,500—I thought it would go smoothly as I had already made almost two hundred buys and I felt my backup team and the men I worked with were the best. Besides, I was invincible—and twenty-four years old.

I pulled my car into a spot around the corner from the location, an apartment house. The weather was springlike, warm, sunny, and calm. I was armed with a .22 Magnum Derringer loaded with twenty-two caliber longs. As I made my way down the street I knew there was a two-man team photographing me from a van somewhere near the entranceway to the building. The tape was running and caught all the sounds—my footsteps, my breathing, kids playing jump rope. Another team or two was riding around in cars covering me as best they could while maintaining a safe distance so as not to be spotted by lookouts. I was alone, just me, the tape, a triple beam-balance scale, and my balls. I entered the lobby, rang, was buzzed in.

I whispered into a small mike taped to my chest as I approached the elevator: "Today's date is April 4, 1974, 11:30 A.M." A pause: "April 4, 11:30 A.M."

Later, when we listened to the tape, we heard all sorts of eerie noises, footsteps, motors, doors slamming from the elevator, clothing rubbing against the mike. As I stepped out onto the third floor, I began walking a long hallway, tiled floors, cement painted walls. I spotted the door leading to the stairwell, which was slightly open. I looked closer and saw a foot, a leather boot, between the door and the brick. Suddenly the door flew open. Out jumped a man in a black patent leather jacket, collar up, wielding a .357 Magnum Western Ruger, six-inch barrel revolver, with a blue ski mask wrapped around his hands. We were two or three feet apart, he in a semi-combat stance, both hands gripping the revolver pointed at my face: "Gimme the money."

I put my hands in the air and tried to stay calm. "All right. OK. Take it easy." I threw the money down.

"All of it," he growled.

"OK, take it easy. Don't panic."

"Way to go, motherfucker."

Boom. Blast. Deafening, reverberating sounds and flame. Smoke, red and yellow, flew at my face. There was a large smoke ring forming around him, growing larger, like the old Camel sign on Broadway and 44th Street. I saw myself standing as a rookie in my new blue uniform. I smelled my fresh new leather gun belt. I saw myself as a boy playing. I jumped, leapt on top of him, and went unconscious.

Next thing I remember, I was on all fours. I jumped up, looking for him, and ran away howling, heaving blood and spit and grunting down the long hall as I pulled out my gun. *There he is.* He turned to fire at me before dashing into the stairwell. I regrouped somehow, saw my shoe heels lying down the hall. I thought, *How'd they come off my shoes?* Blood came shooting into my throat, salty and choking me. I thought, *I'm shot bad.* There's a pain in my right chest. I know I'm shot bad. Fear, anger, hurt, and embarrassment all engulfed my mind. *I gotta get outta here.* I started toward that stairwell. My legs stiffened as I ran down the metal steps. I knew he could be close by but I was too wounded to care. I was on autopilot, half conscious, in shock, with my gun leading the way. My youth, my life, were like the large drops of blood filling my shoes, leaving a trail on the landings and steps. My past was leaking out of me, the years I spent growing up as a kid in an Italian family, all the Christmases at Grandma's house, fun, family, love, playing in the snow with my brother, sleds, years upstate in the apple orchards of the Hudson Valley, rock 'n' roll shows at the Brooklyn Fox, girlfriends, my mom and dad—all pouring out of me in a stream of blood, my promising career issuing in a pool of blood.

Everything turned white, all bright white light, and I was floating. The legs that ran three miles a day were carrying a dead man. When I reached the end of my journey from the third floor out onto the street I fired two shots like a robot walking. Several narcs finally approached me.

Mike Falco, a backup officer shouted, "Angie, Baby, you all right? Ya shot? Oh, shit, take it easy, take it easy, Babe. Lie down, Ang. I'm gonna lay you down." He spoke to me as if I was a person he loved dearly.

I had sustained chest and back wounds, burns to my face, muzzle-flash gunpowder, and loss of hearing.

I never did find out what happened to Mike Falco after he left the job. I miss him. I want to ask him how he is. I have spent thirty-six years trying to regroup. Everything changed. Maybe someday I'll make sense of it.

I am now a single dad with a fifteen-year-old daughter. I'm still a wayfarer seeking my dreams.

Morale Booster

BY CHARLES R. MARTEL

Deputy Sheriff, Harris County Sheriff's Department, Houston, Texas, twenty-five years.

The time was 0700 hours, in late October. A bright sun peeked up over the horizon. Inside the police substation, roll call was about to start. A fresh pot of coffee was brewing its rich aroma filling the air. A large box of donuts, half eaten, sat beside it.

Day-shift patrol was reporting for duty. The squad room was packed with weary officers whose eyes looked as though they were still asleep—too many extra jobs with little or no rest, not to mention administrative changes, low pay, lack of support, citizen complaints, and all the usual crap officers had come to expect. It had gradually taken its toll. The old adage rang true: "A policeman's lot is not a happy one."

The supervisor in charge checked his roster and called out each name. All present. After receiving their unit numbers and patrol assignments, the sullen group of uniformed guardians was ready for work. Sensing their lack of enthusiasm, the sergeant decided to lift their spirits and said, "By the way, in case you're interested, last night three of our brother officers responded to a silent alarm and blew up two members of the 'Bandido' motorcycle gang burglarizing a local sporting goods store on the city's south side.

"They were stealing rifles and shotguns, and attempted to ambush the officers as they entered the building. A gun battle ensued and both suspects were rendered 'DRT' dead right there. None of our guys were hurt."

A raucous cheer went up around the room, followed by hoots, hollers, and thunderous applause. Then, as the noise died down, the sergeant said, "And on that bright note, y'all hit the streets. Have a safe day."

The troops shuffled out the back door toward the parking lot, but with a little more bounce to their step, ready to face the daily perils they might encounter and better prepared to serve and protect. And who said sergeants don't care?

Life Is Precious, Life Is Fragile

DEADLY FORCE

BY CHUCK SPRINGER

Police Officer, Warren PD, Michigan, eight years.

I was starting my shift at midnight on Super Bowl Sunday, a cold February night, when the dispatcher requested units respond to a hotel in the far north end of our city for an attempted pickup. I informed my partner that during the previous night's tour I had received information that the U.S. Marshals Service was attempting to locate and apprehend a serious criminal wanted in connection with a homicide in a neighboring city as well as a felony warrant for weapons violations from the Bureau of Alcohol, Tobacco and Firearms. Apparently, the federal authorities had traced this fugitive's cell phone to the north end of our city, where there are numerous motels. Though they could not pinpoint his location, the Marshals Service did pass out fliers to all the hotel desks. Our information was that the fugitive was armed with an AK-47 assault rifle and considered extremely dangerous.

When I got to the motel, our senior shift sergeant was already speaking to the motel clerk, who believed that he had rented a room to a woman accompanied by the subject in the marshals' flier. We could not, however, find a vehicle belonging to the suspect and the Marshals Service stated that the woman who rented the room did not appear on the fugitive's list of known associates. Also, there was an employee discount applied to the room. After considering all the facts, the agent from the Marshals Service decided that it did not warrant mobilizing his resources. Though I have heard much criticism of the decision, I cannot say that I disagree with it or would have done anything differently if it had been my call; the information was thin.

That being said, I obviously would not be writing this story if there wasn't something to be said for "thin information."

As fate would have it, one of the hotel security guards smelled marijuana smoke emanating from the room that the clerk believed the fugitive was in. (I know how convenient this may sound, but it is absolutely true.) Of course, the hotel security requested our assistance in evicting the occupants from the room. I suggested that instead of knocking on the door, we bring a room key and attempt a stealth entry. As the sergeant pondered this "radical" idea, I pointed out that we were legally justified and that it was better to be safe than sorry. The sergeant conceded my point and allowed me to do it my way. The hotel security guard, our sergeant, and, to the best of my memory, five officers, including me, went to the room.

The room was only a room or two from an exit. Though the hotel staff was doing the eviction, we, too, had possession of the electronic door key since this was a potentially hazardous situation. My partner and another officer went to the exterior window. Another officer and I were on the door. I noticed that the marijuana odor permeated the air as I slipped the door key in the access slot, but instead of a green light showing that the door was unlocked, an amber light appeared. Not good. That meant the deadbolt was engaged and there was no way to unlock the door. The other officer on the door quietly turned the handle, but the door would not open.

The sergeant instructed me to knock on the door. I protested once again and told him that I had another idea. I requested that the sergeant knock on the door as soon as I called him on the radio. I then went back to the window, and my partner's partner for the night took up a position back inside the hotel.

My partner could, and still can, communicate extensively without saying a word. We exchanged a look and he drew his handgun to cover me.

I approached the window and noticed that it could be opened. However, doing it quietly was not going to be possible. Being that it was February and extremely cold, there was rust and ice in the window track that would certainly give us away. As I looked at my partner, I knew he was ready. I opened the window enough to get my fingers inside, and then I slammed the window against the rust and ice, pushing from my right to left several times until it opened. When it did, I heard a male's voice from inside the room demanding to know who was at the window. I then called for the sergeant to knock on the door. One of the officers began to repeatedly kick the door to the room. The diversion worked perfectly and most likely saved my life.

I drew my gun with my right hand and pushed the curtain from my right to left with my left hand. I observed a black male subject on the bed with his hands under the covers, looking frantically from the door to the window and back repeatedly. I knew the moment I saw this subject that he was the fugitive from the Marshals' flier.

I identified myself and ordered the fugitive to raise his hands. He paused for a second, but it seemed like an eternity. Suddenly he rocked back and raised his right hand. In his hand was a semiautomatic handgun. I knew what was coming and instinctively placed my left hand back on my gun to fire. As I did, the curtain closed in front of me and several thunderous blasts roared from inside the room with bullets and glass screaming toward me.

I immediately returned fire. As I fired, I moved to my left across the window to cover. Though I would like to say I planned it that way, I didn't; I just did it. Though not the best tactical decision, since I was closer to the right side of the window, with me on the left and my partner on the right, we could cover most of the room.

It is said that you will always revert back to your training. I didn't realize how true this was until I found myself reaching for a hand grenade. I quickly realized that I had reverted *too* far back in my training and got up to speed. I briefly wondered what the burning sensation was on the right side of my body. It was strange because I could not tell where the burning was coming from other than simply somewhere on my right side.

I remember thinking that the curtain was a serious problem. Just then, the man who wanted me dead asked me for a favor. He yelled that there was a pregnant woman inside the room. He said that she had not done anything wrong and wanted to come out. Though I did not recall seeing a woman inside the room, I knew that a woman had rented the room, and I obviously could not have seen into the bathroom.

First, I yelled for the woman to open the curtain. She did and I could see her but not the suspect. I ordered her to turn around which she did. I then instructed her to lie on the floor, and she complied again.

I yelled into the room and instructed the male subject to do exactly what I told him to, and no harm would come to him.

What the hell, it worked on the woman: Why not try it on the guy?

I ordered the suspect to put down his gun and walk toward the wall away from the bed with his hands up. Almost immediately, the suspect jumped in front of the window, yelled something to the effect of "Fuck that," and began firing at us again. In a combination of shock and fear, I pushed back hard behind the cover of the wall. Though I had been on my right knee, I slipped on the ice and fell flat on my back. I remember thinking that I had given this son of a bitch two chances to give himself up, and on both occasions he had found it necessary to try to kill me. Being that his gun was only three feet away from me, I could once again feel the concussion against my body as the suspect fired widly.

As I got back into a kneeling position, I was joined by another former partner of mine. I will call this Officer "Big Daddy" (because he would like that). Big Daddy and I came up firing together.

I could still feel the concussion from the suspect's gun, which was squared up to the window. Additionally, Big Daddy's gun was roaring in my right ear. We both fired until the suspect fell to the ground. As Big Daddy and I cautiously approached the window, we could see the suspect's .40-caliber Glock at the base of the window as the suspect lay on his back. We entered the room through the window and secured the suspect. We then called for EMS and let the sergeant in from the hallway. I remember telling Big Daddy that I had never wanted to hug another man so bad in my life! It was an unfortunate ending, but one that the suspect chose and forced on us.

The burning sensation on the right side of my body turned out to be from my right hand. It was swollen and had a horizontal red abrasion. I don't know if it was a bullet, a bullet fragment, or a piece of glass, but something grazed me.

The suspect sustained five lethal hits and one nonlethal to his right arm (his gun hand).

I try to take something positive from every situation. In this case, I realized how precious life is . . . especially my own!

That is why I have waited until I was thoroughly enjoying life before writing my story, and that is why it is being written from a lounge chair on a beach in hot and sunny Florida instead of an office in the cold and dreary Midwest.

I Believe

BY RANDY SUTTON

I am a cop and I believe . . .

I believe in my badge and all that it stands for—for courage, for honor, and for compassion. For unity and integrity and sacrifice.

I believe in the men and women who stand beside me with gleaming gold and silver worn proudly on their chests. I know of their triumphs and I know their pain. For cruelty and violence are the acid that corrodes our souls, and it is belief alone that can shield us from being consumed. Our purpose and destinies lie in protecting of others.

I believe that cops are warriors. They are soldiers in one sense, because combat is very real and very personal and never far from their reality. But cops are much more. They are the peacemakers and their courage is tempered by their compassion. Every cop knows that each day may be his or her last. They know that violence may take them and they may fall, and yet they go on. They go on because of belief. Belief in something greater than themselves. They believe in justice. Noble words? You bet they are, and I'm proud to say them, for I'm a cop and I believe.

Justice is not a hypothetical theory to a cop. Nor is it a concept open to debate. It is as real and as visceral as the mournful sound of

"Taps" when another uniform-clad body is laid to rest. It is something to be fought for—and, if necessary, to die for. Yes, I'm a cop, and I believe.

I believe that when my career is over and I no longer shoulder the burdens of my profession, I will look back with pride. Pride in myself and in the knowledge that I did my best. Pride in my brothers and sisters for continuing on. And most of all, pride in my badge and for all that it stands for. I'm a cop. And this is what I believe.